THE COMPLETE BOOK
OF CURRIES

the complete

book of

CURRIES

by

HARVEY DAY

BOOK CLUB ASSOCIATES
LONDON

This edition published 1977 by
Book Club Associates
by arrangement with Kaye & Ward Ltd

Copyright © 1966 Nicholas Kaye Ltd
Revised edition © 1970 Kaye & Ward Ltd

Printed Offset Litho in Great Britain by
Cox & Wyman Ltd, London, Fakenham and Reading

CONTENTS

FOURTH BOOK OF CURRIES

FIFTH BOOK OF CURRIES

COLOUR ILLUSTRATIONS

ACKNOWLEDGEMENTS

Without the very generous help of Elizabeth David Ltd., Indiacraft Ltd., Uneek, Talaware, The Eaton Bag Co., and Jan Oldham, who with great skill prepared the dishes shown in the colour illustrations, and Bryce Attwell of Attwell/Jones, who conjured the photographs, the book in this form would not have been possible. To each my grateful thanks.

H.D.

FOREWORD

THE influx of Indians, Pakistanis, West Indians and other curry-eaters from the Commonwealth into Britain within recent years has seen the sprouting of Indian and Pakistani restaurants like mushrooms on a midden. Which should cause the non-curry eating public to pause, for the popularity of any cult or fashion always brings in its wake a rapacious horde eager to leap on the band waggon.

All who run restaurants where curries are offered to a gullible public are not experts in their native art and the result some achieve on their patrons is a revulsion to curries of every sort. These restaurateurs haven't mastered their art, use only the cheapest ingredients, and are out primarily to make a fast buck.

It cannot be too strongly stressed that the right ingredients must be used if a curry is to be worth eating. Too many of these places seem to serve secondhand food cooked in axle grease and are studiously avoided by connoisseurs of Eastern food. Those taken in once will make a day's march to avoid them.

To get the best results, use fresh vegetables, eggs, fish and meat, and cook in *ghee* or butter, or where expressly advised to do so, in mustard oil or coconut oil. Coconut oil is used mainly in Ceylon and parts of South India; rarely in Central India, the North, or Pakistan.

The idea that tainted fish and meat can safely be used in curries because the power and pungency of spices will disguise the taste and odour, is a mistaken one. Nor should wilting vegetables be used. Nothing but the best is good enough for curries.

A friend of mine bought Robert Carrier's excellent compendium on cookery, at considerable expense, with the intention of astounding his guests. He does just that because he refuses to use the ingredients recommended.

Where a recipe says butter, my friend argues: 'But margarine will do just as well—or lard.' If told to use cream he buys the synthetic stuff used by inferior bakers—because it's so much cheaper. If instructed to make pastry cases for savouries, he rushes out and buys cheap vol-au-vent cases and fills them with messes of his own.

His concoctions are fetching to the eye: cakes and 'cream'-filled pastries which make one's mouth water—till they are sampled. And he wonders why friends refuse his invitations.

Shoddy ingredients always make uneatable food. The best—not always the most costly —ingredients are cheapest in the end, for they are the most satisfactory. And, after all, why insult your stomach? It's a vital possession.

So use the ingredients mentioned in the recipes and no others.

Curries are not meant to be eaten every day but only occasionally, especially in cold weather, and then as dinner or supper dishes, or snacks. Their rich colour, appetising odour, and double warmth in both heat and pungency, make them ideal for winter.

Buy the ingredients in shops that specialize in them and don't put up with substitutes.

The foundation of the curry is the important part. Take a little care with that, and then the curry will more or less look after itself.

The snack-dishes, such as *sambals* and *bhajias* (not to be confused with *bhajjis*) are so easily prepared and quickly cooked that they are ideal for supper on cold nights, and can be eaten with a fork, off a plate on your lap, as you watch TV—without fuss or mess. They can be prepared at any convenient time, put aside and cooked in a few minutes, when needed. They are also excellent for picnics. So are patties, which can be filled with curried meat, vegetables and fish.

As I have had many letters from readers to tell me how much they have liked the curry books it would be base ingratitude not to thank once again all who have rallied so generously to my aid. Their names and addresses are given in different parts of the book, at the end of the recipes they so kindly contributed. I am also indebted to Mrs. May Ewing, who supplied so many of the recipes and to the late Mrs. Mudnani, without whose help the first volume would never have been started.

My thanks are due also to the staff of Nicholas Kaye, without whom I would have been lost.

It all started at a curry supper after a match between the Sportsman's Book Club and the Indian Gymkhana when Stanley Pickard, managing director of Kaye, who was seated next to me, popped some curry into his mouth, looked at me and remarked: 'Delicious! D'you think you could write a book on curries?'

It was a challenge accepted. One never knows how such things end. Neither he nor I dreamt that five books would come out of it!

THE FIRST BOOK
OF CURRIES

WHAT ARE CURRIES MADE FROM?

AN English guest at my club, the Indian Gymkhana, at Osterley, was given a dish of curry compounded by the hands of an expert. 'Very tasty,' was his comment, 'but of course, this is not the real stuff. I had some curry in Bombay in '42 which was so hot that it well nigh took the skin off my tongue. That was *real* curry.'

Far be it from me to disillusion anyone. It would have taken far too long and in any case his mind was made up. *He* had tasted the genuine article—only once, mark you—but now he was an authority. *He* knew, and he wouldn't be put off by base substitutes.

He reminded me of the people who return from Devonshire and say, 'Devon cider is the only cider worth drinking. Two glasses, and you're under the table.'

This book is not for the likes of them.

There are also people who won't eat curry and say they dislike it. When asked what it is about curry they dislike, they explain, 'I don't know—I've never eaten it, but I know I wouldn't like it.'

But if like me, you're willing to try everything once; if you prefer a cider you can enjoy without being carried home on a stretcher, or a curry whose richness and flavour lingers on the palate and fills you with regret that the meal is but a memory, then read on.

Most people in Britain refer to 'curry' as if there were but one dish fit to bear that designation. There are, however, hundreds of curries; curries of meat, fish, prawns, lobsters; bamboo curries and curried fruits; and mixed curries. Some differ vastly in flavour from others. A Madras curry may make a person unused to it imagine that his mouth is on fire; but curries elsewhere can be extremely mild and cause discomfort to none.

India and Pakistan, the home of curries, cover an area as large as Europe, excluding Russia, and it would be surprising if all the inhabitants liked the same sort of food.

Because curries are hot, they are not therefore a concoction of the Devil. Their pungency aids perspiration, one of Nature's ways of cooling the body and at the same time ridding it of toxins, through that important organ, the skin.

In summer the greater part of India (and, of course, Pakistan) has a shade temperature in the region of 100 degrees F. Freshly killed meat bought in the early morning will start to putrefy soon after mid-day if steps are not taken to preserve it, and even cooked meats are barely edible after 12 hours.

The ancients discovered by a process of trial and error that if meats were cooked in certain spices, they would not putrefy for days, and if cooked in special ways in mustard oil, as in the case of vindaloo, not for weeks or months. They learnt to bring together these spices in a multitude of combinations, and it is some of these that form the basis of the curries given here.

3

When you have concocted curries from these recipes you will realize that all curries do not taste alike; that they have as many distinctive bouquets as wines. You can develop into a connoisseur of curries just as you can of the other good things of life.

India is a country largely of vegetarians and originally curries were not eaten at every meal, as they now are. In many parts of India one meal a day—from choice—is the custom. Discriminating people eat fresh fruit, with a curried meal only at night. That is the way to enjoy curries. The palate of the man who eats only curries, soon loses its sensitivity.

The British reader, for whom this book is primarily meant, is urged to make curries only occasionally. These he will enjoy to a far greater degree than if he eats curries every day.

Curries should be a change from the normal fare; not a substitute for it.

Only simple, easy-to-make curries are described here; curries for which all the ingredients may be bought in shops that specialize in such spices, as well as in the multiple stores like Express Dairies shops, and in vast emporia like Harrod's and Selfridge's (*see also list on pp. 249–250*).

There exists an impression, difficult to eradicate, that curry eating is bad for you; that it causes dyspepsia, makes you evil-tempered and tends to shorten your life. This impression has been fostered by writers who depict purple-faced, curry-eating colonels who retire to rural England and vent their spleen on the natives.

That such characters exist is no figment of the writers' imagination; but curries are not the criminals. Prolonged existence in an army mess is sufficient to drive any mortal to the verge of apoplexy, particularly if the mess is situated in a torrid zone and the food concocted by an army cook. And if generous doses of whisky are poured into the victim (after sundown) the result, in ninety-nine cases out of every hundred, is bound to be a volcanic colonel (or major) in a state of perpetual eruption, who doesn't even need a bar of soap to start him off.

Curries—will this astonish you?—are foods *for health*.

Every spice used in their making is a preservative. All have some antiseptic value and many are carminatives: that is, they tend to reduce flatulence, as do dill and caraway, which are so innocuous that they are given to babies.

Curries have been eaten for centuries. The discovery of vitamins was broadcast to the world by Sir Frederick Gowland Hopkins in 1911. But no one realized that the spices used to make curries are rich in vitamins, though part of some of the vitamins is killed in cooking. The paprika and chilli families are extremely rich in vitamin C, an antiscorbutic vitamin, which is good for the skin. This may be one reason why so many Indian women have such remarkably clear skins.

In 1926 Szent Gyorgyi and his co-workers isolated a vitamin from paprika juice which is superior even to ascorbic acid in the prevention of capillary bleeding. He wrote, 'I called it vitamin P in honour of Paprika and Permeability'.

Of the curry spices, ginger has long been used as a medicine by Chinese and Indians and is mentioned in Chinese medical books, in Sanskrit literature and the Talmud. It is supposed to have aphrodisiac qualities and was highly esteemed, among others, by Henry VIII. In Britain ginger wine is still taken as a cordial for keeping out the cold, and in the seventeenth century a preparation of aromatic herbs, ginger wine and other spices, known as 'Dr. Stevens' Water', found a place in every medicine chest.

4

Turmeric, too, is used widely in the East for skin diseases, healing bruises, leech-bites, and as a carminative.

Both garlic and onions are blood cleansers and ward off colds in winter. On the Continent both are eaten uncooked. Unhappily, like many things that are 'good for one', they have an unpleasant reaction and make the breath smell offensively because of the sulphur they contain. Garlic is rich in vitamins B, C and D, and onion in C. During the 1914 war, distilled onion juice was given in blood transfusions with excellent results. Both are Nature's medicines.

When cooked in curries, garlic and onions add to their flavour and aroma, but do *not* taint the breath. As an internal cleanser garlic has few equals.

Recent experiments carried out at the University of California prove that onions contain allyl aldehyde, and that garlic contains crotonic aldehyde, both potent germ destroyers.

Onions and garlic are rich in the trace elements zinc, copper, aluminium, manganese, sulphur and iron which, scientists have now discovered, keep away disease.

Cinnamon is an extremely powerful germicide. Some years ago the scientist Cavel infected beef tea with water taken from the collecting tank of a sewage system. To one sample was added cinnamon oil diluted to 4 parts in 1,000; to another, oil of cloves diluted to 2 parts in 1,000. The germs in each sample were destroyed. But when carbolic acid was used the strength of the solution had to be increased to 5·6 parts in 1,000 to be equally effective.

Yet how many people realize that clove and cinnamon oils are more powerfully antiseptic than carbolic acid?

Coriander seed is also an antiseptic and a carminative. In the Middle Ages cordials were made from it, the best known being the renowned Eau de Carmes, prepared in the pharmacy of the Carmelite monks from lemon peel, coriander seed, nutmeg, cloves, cinnamon, angelica root and spirits of wine.

From both nutmeg and mace a volatile oil is produced for use in cases of renal or hepatic colic, and for certain nervous maladies. Nutmeg oil aids digestion, is a carminative, is used to stop vomiting, is sometimes given in cases of dysentery and to counteract the effect of certain poisons. For centuries Orientals have applied it to their temples to induce sleep, and in England an infusion called nutmeg tea was used in the past to cure insomnia.

Mace, a herb known to English cooks, has many qualities common to nutmeg.

The peppers, too, have been valued for centuries because of their medicinal properties. Black pepper was administered to fever patients in doses of six to ten grains in the form of pills. It did not suppress fever as quinine does, but caused the patient to perspire profusely. Unlike fevers cured by quinine, these did not recur and there was never any harmful after-effect, such as deafness. In Europe pepper was once considered so valuable that when Alaric the Goth conquered Rome in 400 A.D. he demanded 3,000 lb. of pepper as part of the city's ransom!

Into this category we also place allspice or pimento, so called because it has a flavour resembling a mixture of cloves, cinnamon and nutmeg.

Mustard seed is not only an ingredient of some curries, but the oil is sometimes used for cooking them. According to *Diet and Diet Reform* by M. K. Gandhi, that modern saint, it contains 98–99 per cent fat as well as minute traces of manganese, nickel, cobalt; and if the skin, which contains ergosterol, is rubbed with mustard oil and exposed to the sun, the sunlight is converted into vitamin D. Without knowing these facts Bengali mothers have, since time immemorial, rubbed their babies with mustard oil and put them out into the sun.

Mustard oil forms the base of many unguents and embrocations. Pliny writes: 'It is so pungent in flavour that it burns like fire, though at the same time it is remarkably wholesome for the body'. Pythagoras claimed it as a cure of scorpion bites and in Old England a potent cough cure was concocted by boiling powdered mustard with dried figs in strong ale.

Aniseed has long been prized for its many virtues, both real and imaginary. It was eaten to promote appetite and still forms the base of innumerable cough mixtures and lozenges.

Fennel, also used in curries, was once much esteemed by both the Welsh and Anglo-Saxons. There is an old Welsh saying: 'He who sees fennel and gathers it not, is not a man, but a devil'. In the eighteenth century a concoction known as 'Stephens' Cure', which had fennel as its base, achieved such a reputation that in 1739 an Act of Parliament was passed to ensure that the secret of this preparation might be known to the nation. Mrs. Stephens, the inventor, was given an award of £5,000 and the recipe was published in *The London Gazette* of 19th June 1739. (Wootton—*Chron. Pharm.* vol. 2, pp. 199–203).

Saffron as well as turmeric is used in the making of curries. They both impart colour and flavour. Once, before cheap synthetic dyes ousted it from favour, saffron was widely used in England. It was cultivated mainly in Essex, the town of Saffron Walden being the centre of the industry.

The cardamom is a neglected spice in Britain. The seeds, either ground or whole, are used in certain curries and sweetmeats. It is such a pleasant spice that housewives should make themselves acquainted with it; nothing, for instance, gives rice pudding such a distinctive flavour and aroma as a few cardamom seeds. The oil is mixed into medicines and is used in combination with purgatives. It is also a digestive and a carminative and in India it is customary after a meal for a dish bearing cardamoms and betel (areca nut) to be placed before guests.

Cardamom oil is strongly antiseptic and is used also in the manufacture of many perfumes. The Germans are the biggest users of cardamoms in Europe.

It is obvious from all this that curry ingredients are not strange, exotic spices shrouded in mystery. With the exception of chillis and paprika, which are now coming into general use, all the curry spices have been used or known in Britain for centuries. The only ones that have never been used, except in medicines, are fenugreek, asafoetida and poppy seed.

The first two are unpleasant on their own, but when combined with other spices, change in character. Poppy seed has never been popular in Britain though it has been eaten in cakes and sweets in Russia for centuries. It was taken to America by emigrants, where it is well liked, and recently dieticians have discovered that it is rich in fat and protein.

But spices are not the only ingredients giving to curries their special nature. The flesh of the coconut, as well as coconut milk, is enlisted to give certain curries—especially fish—a delicious, individual flavour. And so are lime or lemon juice, and tamarind. Various leaves, such as bay, are also added.

No one seems to know why curries have not been more popular in Europe, for the ingredients have been available for centuries. It may be that the pace at which we live does not allow time for their making, every day—for good curries do demand a certain degree of attention. In the East there has always been more leisure. Eating and conversation are arts that have been cultivated. Men are on friendlier terms with their stomachs than they are in Britain. They treat them better, look after them more, and consequently are freer from digestive as well as nervous troubles, for the two go hand in hand.

The aim of the curry eater is not to bolt his food, but to savour it. Flavour then, is all important. This enjoyment of food has a stronger psychological bearing on health than we realize.

First, there is anticipation, caused by the appetizing *aroma* of curry. Digestive juices are secreted in the mouth. Then follows the real pleasure of eating with enjoyment. Contentment, naturally, is the result, and in its train, sound health.

Indians who suffer the torments of dyspepsia are invariably those who overeat. Therein lies the sole disadvantage of curries. They tend to turn you from a gourmet into a gourmand.

Before you embark upon the unknown sea let me remind you that curry is best made in an earthenware dish or casserole. The less metal that comes into contact with curry spices, the better. But if you must cook in metal utensils, use good enamelware in preference to aluminium.

Use wooden spoons for mixing your curries, and keep those spoons for curry-making and nothing else.

When eating curry and rice, use a dessertspoon and fork. In their homes, Indians and Pakistanis use their fingers, but they are experts, and if you attempt to do so in public you will in all probability get yourself into a dreadful mess.

THIS IS IMPORTANT TO REMEMBER. If you make too much curry, don't worry. Curries always taste better next day or the day after. Keep in a cool place, re-heat and eat with rice, Indian bread, or slices from your baker's loaf. Rice and Indian bread do not improve with keeping. Both set hard and dry.

A WORD ABOUT KINDS OF CURRY

THE European with only a passing acquaintance of curries, gained possibly at an Indian restaurant or on a tour of India as a guest of the Army, does not realize that some of the cooking processes employed by Hindus and Moslems differ almost as widely as plain English cooking does from French cuisine. And even among Hindus, tastes are by no means alike.

Madras cooking, for instance, is very much more pungent than anything in Hindustan, and Madrassi curries are thinner and more watery. Bengalis specialize in fish and bamboo curries cooked in mustard oil, and in rice. In the Punjab the flat unleavened bread of whole wheat often replaces rice, and lentils of great variety are eaten. The food in Bombay is perhaps the most cosmopolitan of all—and so on.

In the past Hindus must have been strictly vegetarian, for Sanskrit recipes make no mention of meat; whereas in the Koran, the Niamut and other Persian works, there are glowing descriptions of dishes consisting of game, fish, fowl, mutton and beef. Pork is tabu, of course, to the True Believer.

Hindus specialize in cakes of wheat and various grains; in rice prepared in a score of different ways; in curries called 'bhajjis' made from vegetables, eaten with chutneys, pickles, oil, vinegar, salt, mustard and tyre.

Moslem cooking is more substantial. Because it makes use of meat into which you can get your teeth, it is more suited to European palates. Their food is much drier, often rendering knives and forks superfluous. In their meat recipes one is told to 'bogharer' the meat; that is, fry it before cooking in spices, an operation which transforms a merely tasty dish into one that is delicious. They also brought to India many Persian dishes, among them being the pilau (pillau, pillow), or as it is sometimes written in English, pilauf.

A pilau has rice as its base. It is cooked in ghee (clarified butter) or butter, is heavily spiced and sometimes contains sultanas, raisins and almonds.

Birianees are a form of pilau; a cross between a pilau and a curry.

Ashes contain meat, flour, lentils and vegetables, and even fruit, sugar, milk and tyre (yogurt).

Kababs, or to use the English corruption, kabobs, consist of meat and vegetables, heavily spiced, cut into slices or chunks, or moulded into segments and then skewered on wooden, steel or wire skewers and roasted over an open fire.

This does not mean that Hindus do not eat Moslem dishes, or that Moslems disdain Hindu fare. As is natural when communities have lived together for centuries, some of the food habits of each are adopted by the other. Generally speaking, however, Hindu dishes are vegetarian, whereas Moslem dishes have a foundation of meat or game.

A word as to curry ingredients. The reader will see from the recipes that not all curries are made in the same way; even when curry powder or curry paste is mentioned, these may vary considerably. For those who do not wish to experiment, there are some excellent curry pastes and powders available in this country. The most expensive are not always the best. Try them all and see which suit your palate best.

But there must also be many who would like to concoct their own curry ingredients. For these adventurous souls a list of curry ingredients is given, together with three different recipes for making curry powders and a paste.

Curry ingredients may be bought either whole, as in the case of chillis, ginger in the root, peppercorns, cardamom and cinnamon; or ground. If you wish to grind your own curry-stuffs you may do so in a small mill, such as a coffee grinder, though the same grinder must not be used for coffee as the aroma and taste of curry spices are strong and linger, and cannot always be washed out.

In India, where curry spices are bought every few days fresh from the market, the cook pounds them on a large, flat stone slab (the surface of which is specially treated to make it rough) called a 'seel', or mashes them in a 'hummumdusta' (mortar) with a 'hummumdusta ka duntee' (pestle). But this is merely by way of digression.

Given below are not only the names of the various spices in English, but their Indian and botanical equivalents, because one day you may blossom into an expert in the art of making curries, and as an expert you must know the proper jargon in which to air your specialized knowledge.

If at first making you find any of the dishes too pungent, reduce the number of chillis or the amount of curry powder to suit your palate.

CURRY INGREDIENTS

INDIAN	ENGLISH	BOTANICAL
souf	aniseed	*Pimpinella Anisum*
seetul	allspice	*Myrtus Pimenta*
eelachie	cardamom	*Elelbaria Cardamomum*
jawatrie	mace	*Myristica Moschata*
jauphull	nutmeg	*Myristica Moschata*
kulmie darchini	cinnamon	*Laurus Cinnamonum*
dhunnia or kotimear	coriander	*Doriandrum Sativum*
laoong	cloves	*Engenia Caryophyllata*
zeera or jeera	cummin seed	*Cuminum Cyminum*
kala mirchi	black pepper	*Piper Nigrum*
rai	mustard seed	*Sinopis Chinesis*
lal mirchi	chillis	*Capsicum Frutescens*
huldie	turmeric	*Curcuma Longa*
mayti	fenugreek	*Trigonella Foenum Craecum*
lassoon	garlic	*Alium Sativum*
sont	ginger (dry)	*Amomum Zingiber*
udruck	ginger (green)	*Amomum Zingiber*
khush-khush	poppy seed	*Papaver Somniferum*

9

INDIAN	ENGLISH	BOTANICAL
pipel	long pepper	*Piper Longum*
hing	asafoetida	*Ferula Asafoetida*
chironji	chironji nut	*Buchanonia Latifolia*
badam	almond	*Amygdalia Communis*
nareul	coconut	*Cocus Nufifera*

In addition to the above ingredients, yogurt, vindaloo, coconut milk or cream, and tamarind are used in certain curries. Yogurt may be bought in Greater London from either the Express Dairy or the United Dairies in 5-oz. bottles; or it can be made at home. Vindaloo and tamarind may be bought at shops that specialize in Indian spices (and see page 249), and so may coconut cream. Coconut milk is made by mixing or mashing desiccated coconut in boiling water and then straining through fine muslin.

SAROJINI MUDNANI'S CURRY POWDERS

INGREDIENTS

2 oz. cummin seed	6 oz. coriander seed
1 oz. black pepper	½ oz. fenugreek

METHOD

Roast these ingredients until a rich aroma is given off, but take care not to burn. Then grind in a hand mill and pass through a fine sieve, ready for blending as described in the second part, for which you need:

INGREDIENTS

1 oz. cloves	2 oz. cinnamon
1 oz. cardamom	1 oz. mace
2 oz. red chillis	

METHOD

Grind these five ingredients or they may be bought ground at a shop specializing in spices. If you grind them, put them through a fine sieve afterwards. Then mix these together with the roasted ingredients, very thoroughly, and store them in a jar or large bottle with an airtight stopper. These quantities will make from 25–30 dessertspoons. Don't worry about making a large quantity, as curry powder, if kept in an airtight jar, *improves* in quality and aroma.

INGREDIENTS

4 oz. cloves	1 oz. cardamom
1 oz. cinnamon	4 oz. cummin seed
4 oz. black pepper	½ oz. bay leaves
1 oz. mace	

METHOD

Roast these ingredients as instructed in the recipe above, then grind thoroughly and pass through a fine sieve. Store in an airtight jar. Quantity: 25–30 dessertspoons.

NOTE: The second recipe will seem milder and more mellow to those not used to the pungency of curries, though the coriander and fenugreek will give the first a distinctive flavour.

HARVEY DAY'S CURRY POWDER

INGREDIENTS

4 oz. turmeric	½ lb. coriander seed
2 oz. cummin seed	1 oz. poppy seed
2 oz. fenugreek	1 oz. dry ginger
½ oz. mustard seed	1 oz. dry chillis
1 oz. black peppercorns	

METHOD

This is not as pungent as the first recipe and, for some, has more flavour. It is best, when compounding this curry powder, to buy ground spices. Some of the seeds, like coriander, *must* be roasted before being ground as they contain a considerable amount of oil and, when bought ready for use, this part of the work has been done, by experts, before the grinding. Will make 25 dessertspoons of powder.

MADRAS CURRY PASTE

INGREDIENTS

4 oz. coriander seed	2 oz. salt
1 oz. mustard seed	½ gill vinegar
1 oz. garlic	2 dried chillis
1 oz. cummin seed	½ oz. dried ginger
1 oz. saffron	2 oz. Bengal gram
1 oz. pepper	¼ cup butter or ghee

METHOD

Buy the ingredients already ground. Pass through a fine muslin sieve and mix into a thick paste with butter or ghee and vinegar; then bottle. This will make about 25 dessertspoonful. Bengal gram, a type of large pea, may be bought from any store specializing in curry ingredients. In India, curry ingredients are always made up fresh, and used in paste form.

A Word About Fats

IN India ghee and mustard oil are—or were—the two main cooking fats. Ghee is clarified butter; that is, butter treated with steam to remove impurities. It tastes quite different from butter.

Mustard oil (grocer's) must always be heated till a wisp of blue smoke rises from its surface before adding ingredients.

For the best results, use ghee, butter, mustard oil or olive oil; but lard, dripping, peanut, coconut or soya-bean oil are all permissible. If you find the quantities given too much, use less.

LAMB-RICE BIRIANEE (For the Beginner)

As beginners are often baffled by curry recipes Mrs. Cynthia Wixey (now in England), who learnt the art in India, has devised a simple recipe to ensure success the very first time.

INGREDIENTS

1 lb. lamb	1 large onion
2 cups Patna rice	10 oz. 'natural' or unflavoured yogurt
1 cup boiled peas (canned *garden* peas will do)	1½ teaspoons of salt
2 tablespoons good curry powder such as Bolst's,	1 teaspoon garlic salt
Halford's or Vengatachellum's, which	2 tablespoons Cookeen, ghee,
can be bought almost anywhere	butter, or cooking oil

METHOD

Place the rice in a deep pan, cover with water and boil till the grains are soft if felt with the fingers, but not squashy. Now drain the rice in a colander and pour two cups of cold water over it to separate the grains.

Melt the cooking fat in another pan; chop the onion and fry it till golden brown. Add the curry powder, salt, and garlic salt mixed in a cup of water, add to the onions and fat and cook for three or four minutes.

Cut the lamb into cubes, put into the fat and water, and fry till thoroughly tender. The water will soon evaporate. Then add the yogurt and mix thoroughly. Cook till lamb is tender, and if more water is needed, add a little.

Now put the rice into a large casserole, then some curry mixture, and then some peas. Keep some rice apart, so that the top layer can be one of rice. Sprinkle with water, cover and place in a warm oven for 25 minutes, till rice is tender. Chicken may be used instead of lamb.

Mrs. Cynthia Wixey,
30 Litherland,
Sale,
Cheshire.

PANCH PHORA

Curry spices are not necessarily used as powder that has been roasted or made into paste. Nor need curries be in the least bit pungent.

Many curries are made with *panch phora*. *Panch* means five: the Punjab, a word derived from *panch,* five, and *ab*, river, means the land of five rivers, Jhelum, Beas, Ravi, Chenab and Sutlej, which combine to form the Indus. *Panch phora* is a combination of five spices in equal quantities. The most popular are: mustard seed, aniseed, cummin, cassia leaves and red chillis; and cummin, fenugreek, aniseed, mustard seed, and black cummin.

Panch phora need not be ground; more often than not it isn't, but one or two teaspoons are added to chopped or diced vegetables. The usual method is to slice an onion or two finely, fry in fat, add vegetables and *panch phora*, cover with water and simmer till the vegetables are soft. Then eat with either rice or poorees, with or without pickle or chutney.

Panch phora, if added to stews or plain boiled vegetables, will give them a distinctive aroma and a pleasant unusual flavour. Many who never accustom themselves either to the richness or pungency of curries like the addition of *panch phora* to their food.

Here are two recipes for vegetable dishes which specify *panch phora* as an ingredient.

POTATO FRITTERS

INGREDIENTS

Cold potato, left over from a meal may be used.	$\frac{1}{2}$ teaspoon baking powder
2 heaped tablespoons mashed potato	1 teaspoon green chillis, chopped
2 tablespoons minced cold meat	1 dessertspoon onion, finely sliced
1 tablespoon butter or cooking fat	3 eggs
1 teaspoon minced vinegar pickle or	1 tablespoon milk
1 heaped teaspoon **panch phora**	Pepper, nutmeg and salt for seasoning

METHOD

Beat the eggs thoroughly, then mix in all the ingredients except the butter or cooking fat.

When the fat is very hot, drop in a dessertspoon of the mixture, and when light brown on both sides, remove and drain in a wire basket. The fritters are tastier when **panch phora** is used instead of pickle, and the amount of **panch phora** may be increased if you wish.

These quantities make about 16 fritters and form a tasty supper snack on a cold winter's night.

BAKED TOMATOES

INGREDIENTS

6 very large tomatoes	2 tablespoons breadcrumbs
2 eggs	1 medium size onion
1 teaspoon tarragon	1 teaspoon **panch phora**
3 or 4 cloves of garlic	1 teaspoon turmeric
4 oz. butter or cooking fat	

METHOD

Slice the tops off the tomatoes and put the tops aside.

Scoop out the insides and put it into a bowl. Chop finely the onion and garlic and mix with the breadcrumb, **panch phora, tarragon** and **turmeric**; then whip the eggs and add them and the crumb mixture together. Mix thoroughly and stuff into the tomatoes. Put on the tomato lids, and if any mixture is over, pour over the top. Bake in a medium oven for an hour in the cooking fat.

MEAT, GAME, EGG CURRIES

CHICKEN CURRY

INGREDIENTS

1 chicken, jointed	1 two-in. stick of cinnamon
2 onions, finely sliced	*1 dessertspoon ground coriander
4 cloves garlic, sliced	*½ teaspoon ground turmeric
2 oz. cooking fat	½ teaspoon ground ginger
2 cardamoms	½ teaspoon ground cummin
2 cloves	½ teaspoon ground chillis (or less)
Salt, to taste	

METHOD

Fry onions, garlic, cloves, cardamoms and cinnamon in fat and when onions are golden-brown, add other ingredients.

Mix well and cook on low flame for 5 minutes. Then add pieces of chicken and fry in curry mixture, stirring occasionally to prevent burning.

Add enough water to form thick gravy, then cover pan and simmer till chicken is soft. Squeeze lemon juice over the curry before serving.

Enough for six

* NOTE. Here, and throughout the book, the use of the word 'spoon' implies a FLAT, and not a heaped, spoonful; similarly '½ spoon' indicates half a flat measure.

CHICKEN CURRY WITH GREENS

INGREDIENTS

1 chicken, jointed	2 oz. cooking fat
2 onions, finely chopped	1 dessertspoon curry paste
2 tomatoes, finely sliced	2 cardamoms
2 cloves garlic, finely sliced	2 cloves
1 two-in. stick cinnamon	1 dessertspoon ground almonds
(1 teaspoon of poppy seed may be used instead of almonds)	

Fry onions, garlic, tomatoes and spices in cooking fat. Then add curry paste and ground almonds. Mix thoroughly and continue to fry for 5 minutes. Add pieces of chicken and mix again. Then cover pan and simmer gently for 10–15 minutes, making sure that the contents do not burn. If too dry, add a little water. Finally, add a pound of spinach or other greens (well washed and drained), and mixing occasionally, simmer till chicken is soft. Salt to taste.

Enough for six

LAMB, BEEF OR CHICKEN CURRY (DRY)

INGREDIENTS

1 chicken, jointed; or 1½ lb. lamb or beef	2 dessertspoons curry paste
3 onions, finely chopped	1 dessertspoon tomato paste or purée
2 cloves garlic, finely chopped	2 oz. cooking fat

METHOD

Fry onions and garlic lightly in fat for 4 minutes. Add curry paste as well as tomato paste, and fry for 4 minutes more. Now add chicken (or lamb or beef); beef or lamb must be cut into cubes. Mix well, cover pan with close-fitting lid and simmer till chicken (or meat) is tender.

Watch contents to prevent burning, and if this seems likely add a *little* water. Shortly before serving, add salt and lemon juice as well as a tablespoon of desiccated coconut, which will quickly absorb any excess of gravy.

Enough for six

COLD POULTRY OR GAME CURRY

INGREDIENTS

Legs of cold poultry or game	1 tablespoon curry powder
2 onions, finely chopped	OR 2 tablespoons curry paste
½ teaspoon chopped garlic	Heaped dessertspoon tomato paste or purée
2 oz. fat	Pinch salt
Juice of a lemon	

METHOD

The legs of cold chicken, duck, turkey or geese (or other game) may be used for this dish. First make a thick sauce from the following ingredients; then add the game and gradually heat up the dish.

Fry 2 finely chopped onions and ½ teaspoon of chopped garlic in 2 oz. fat, till golden brown. To this add a tablespoon of curry powder, or if a rich curry is preferred, 2 dessert-

15

spoons of curry paste. Blend thoroughly with onions and garlic and cook for 5 minutes. Now mix in well a heaped dessertspoon of tomato paste or purée, and thin down with a little water. This makes a rich sauce. Add salt and the juice of a lemon and simmer for 10 minutes before putting in the legs of poultry or game.

The legs of a single chicken will make enough for one person.

DUCK AND GREEN PEA CURRY

INGREDIENTS

1 duck cut into convenient pieces	4 cloves of garlic, finely minced
1 breakfast cup of green peas	2 large onions, finely minced
½ lb. tomatoes	2 dessertspoons curry powder
2 oz. cooking fat	Juice of a lemon

METHOD

Fry onions and garlic for 5 minutes in cooking fat, till golden. Add curry powder, mix well and continue to cook for 4 minutes more over a low flame. Peel and chop tomatoes and put them in, together with about a pint of water—less rather than more. Mix well and add pieces of duck, then cover pan and cook slowly till duck is tender. Now add green peas and simmer for 15 minutes on a slow fire. Add salt to taste and squeeze in the juice of a lemon.

Enough for six

KEEMA CURRY

INGREDIENTS

1 lb. finely minced beef or mutton	1 teaspoon tomato purée
Two cloves of garlic	OR 3 large fresh tomatoes
2 oz. cooking fat	1 tablespoon yogurt OR 1 5-oz. bottle
1 tablespoon curry powder	1 small onion

METHOD

Mince finely two cloves garlic and one small onion, and fry for 4 minutes in 2 oz. cooking fat, till golden. To this add one tablespoon of curry powder and one teaspoon of tomato purée, or three large fresh tomatoes, finely sliced. Mix thoroughly and cook mixture on a fairly high flame for 3–4 minutes more; then add 1 lb. finely minced fresh beef or mutton and a tablespoon of yogurt (one 5 oz. bottle if you like), or milk that has curdled and turned almost solid. Mix well and cook slowly till done, which should be in about an hour and a quarter. This curry should not be quite dry, but fairly moist, though there should not be any gravy.

Enough for four

KEEMA AND LETTUCE CURRY

INGREDIENTS

½ lb. finely minced meat of any kind, free of skin and fat

2 cloves garlic, finely chopped

1 large onion, finely chopped

1 oz. cooking fat

2 large fresh tomatoes

1 dessertspoon ground coriander

½ teaspoon ground turmeric

½ teaspoon ground ginger

½ teaspoon ground cummin

½ teaspoon ground chillis

1 small lettuce

METHOD

Fry onion and garlic in cooking fat till golden in colour. Add tomatoes, quartered or sliced; they provide the necessary moisture and flavour. Add ground spices, mix thoroughly and cook for from 5–7 minutes over good flame. Then shred a small lettuce coarsely and mix it into curry. Simmer for 10 minutes, add meat and salt, and when meat is well cooked through and soft, the keema is ready.

Enough for two

KOBI KEEMA (Cabbage and Mince)

INGREDIENTS

1 lb. minced meat

1 small cabbage

1 teaspoon salt

2 oz. fat

2 onions, finely chopped

2 cloves garlic, finely chopped

½ teaspoon ground chilli

¼ teaspoon ground turmeric

¼ teaspoon ground coriander

¼ teaspoon ground cummin

Pinch each of ground cloves and cinnamon

½ teaspoon ground ginger

METHOD

Fry onions in fat till light brown. Add mince and all the spices, including garlic and salt. Stir well and cook for 30 minutes. Don't add water. Shred cabbage and add to mince; cook till cabbage is tender. Alternatively, either aubergine or cauliflower may be used instead of cabbage.

Enough for two or three

PORK VINDALOO (pronounced vin-dá-loo)

INGREDIENTS

1 lb. fat pork, cut into inch cubes

4 cloves garlic, finely chopped

2 large onions, finely chopped

2 tablespoons vindaloo paste

2 tablespoons vinegar

2 oz. cooking fat and salt to taste

17

METHOD

Put the fat into stewpan with onions and garlic. Cook till onions begin to change colour, then add vindaloo paste and vinegar. Stir well and cook for 4 minutes on a slow fire, making sure that the contents do not burn. Now add the pork and mix the whole thoroughly. Then cover pan with well-fitting lid and cook over a low flame till pork is tender. This dish needs constant watching, and if necessary a little water can be added to form a rich gravy. Salt to taste.

Enough for four

MADRAS BEEF CURRY

INGREDIENTS

1 lb. beef cut into 1–1½ inch cubes	1 oz. cooking fat
2 cloves garlic, finely chopped	1 tablespoon curry powder
2 onions, finely chopped	2 teaspoons salt
2 dry (red) chillis, with seeds removed, finely chopped	Juice of lemon
1 dessertspoon tomato paste or purée,	3 potatoes, diced (optional)
or 4 fresh tomatoes peeled and sliced	

METHOD

Fry chopped ingredients in fat for four minutes, then add curry powder. Stir and fry for 4 minutes more. Add meat, mix well and cook for 10 minutes longer. Then add paste, purée or fresh tomatoes and ½ pint of water. Cover pan, bring mixture to the boil and simmer gently till meat is tender—about 1¼ hours, when the gravy should thicken. Add salt and juice of a lemon. Diced potatoes may be added half an hour after meat is put in.

Enough for four

BEEF AND DHALL CURRY

INGREDIENTS

1 lb. lean beef cut into 1½–2 inch pieces	1 dessertspoon curry powder
2 dry (red) chillis with seeds removed	¼ lb. lentils
2 cloves garlic, finely chopped	2 cloves
2 large onions, finely chopped	2 oz. ghee
Vinegar	1 1-inch stick of cinnamon
1 dessertspoon tomato paste	Salt

METHOD

Fry garlic, onion and spices lightly in ghee for 7 minutes then add curry powder and cook for 5 minutes more. Mix in tomato paste, add meat and cook for 4 minutes. Then boil lentils till soft and add water in which they've been boiled. Bring the whole to the boil, cover pan and simmer gently till meat is nearly cooked (about 1 hour). Now add parboiled

18

lentils, and a teaspoon each of vinegar and salt. Cover pan and continue to cook till meat is tender and lentils have disintegrated, when the dish will be ready to serve.

Enough for four

PORK OR BEEF KORMA

INGREDIENTS

1 lb. pork or beef cut into 1–1½ inch cubes	5 large ripe tomatoes, halved
3 onions, finely sliced	½ teaspoon ground ginger
4 cloves garlic, finely sliced	¼ teaspoon ground black pepper
¼ teaspoon ground cummin	12 cloves
2–3 1 inch sticks cinnamon	6–7 cardamoms
3–4 bay leaves	4 oz. cooking fat or mustard oil, but *not* lard
2 five-oz. bottles plain yogurt	

METHOD

Fry onions and garlic in cooking fat or oil till golden brown. Put the meat into pan, mix and let it simmer till the whole is a nice, rich brown. Add half a cup of water together with ginger, pepper, cummin seed, cloves, cardamoms, cinnamon, bay leaves and tomatoes. Bring to the boil, then simmer over a low flame till meat is soft. If you like, add a few small, unpeeled potatoes, well scrubbed. Now pour in yogurt and mix occasionally to prevent the korma from burning. The dish is ready when the meat is soft.

Enough for four

AK-NI KORMA

INGREDIENTS

1 lb. lean mutton	2 cardamoms
1 large onion cut in thick slices	½ teaspoon cummin seed
¼ oz. coriander powder	1 oz. butter
¼ oz. green ginger	1 bottle plain yogurt
4 cloves garlic	½ teaspoon saffron
1 1-inch stick cinnamon	2 teaspoons salt
2 cloves	

AK-NI SPICES: (¼ oz. fennel seed; ¼ oz. green ginger; 4 cloves garlic; ¼ oz. coriander seed; 1 small onion).

METHOD

Cut meat into 1½-in. cubes; place in pan with 1 pint of water. Put Ak-Ni spices into small muslin bag, and add. Boil meat and spices till well cooked. Meat must be tender and water reduced to about ½ pint. Now brown onion in butter and to it add spices and yogurt. Fry for 10 minutes; then put in meat and Ak-Ni liquid. Mix saffron into thin paste with boiling water and sprinkle over. Add salt. After Ak-Ni spices have been well boiled, the bag should be removed ånd discarded.

Enough for four

19

POTATO CHOPS

INGREDIENTS

Cold meat

Onion

Salt and pepper

½ teaspoon ground cummin seed

Chopped red or green chillis

A pinch of turmeric and saffron (optional)

Juice of a lemon

Cooking fat or dripping

Egg and breadcrumbs (for coating)

METHOD

This is a tasty supper dish and a favourite among the Anglo-Indian community in India. It is also an easy way of using cold meat that is left over from a 'Sunday joint'.

Mince any cold meat that is available. Add to it about half as much finely chopped onion. Season with salt, black pepper, chopped red or green chillis or chilli powder (½ teaspoon to a pound of meat), half a teaspoon of ground cummin seed and a pinch of turmeric or saffron (optional). Squeeze in the juice of a lemon and mix well.

Place a dessertspoon of the mixture on a thick layer of cold mashed potato and cover with another layer of mashed potato. Press top and bottom layers together and join the edges so that meat and onion mixture is perfectly sealed. Sprinkle with flour, brush with beaten egg and coat with breadcrumbs. Fry in hot dripping and serve with parsley.

If ½ lb. meat is used, enough for two

VADAIS

INGREDIENTS

1 breakfast cup red lentils

½ teaspoon salt

2 large onions, finely sliced

1 teaspoon turmeric

4 green chillis, chopped

1 egg

METHOD

Throw lentils into half a pan of boiling water, add turmeric and boil briskly till lentils are soft. Now put in raw onion, chillis and beaten egg. Mix well, form into little cakes and fry in boiling fat. N.B. One large breakfastcup of lentils will absorb, completely, about a pint of water. Use less water rather than more, and watch lentils while boiling as they are apt to stick to the pan. Keep stirring.

Enough for two

JHAL FARAZI (Dry)

INGREDIENTS

¼ lb. cold meat from Sunday's joint

6 peppercorns, finely ground

½ teaspoon ground chillis or powder

1 teaspoon salt

2 oz. butter or fat

½ lb. potatoes

1 large onion, finely chopped

20

METHOD

Fry onions lightly in butter or cooking fat. Dice meat and potatoes and fold in. Add salt, ground peppercorns and chilli powder and mix well. Fry till almost dry.

Enough for two

JHAL FARAZI (With Gravy)

METHOD

If Jhal Farazi with gravy is wanted, take the same amounts as above of meat and potatoes, onion, peppercorns and chillis, and as well a ¼ teaspoon powdered ginger and 3 cloves of garlic.

Mash onion, garlic and other spices together with pestle and mortar. This prevents the onion from frying crisply and helps to form the gravy.

When butter is hot, put in one sliced onion and cook till brown. If the concoction is too dry, add a cupful of vegetable or meat stock. Add garlic, ginger, peppercorns, onion, and chilli powder—all mashed together—and cook for 10 minutes more. Now add diced meat and potatoes, and when the potatoes are cooked, the dish is ready.

This is an infinitely more appetizing dish than the eternal cold meat and pickles eaten for supper in thousands of British homes on Mondays and Tuesdays.

Enough for two

KOAFTAH CURRY

INGREDIENTS

1 lb. meat finely minced   4 cloves garlic finely minced

1 onion finely minced

METHOD

A pinch each of black pepper, ground cinnamon, ground cloves, ground cardamoms, and 2 green chillis finely chopped. Also, 2 boiled potatoes, medium size, well mashed—and 1 teaspoon salt.

Blend these ingredients together with an egg and a pinch of salt.

With lightly floured hands, form the meat into balls the size of an apricot. Fry these to a light brown in cooking fat, then drain away fat. Now, using some of the drained fat, fry a large finely chopped onion and 3 finely chopped tomatoes. To this add:

1 teaspoon ground coriander   ½ teaspoon ground cummin seed

½ teaspoon ground turmeric   ½ teaspoon ground ginger

¼ teaspoon ground chillis

Cook these ingredients lightly for 5 minutes, and to the mixture add a cup of thin coconut milk, ¼ teaspoon salt and a generous squeeze of lemon juice.

Now put the balls of meat into this mixture and simmer gently for half an hour, shaking the pan (not violently, for the balls may break up) from time to time to ensure that they do not stick or burn.

This recipe may appear a trifle complicated, but koaftah curry is quite simple to make and is a universal favourite all over India and Pakistan. You will find it well worth the trouble.

Enough for four

HARA MIRCHA (CAPSICUM) CURRY

Though capsicum is a member of the chilli family, it has none of its biting pungency, and large green capsicums are ideal for stuffing with meat.

INGREDIENTS

6 large green capsicums	1 dessertspoon ground coriander
1 lb. minced meat (any kind)	2 oz. butter or cooking fat
2 small green chillis	6 cloves
1 oz. green ginger	6 cardamoms
2 large onions	Salt
6 cloves garlic	1 teaspoon cummin

METHOD

Butter (unsalted) is always preferable to cooking fat for dishes that are entirely vegetable, but if too costly, use cooking fat.

Slice ginger, onions and chillis and brown in butter. Then add mince, coriander, cardamoms, cloves, cummin and salt to taste, and fry.

Mash garlic, mix it into a cup of water and sprinkle over the cooking spices. Cook till the mince is soft; then place the mixture on one side.

Wash capsicums and split carefully down one side; then stuff with mince, and close. Place in a buttered baking tin or casserole (line tin or casserole with dripping if you prefer) and cook for 15 minutes in pre-heated, slow oven. This dish is always better hot than cold. Aubergines, pumpkins and very large tomatoes may be stuffed in the same way.

Enough for four

COUNTRY CAPTAIN

INGREDIENTS

1 chicken, jointed	3 green or red chillis
Cooking fat or dripping	Pinch of black pepper
5 or 6 slices of green ginger	1 teaspoon salt
1 large onion, finely sliced	

METHOD

The name of this curry is somewhat misleading, for the word 'captain' is obviously a corruption of 'capon'. But that is what it is called by Moslem cooks throughout the country.

Fry a jointed chicken in a little fat till light brown. Remove the pieces of chicken and in

22

Curry Ingredients
(See page 9)

the same fat fry 5 or 6 slices of green ginger, a large finely sliced onion, and 3 green or red chillis cut lengthwise. Add a pinch of black pepper.

Now put in the chicken and just enough water for it to cook till tender. Add salt.

Enough for four

KHARI MOORGHI (Parsee Chicken Curry)

INGREDIENTS

1 jointed chicken	4 slices fresh ginger, finely chopped
4 medium-sized onions, finely chopped	3 oz. fat
4 cloves garlic, finely chopped	½ teaspoon chilli powder
5 tomatoes, finely chopped	2 teaspoons salt
4 green chillis cut lengthwise	

METHOD

Fry the onions to a golden brown and to them add the tomatoes, garlic and ginger. When the mixture is well browned, add the pieces of chicken, ground chilli, salt and a breakfast cup of water. When the chicken is tender, add the green chillis, and if you wish, a cupful of fried potato chips. But this is optional. Cook fairly fast for 3 or 4 minutes, then serve.

Enough for six

EGG CURRY

INGREDIENTS

6 eggs	½ teaspoon ground cummin
2 onions, finely chopped	½ teaspoon ground chilli
2 cloves garlic, finely chopped	¼ teaspoon ground turmeric
2 green chillis	½ oz. tamarind
½ teaspoon ground coriander	3 tomatoes, sliced

METHOD

The tamarind is necessary as it lends a piquancy to the curry that cannot be obtained otherwise.

Fry the onions in 2 oz. cooking fat and when lightly browned add tomatoes, garlic and other ingredients—except tamarind. Cook over a low flame with one cup of water for 7–10 minutes.

Put tamarind in half a cupful of water and mix thoroughly. Squeeze and break it up with a spoon. Then drain the juice through a fine muslin and discard the residue. Add the tamarind juice to the gravy and salt to taste.

Now break the eggs, one at a time, into the gravy and simmer for 3 minutes, till they are set; but do not stir.

An alternative method is to hard-boil the eggs, cut them into halves and cook them gently in the gravy. *Enough for three*

N.B. In this, as in other recipes where chillis are used, it is advisable, if curries have never been eaten before, to put in rather less than the amount mentioned, and to discard the seeds of red chillis. If the curry is not hot enough, more chilli can be added, but it is as well to err on the side of caution.

ALOO ANDA (Egg on Potatoes)

INGREDIENTS

4 eggs	2 oz. fat
1 lb. potatoes	½ teaspoon ground chilli
2 onions, finely chopped	¼ teaspoon ground turmeric

METHOD

Fry the onions in fat for 4 minutes and add potatoes cut into small pieces, together with chilli powder and turmeric. Cook till potatoes are tender. Break the eggs into a bowl and beat thoroughly, then pour them on to the potatoes and cook till the egg is light brown in colour. Add salt to taste.

Enough for two

ALOO MUTTER (Potatoes with Peas)

INGREDIENTS

1 lb. green peas	½ teaspoon ground chilli
½ lb. potatoes	¼ teaspoon ground turmeric
2 onions	¼ teaspoon ground coriander
2 tomatoes	¼ teaspoon ground cummin
2 oz. cooking fat	2 teaspoons salt

METHOD

Fry the onions to a golden brown, then add tomatoes and fry for 4 minutes more. Now put in the potatoes, peas and all the spices, with salt. Simmer over a low flame till the peas are tender, by which time, of course, the potatoes will also be done.

If tinned peas are used, it is as well to use the processed variety, which do not break up under prolonged cooking as do the garden variety.

This makes a simple and tasty supper dish for three or four people, and should be eaten with either chappattis or parrattas.

ANDA JHEENGA CURRY

INGREDIENTS

4 hard-boiled eggs cut lengthwise into halves	2 green chillis cut lengthwise
12 prawns, large, if possible—cooked	1 teaspoon curry powder
1 teaspoon salt	1 dessertspoon tomato paste
4 cloves garlic, finely chopped	The juice of a lemon
2 onions, finely chopped	1 oz. thick coconut milk

METHOD

Fry onions, garlic and chilli lightly in fat for 4 minutes. Add curry powder and tomato paste. Stir thoroughly and cook slowly for six minutes more. Thin this mixture down to a thickish gravy by adding a little water; then simmer gently, add salt and lemon juice, the coconut milk, and finally, the eggs and prawns.

The gravy must be thick enough to adhere to the eggs.

The cocnut milk (or 'coconut cream' as it is called in the shops that sell curry ingredients) is *most* necessary, as it makes all the difference in the world to the flavour.

Enough for four

FISH CURRIES

For some reason beyond our comprehension fish, except when eaten with chips out of a newspaper on a rainy night, in company with a number of convivial souls, is not regarded with favour by the British male.

Most rugged Britons, in short, regard fish as a somewhat emasculate dish. No body in it. Fish, they feel, puts the finishing touch to a high tea or supper, but should never be the *pièce de résistance* of any dinner. Not solid enough; too many bones; no taste. And when it is eaten in British homes, fish is usually swamped by tomato ketchup, or sweet chutney.

Let us then dispose of the first charge laid at its door, that fish, having 'no body'—that is, not being as tough as leather—lacks nutrition.

Average sea fish contains 18 per cent protein, the same amount as that contained in beef. Protein is that part of food that repairs wear and tear. There are 60 parts of mineral matter in every thousand of fish, and only 41 in beef. It is these 'trace elements'—potash, sodium, calcium, manganese, iron, phosphorus, sulphur, silicon, chlorine, and fluorine—that enrich the blood, build strong bones and teeth and give us the resistance to keep disease at bay.

Not long ago an American dental surgeon, Dr Weston Price, toured the world to find out what people ate and what it is that keeps them fit. He discovered that where people ate a good deal of sea fish, which is rich in oil, and wholemeal flour instead of white, they had splendid teeth. In Britain he found the strongest and most perfect teeth in the Hebrides, where only 1·3 per cent of the children had dental caries. How different is this from Derbyshire, where 85 per cent of the children are sadly in need of dental treatment, and Lancashire where the percentage is no less than 78!

The crofters in the Hebrides live mainly on herrings, cod and oats grown in soil fertilized by smoke-impregnated thatch. And fish oil, incidentally, is the finest known source of vitamin D—apart from direct sunshine.

So don't run away with the idea that fish as a food is fit only for women and weaklings!

Some of the toughest people in the world are seafarers and those who live in coastal areas—despised fish-eaters. Coastal Indians are no exception to the rule. But for centuries they have curried their fish and so transformed it into food fit for the gods.

You can do likewise with cod and humble herring, which weight for weight and in proportion to its price, is the finest food on the British table. If only herrings were a guinea a pound, there would be a mad scramble for them at the Ritz.

Those who know their curries swear that there is no food to touch fish cooked with the spices of the East and blended with coconut milk. In India, fish is also curried with bamboo shoots—another succulent dish.

We feel sure, however, that when you have taken the trouble to compound your spices, have impregnated the fish with them as instructed, and cooked it gently in coconut milk, you will agree that it stands in a class on its own.

Fish curries—and this is a point in their favour in a country where the housewife has so little leisure and so much to do—have the advantage of being the quickest of all to make.

KHARI MACHHLI

This is a fish curry that can be prepared from either halibut, turbot, plaice or mullet.

INGREDIENTS

2 lb. of any of the above fish, sliced	½ teaspoon ground chilli
2 large onions, sliced	¼ teaspoon ground turmeric
4 cloves garlic, sliced	½ teaspoon ground coriander
2 oz. cooking fat	¼ teaspoon ground mustard
½ teaspoon ground ginger or 6 slices of ginger	1 dessertspoon tomato purée

METHOD

Fry the fish in fat for 2–3 minutes and then remove from the pan. In the same fat, fry onions, garlic and ginger to a golden brown. Now add the tomato purée and other spices, including salt, and gently pour on ½ cup of water. Allow the whole to simmer till the gravy is well blended, then add fish and cook slowly for 4 minutes before serving.

Enough for four

MACHHLI KA SALNA

INGREDIENTS

Fillets of fish	1 teaspoon of curry powder
2 onions	1 dessertspoon tomato purée
2 cloves of garlic	OR ½ lb. fresh chopped tomatoes
2 oz. fat	½ cup of water

METHOD

Finely chop 2 onions and 2 cloves of garlic and fry lightly in 2 oz. of fat. To this add one teaspoon of curry powder and stir over a brisk flame for four minutes. Now put in either one dessertspoon of tomato purée or ½ lb. fresh, chopped tomatoes. Stir and cook for four minutes more. Then pour in half a cup of water to form a thickish gravy, and bring to the boil. Into this slide fillets or slices of fish (of any kind), and cook till done. Once the fish is in, don't stir, but agitate the pan gently to prevent fish sticking to the bottom.

Four fillets will provide a dish for four

MACHHLI KA BHUJNA (Bombay Fish Curry)

INGREDIENTS

2 lb. of any kind of fish, sliced or filleted	½ pint coconut milk
2 oz. fat	1 teaspoon rice flour
2 cloves garlic, sliced	1 onion, chopped
1 teaspoon ground coriander	½ teaspoon ground turmeric
½ teaspoon ground chilli	½ teaspoon ground mustard seed
Juice of 1 lemon	2 dried chillis cut lengthwise, with seeds removed

METHOD

Brown the onion lightly in fat and add to it garlic, chilli and ground spices. Mix coconut milk with a teaspoon of rice flour and pour in. Squeeze in the juice of a lemon and add salt. Cook over a low flame till mixture thickens, then slide in the fish and cover it with the curry sauce. The curry is ready as soon as the fish is tender. *Enough for four*

HINDUSTAN FRIED FISH

INGREDIENTS

2 lb. of fish	4 cloves of garlic
1 teaspoon ground chillis	Wholemeal flour or bread crumbs (for coating)
½ teaspoon ground turmeric	Cooking fat or dripping

METHOD

Mix thoroughly 1 teaspoon of ground chillis, ½ teaspoon of ground turmeric, and 4 cloves of garlic finely minced. It is better to place the garlic in bowl and press to pulp with a fork or spoon and then, mixed with chilli and turmeric, a thickish paste can be formed. Rub this paste thoroughly over and into the fish and allow it to stand for 30–45 minutes. Then the fish will be well impregnated. This done, dip each piece of fish into either wholemeal flour or breadcrumbs and fry in either very hot fat or oil. This dish is far more acceptable to the Indian palate when fried in mustard oil, which gives it a distinctive flavour.

All who like a tasty supper tit-bit find this a welcome alternative to the usual boiled or fried fish done in batter.

Two pounds of fish will provide enough for four

DRY BOMBAY DUCK AND BRINJAL CURRY (Boomla Begga Ka Salna)

Bombay duck bears no relation to the fowls of the air. It is a species of cured fish, popular not only in Bombay but in every corner of India, and over here tins or packets of Bombay duck may be bought anywhere in shops that specialize in Indian spices and chutneys. Don't be put off by the smell of Bombay duck. When cooked, the transformation is complete. Don't be like the Englishman, who when told it was 'cured' fish, exclaimed: 'Cured! Why, it seems to me that it's been dead a long time!'

Brinjal is the Indian name for aubergine.

INGREDIENTS

1 brinjal cut lengthwise in half and then crosswise in slices, each slice about an inch thick	$\frac{1}{2}$ teaspoon salt
	12 pieces Bombay duck
2 tablespoons desiccated coconut	4 cloves garlic, finely sliced
1 large onion, finely sliced	$\frac{1}{2}$ teaspoon ground turmeric
1 teaspoon ground coriander	$\frac{1}{4}$ teaspoon ground chilli
$\frac{1}{2}$ teaspoon ground cummin	Juice of lemon

METHOD

Fry the onion and garlic till well browned in 3 tablespoons of good oil, preferably mustard, which can be bought for that purpose. Don't buy the embrocation type of mustard oil from the chemist, but that meant for cooking purposes from a curry shop!

Add all spices except coconut and cook for 5 minutes more. Then slip in the slices of brinjal and $\frac{1}{2}$ pint of water. Salt to taste. Simmer till the brinjal is cooked. It is done when a sharp knife slides easily through the flesh. Now add 12 pieces of Bombay duck, each cut into four. Put in the coconut, squeeze the juice of a lemon over the concoction and cook for 5 minutes before serving.

One large aubergine will make enough for two

ALOO KOLBI

INGREDIENTS

2 lb. prawns, shelled	2 large onions finely chopped
3 large potatoes	2 green chillis cut lengthwise
$\frac{1}{4}$ teaspoon ground chilli	4 tomatoes cut into small pieces
$\frac{1}{4}$ teaspoon ground turmeric	4 cloves garlic, finely chopped
2 tablespoons desiccated coconut	1 teaspoon salt

METHOD

Brown onions and garlic in 2 oz. fat and put in tomatoes. Add a cup of water and all the spices except coconut. Salt and simmer for 4 minutes. Now drop in potatoes, chillis and prawns and cook till the potatoes are done. Add the coconut, stir, simmer gently and serve. If potatoes are well scrubbed and their skins clear, don't peel. Some think their flavour is improved this way.

Enough for six

PRAWN OR LOBSTER MOLEE

INGREDIENTS

1 lobster or 2 lb. of prawns, shelled	3 fresh or dried chillis, cut lengthwise, then in halves
2 oz. fat	
1 large onion, chopped	6 thin slices fresh or pickled ginger
4 cloves of garlic, sliced	$\frac{1}{2}$ pint thick coconut milk
$\frac{1}{4}$ teaspoon ground turmeric	1 teaspoon salt

28

METHOD

Fry onions and garlic to a golden brown. Add turmeric, ginger, coconut milk and chillis. Simmer for 10 minutes and add salt. Then mix in as many prawns or as much lobster as will be covered by the amount of curried sauce, and cook gently for 10 minutes more. The pan must not be covered during cooking.

Enough for six

TURBOT, HALIBUT OR SALMON, WITH SPINACH

INGREDIENTS

½ lb. of any of the above fish, cut into slices	½ teaspoon ground chilli
4 cloves garlic	¼ teaspoon ground cummin
2 lb. fresh spinach well washed and chopped	A pinch of ground cloves
2 oz. fat	¼ teaspoon ground turmeric
1 teaspoon salt	¼ teaspoon ground coriander
2 large onions, sliced	A pinch of ground cinnamon
4 large tomatoes cut into quarters	

METHOD

Fry onions, garlic and tomatoes lightly. When well blended, add all spices, including salt. Cook on a low flame for 4 minutes, then add spinach and cook for 10 minutes more. Now put in the fish and continue cooking till it is soft enough to be eaten. Do not stir the pan but shake gently to prevent burning and sticking.

Enough for two

PICKLED FISH

INGREDIENTS

2 lb. halibut, turbot, salmon or prawns	4 tablespoons olive oil
2 teaspoons ground chilli	½ teaspoon mustard seed
1 teaspoon ground turmeric	½ teaspoon fenugreek seed
¼ teaspoon salt	Pinch of asafoetida
Juice of 4 lemons	

METHOD

Fish pickled according to these instructions will keep in perfect condition for a fortnight, and in very cold weather for much longer. This dish must not be confused with pickle, as such, and it makes an excellent adjunct to boiled rice and dhall curry.

2 lb. halibut, turbot, salmon or prawns. Fish must be cut into small pieces, about 2 inches square; prawns must be shelled.

Make a paste consisting of 2 teaspoons ground chilli, 1 teaspoon ground turmeric, ¼ teaspoon salt and the juice of 4 lemons. Rub this well over the fish and let it soak in for 2–3 hours.

Pour 4 tablespoons of olive oil into a pan and heat it. To this add the whole mustard seed; $\frac{1}{2}$ teaspoon of whole fenugreek seed and a pinch of asafoetida. The whole seeds will make a popping noise in the hot oil. Put in the pieces of impregnated fish and cook for 15 minutes, when it will be ready to serve.

Enough for four

KOLBI PATIA (Prawn Curry, Parsee Style)

INGREDIENTS

$\frac{1}{2}$ lb. prawns	$\frac{1}{2}$ teaspoon ground ginger
2 large onions, finely sliced	$\frac{1}{4}$ teaspoon ground chilli
2 large tomatoes or one dessertspoon	$\frac{1}{4}$ teaspoon ground turmeric
tomato purée	4 green chillis cut lengthwise
4 cloves garlic, finely chopped	2 oz. fat
6 pieces fresh ginger, chopped	1 teaspoon salt

METHOD

Fry onions in fat till golden brown, then add fresh tomatoes (or puree), garlic and ginger. Cook for 10 minutes over a low flame. If too dry, add $\frac{1}{2}$ cupful of water; then put in prawns, ground spices and green chillis. Cook for 10 minutes and salt to taste. This is best eaten with boiled rice and Bombay duck. Bombay duck may be grilled or baked, but must be crisp and crumbly.

Enough for two

RICE DISHES

THE mention of rice to an Englishman calls to mind rice pudding, which can be creamy and delicious, but is more often than not a glutinous mess surrounded by a dark brown crust ornamented by a blob of red jam. Alternatively it is eaten with prunes, also boiled.

Rice rarely conjures up an attractive vision; nor does the picture automatically set the salivary glands to work. One's mouth never waters for rice pudding served in the average English café. It is a sweet over which few people linger.

This is, of course, in keeping with the modern tradition of 'canned cookery', frozen food and the stern English character through which runs a Puritan streak. The Englishman feels that enjoyment of any sort, be it ever so innocent, is ungodly and must be paid for later with fasting, prayer and shirts of horse hair.

This desire for self-immolation has created an incredibly tough race that will queue for hours in the rain on a bitter winter's day for the doubtful pleasure of watching twenty-two men agitate a bag of wind. It has helped to make the Island Race the hardiest in the world, so impervious to wind and weather that an ordeal like Dunkirk, which would have quelled any other race, was accepted as almost another frolic.

Rice pudding and inclement weather have contributed much to the average Englishman's stoicism and to Britain's success as a great power. There is little doubt that many of her Empire Builders fled these shores for balmier lands because they could no longer stomach rice pudding and cold mutton, and far across the sea they learnt that rice could be concocted in more delectable ways.

Now that the hydrogen bomb bids fair to make wars suicidal, the hardy Englishman at home may be tempted to eat and enjoy rice in some of its more palatable forms. And of these there is no end.

Rice is the staple food of more than one thousand million leisure- and luxury-loving peoples of the East. They eat rice not as a grim duty, but because they like it.

They boil it and drain away the water and eat it with curries. The firm, soft, snowy grains temper the acid and pungency of curries.

Sometimes, as in Burma, it is steamed and there is no water to be discarded.

It can be made into a delicious soup called mulligatawny, famous throughout the world, though the 'mulegoo-tunne' of South India bears little relation to the product we find in the tins.

It may be cooked with dhall (lentils) and in this guise goes under the name of khichiri (khedgeree).

Or fried in butter or ghee and interlarded with spices, raisins and nuts, when it is known as pilau.

And with all these, together with meats and vegetables, it may be known as birianee.

31

Finally, there are sweet dishes made with rice and milk and spices.

Rice is to the native of India what bread is to the Briton. You eat bread daily and never tire of it. The Indian eats rice every day and it sustains him, for rice contains 8 per cent protein and nearly 80 per cent carbohydrates—and unpolished rice about four times the mineral matter of polished rice.

Much of the rice eaten in the East has a tissue-like red covering, such as one finds on the peanut. This skin is rich in aneurin or vitamin B-1, which prevents beri-beri. If one's diet consists mainly of rice as is the case with millions of the poor all over the East, then this skin must be retained, otherwise one falls a prey to deficiency diseases.

But the Englishman's diet is rich and varied, so he need have no fear on that score. He can eat his rice as white and fluffy as any chorus girl.

Rice is every bit as good a filler as bread and when you have cooked your husband rice in some of its many forms, he may even grow to be an addict.

There are many varieties of rice: the stubby-grained 'table' rice from Carolina; long, thin rice from Patna; Burma rice, pilau rice, Chinese rice, etc. The best general type of rice for use with curries is Patna rice, which can be bought from any good grocer.

Incidentally, most people add salt to the water when boiling rice. I do not, and guests at our table don't seem to notice the difference. But you can cook a pound of rice in water to which as much as a tablespoon of salt has been added, for the salt drains away with the water. Rheumatic sufferers and those afflicted with high blood pressure or heart complaints should avoid salt.

It is one of the easiest and quickest dishes to cook and when well made, delicious. And now we hope to initiate you into some of its mysteries. But first, a word about mulligatawny.

This is a South Indian dish, the name being derived from two Tamil words: *molegoo* (pepper) and *tunnee* (water). Thus, 'pepper-water', which is made by pounding a dessert-spoon of tamarind, 6 red chillis, 6 cloves of garlic, a teaspoon of mustard seed, a saltspoon of fenugreek seed, 12 black peppercorns, a teaspoon of salt and 6 leaves of *karay-pauk*, *kurreaphool* or *kodia-neem* (all different names for the same thing).

This is worked into a paste, a pint of water added and the mixture boiled for 15 minutes. Then 2 small onions are sliced, put into a pan with a dessertspoon of clarified butter (ghee) and fried. The soup is then strained, poured over the fried onions and cooked vigorously for 5 minutes. This pepper-water is extremely pungent and is always eaten with a large quantity of rice.

But if you wish to make a good mulligatawny, which is really a soup, put into a muslin bag 2 oz. of coriander seed, 1 oz. cummin seed, 1 oz. fenugreek, $\frac{1}{2}$ oz. mustard seed, 2 cloves of garlic, 12 black peppercorns and 5 *kurreaphool* leaves. Boil for half an hour in meat or vegetable stock to produce 3 pints of soup. A teaspoon of tamarind will impart a distinctive flavour.

PLAIN BOILED RICE

Rice should be cooked till each grain is dry and separate from all the others, for nothing puts one off rice dishes so much as lumpy, clogging, cloying rice. It takes one back to school when a similar nauseous mess had to be eaten with prunes. The British Empire was, of course, built on this sort of food but now that we are shedding the last vestiges of Empire it is time to relegate soggy rice to the place it belongs—the dustbin. So let me show you how rice should be cooked. It's easy enough if someone hasn't already told you that it's an incredibly complicated ritual.

Method 1
Plain boiled rice is one of the easiest dishes to make. Wash the rice till it is clean and drain off the water. Then three parts fill a large saucepan with water and bring it to the boil. Add a teaspoon of salt and sprinkle in the rice by hand. Always use a good deal of water as rice swells alarmingly. Boil *hard* for 10–12 minutes, then take out a few grains and test between finger and thumb. If necessary, cook a little longer. When soft but *still firm*, take the pan off the heat, hold it under a tap and pour in cold water. This separates the grains from each other. Now strain into a sieve or colander. Then lightly butter the bottom of a warm dish and shake the rice into it. Riffle lightly with a fork to let the air circulate, and set the dish in a warm place (a pre-heated oven) but not on a flame. If in an oven, keep the door slightly open and cut off the heat. In 5–10 minutes the rice should be ready for the table. One breakfast cup of rice is ample for two people.

This method is foolproof except for the most ham-handed. By following the directions, those who have hitherto turned out a gluey mess will produce a pile of firm, snowy grains.

Method 2
Measure (with cups) the quantity of rice needed. One cup is usually sufficient for two people. Measure accurately, twice the volume of water as of rice. Place rice and water in a thick-bottomed pan and soak for at least half an hour.

Bring rice and water to the boil, then turn down the flame and simmer on a very low heat till every particle of water has been absorbed. When this is done the rice should be perfectly cooked and each grain separate from the others. Make sure that you use a pan with a tightly fitting lid, otherwise steam will escape, the rice will not be quite ready by the time the water has evaporated, and you will have to add more.

KHICHIRI OR KHICHIDI (KHEDGEREE)

INGREDIENTS

1 lb. rice	2 oz. fat
½ lb. lentils	2 teaspoons salt
½ teaspoon cummin seed	

METHOD

Wash rice and lentils and cook in 3 pints of water till the lentils are soft. Add salt before cooking.

Heat 2 oz. of fat in a frying pan and drop in ½ teaspoon of cummin seed which will soon start popping and jumping with the heat. When it does this, take pan off the flame and pour fat and cummin seed over rice and lentils. Mix thoroughly.

This dish is best eaten with yogurt (which can be bought or made at home) and mango or lemon pickle.

Enough for six

BIRIANEE

This birianee, though somewhat complicated, is well worth attempting, for it is very tasty and a favourite with Moslems.

INGREDIENTS

3 lb. lamb cut into cubes
 or one roasting chicken, jointed
1 lb. Patna rice washed and
 soaked in water for two hours
6 large onions, finely sliced
½ lb. butter, margarine or
 cooking fat
6–10 cloves garlic, chopped
2 large lemons

½ teaspoon ground cloves
¼ teaspoon ground cardamom
¼ teaspoon ground chilli
6 thin slices ginger, chopped
1 teaspoon ground cummin
½ teaspoon ground cinnamon
½ teaspoon ground black pepper
2 5-oz. bottles yogurt
1 teaspoon ground coriander

METHOD

Wash the meat (or chicken), put it into a pan with ground spices, garlic, ginger, yogurt, lemon juice and salt to taste. Mix meat and spices thoroughly and set the dish on one side. Fry the onions in a generous quantity of fat till crisp and brown. Divide into two portions. Crush one portion thoroughly and mix with meat and spices. Set aside the remainder for the rice.

PREPARING THE RICE FOR THE BIRIANEE

INGREDIENTS

10–12 whole cloves
10–12 whole black peppercorns
7–8 bay leaves

10–12 whole cardamoms
7–8 sticks cinnamon
½ teaspoon saffron or turmeric

METHOD

Take a large saucepan, fill it three parts full with water and put in the spices with one dessertspoon of salt. (The salt will eventually drain off.) When the water comes to the boil put in the Patna rice. When parboiled and the grains still hard, remove from heat and drain through a fine sieve. Do not remove spices from the rice. When completely drained place rice on a tray to cool.

Now mix saffron (or turmeric) into two teaspoons of hot milk. When the rice has been drained, empty half of it over the meat and spices, and pour over it the remainder of the onions, and then pour on the saffron (or turmeric) and milk.

Then cover the pan with a tightly fitting lid and bring the contents to the boil. Immediately it boils, turn down the heat as low as possible and simmer for 1½ hours, when the meat should be soft.

Cook the remainder of the rice till soft but the grains separate from each other, drain and, when dry, spread on a large flat dish. Over this, ladle the meat and rice mixture, and decorate with sliced, boiled eggs, or fried almonds, cashews and sultanas—or some of each. Garnish, if you like, with parsley.

As the cooking time for this dish is about 4 hours, it is not something you should attempt to toss off on the spur of the moment. It is meant for the big occasion when you want to do someone really well, like the boss who, you hope, will give your husband a rise, or the rich uncle who could leave you a packet in his will. If well made, it is so delicious that he'll eat more than he ought, and that will put paid to him! So, you can see it's well worth any amount of trouble.

Enough for six

MUTTON PILAU

INGREDIENTS

2 lb. bony mutton	5 medium onions
6 cloves garlic	2 large onions
3 1-inch sticks cinnamon	12 cloves
4½ cups Patna rice	12 cardamoms
6 carrots	12 black peppers
8 oz. cooking fat	4 oz. margarine

METHOD

Place the spices, but not onions, in a small muslin bag. Empty 12 breakfast cups of water into a pan. Cut up 2 lb. of bony mutton and add it to the water. Drop in the spices, together with the 2 onions, peeled. Boil till meat is tender and you have a tasty soup.

Now remove meat and bones from the liquid and take out and discard the bag of spices; but leave the onion.

This accomplished, heat 8 oz. cooking fat and 4 oz. margarine in another pan. Slice five medium-sized onions finely and introduce them, together with ¼ cup of water, to the warm fat. Bring fat to the boil and fry till onions are golden.

To this add the bony mutton that was removed from the soup, together with 4½ cups of Patna rice and six carrots shredded into long strips. Fry the lot.

When the rice has a golden tint, pour on the soup, add salt to taste, and simmer on a very low flame with lid tightly on, till all water is absorbed.

If due to evaporation the soup that you add to the onion and fat is less than 10 cups, make up the deficiency with water. When the water is absorbed the pilau is ready, and each grain should be separate and firm. If you have never made this dish, remove the lid occasionally to see how it is progressing.

Enough for eight

PILAU (Sindhi Style)

INGREDIENTS

2 lb. meat cut into small pieces	2 teaspoons salt
4 onions, finely cut, lengthwise	½ lb. Patna rice
4–5 whole cardamoms	4–5 black peppercorns
4–5 whole cloves	4–5 sticks cinnamon (1 inch each)
½ lb. fat	

METHOD

Place spices in a small muslin bag and put spices and meat into a pan containing 2 pints water. Boil meat till tender.

Fry onions to a deep brown in fat, put in rice, and salt to taste. Fry the rice for 10 minutes over brisk flame; then add the pieces of meat and broth. Stir well, add salt and a cupful of milk. The rice will soon absorb the liquid, and if you think it is not sufficient to cook the rice without burning it, add a little water or milk. Cook *on a very low flame* till rice is soft. Cooking time should be about 1½ hours.

Enough for four

MUTTER PILAU (Peas and Rice)

INGREDIENTS

½ lb. rice	1 teaspoon salt
1½ lb. fresh or 1 lb. frozen peas	4 whole black peppercorns
4 oz. fat	4 whole cardamoms
2 onions, sliced lengthwise	4 sticks cinnamon, each about an inch long
4 whole cloves	

METHOD

Fry onions to a golden brown, then add salt and spices and continue to fry till onions are well browned.

Wash rice and peas and add them to the fried onions, and fry for 10 minutes. Now pour in 2 pints of boiling water and cook over a very low flame till the rice is soft, but each grain separate. Fried potatoes or fried cauliflower may be used instead of peas. Total cooking time about 45 minutes.

Enough for two or three

PRAWN RICE

INGREDIENTS

2 pints prawns, shelled	½ lb. Patna rice
2 large onions, chopped	1 cup green peas, fresh or frozen
1 teaspoon ground chilli	½ teaspoon ground turmeric
¼ teaspoon ground cloves	¼ teaspoon ground cinnamon
4 oz. butter or margarine	¼ teaspoon ground cardamoms
1 pint coconut milk	2 teaspoons salt

METHOD

Wash rice and set it aside to soak for an hour. Fry onions lightly, but do not brown. Add to them the peas and prawns and cook over a low flame for 10 minutes. Put rice into this and fry well, till colour changes to light brown. Now pour in a pint of coconut milk, add chilli powder, turmeric powder and salt. Stir well, place lid on pan and cook for 10 minutes till rice is half done. Add remaining spices, mix well and cook for a further 10 minutes on a very low flame till every drop of water has been absorbed, the rice is thoroughly cooked through and each grain is separate.

It is advisable when cooking curries, and rice especially, to use pans with thick bottoms, which retain heat and do not burn the contents.

Enough for four

BADAMI RUNG RICE (Brown Rice—a Parsee dish)

INGREDIENTS

1 lb. Patna rice	3 oz. fat
1 onion, finely chopped	2 teaspoons salt (approx.)

METHOD

Fry the onion till brown, then add the rice and fry for a further 10 minutes. Now pour rice, fat and fried onion into a pan in which a quart of water is already boiling, together with enough salt to flavour. Lower flame and cook very gently till rice is done. Keep lid on pan and test grains of rice from time to time. Brown rice is best accompanied by Dhan Sag, the recipe for which is given below. Cook on a very low flame, otherwise rice is apt to burn.

Enough for six

DHAN SAG

INGREDIENTS

2 lb. lamb or one roasting chicken, jointed	$\frac{1}{2}$ teaspoon ground chilli
$\frac{1}{2}$ lb. lentils	$\frac{1}{2}$ teaspoon ground coriander
3 onions cut into pieces	A pinch of ground cinnamon
2 large potatoes cut into pieces	$\frac{1}{2}$ teaspoon ground turmeric
4 tomatoes	$\frac{1}{2}$ teaspoon ground cummin
1 aubergine	A pinch of ground cloves
2 oz. fat	2 green chillis
Juice of a lemon	2–3 sprigs of fresh mint
3 teaspoons salt	

METHOD

Wash meat and lentils and put them into 2 pints boiling water. Add potatoes, tomatoes, onions and aubergine and cook till meat is tender.

Now remove meat, strain the liquid through a sieve, and after squashing, discard the residue. Return the meat to the gravy, add chilli, coriander, cinnamon, turmeric, cummin, cloves, mint and green chillis, 2 oz. fat, the juice of a lemon and salt. Cook for 15 minutes. Total cooking time about 2 hours. Serve with Badami Rung rice, prepared as above.

Enough for six

VEGETABLE DISHES (BHAJJIS)

DHALL (Lentils)

INGREDIENTS

½ lb. lentils (any kind)

3 tomatoes, quartered

1 oz. fat

2 onions, finely chopped

½ teaspoon ground chilli

1 teaspoon salt

¼ teaspoon ground turmeric

METHOD

Put lentils, turmeric, ground chilli and salt into a quart of *boiling* water, and cook till tender.

Fry onions and tomatoes together in fat till onions are brown, then add them to the lentils. Cook for 5 minutes more. The dhall should be neither too thick, nor like clear soup. It should have the consistency of thick sauce and is best eaten with boiled rice. This simple dish is eaten by the poorest as well as the most wealthy, because it is cheap, sustaining and tasty.

Enough for two

In Britain split peas are used mainly for pease pudding and lentils as a thickening for meat stews. But cooked like this they make an ideal supper dish for a cold night. Lentils contain 25 per cent protein (lean meat has 18–20 per cent) and are rich in aneurin and riboflavin (vitamins B-1 and B-2).

BYGAN DHALL

INGREDIENTS

½ lb. lentils

2 onions, finely chopped

2 green chillis

¼ teaspoon ground chillis

¼ teaspoon ground turmeric

¼ teaspoon ground coriander

¼ teaspoon ground cummin

1 aubergine cut into small pieces

1 oz. fat

1 teaspoon salt

METHOD

Boil lentils and onions in 3 pints water. When lentils are tender, add the spices, aubergine and salt. Cook till aubergine is tender, then warm fat in a frying pan and put into it ½ teaspoon of whole mustard seed and a pinch of asafoetida. When the mustard starts popping, pour contents of pan into lentils, mix well, and cover. A squeeze of lemon before serving adds piquancy, but is optional. Total cooking time 45 minutes.

Enough for three

KOBI SABJI

INGREDIENTS

1 small cabbage, finely chopped	2 green chillis
2 onions, finely chopped	2 oz. fat
1 teaspoon salt	$\frac{1}{4}$ teaspoon ground turmeric
2 tomatoes cut into small pieces	$\frac{1}{2}$ teaspoon whole mustard seed

METHOD

Heat cooking fat, add mustard seed and fry till they pop. Add onions and tomatoes and cook for 10 minutes more, then fold in cabbage, chillis and turmeric and cook till cabbage is tender. Add salt. While cabbage is cooking you may, if you wish, add a tablespoon of desiccated coconut, but *no water*.

Enough for four

KOBI BHANAVLI

INGREDIENTS

1 cabbage, finely chopped	$\frac{1}{2}$ teaspoon ground chilli
2 onions, finely chopped	$\frac{1}{4}$ teaspoon ground turmeric
1 teaspoon salt	2 tablespoons basun (Indian pea flour)
2 tablespoons desiccated coconut	Pinch of baking powder
2 green chillis, chopped	3 eggs, well beaten

METHOD

Mix all the ingredients together with eggs, flour and salt. Add $\frac{1}{4}$ breakfast cup of water. Grease a casserole, put in mixed ingredients and bake for 45 minutes in medium oven. Cabbage should be well browned on top. This is an excellent savoury for high tea.

Enough for four

BENGALI BHAJJI

INGREDIENTS

$\frac{1}{2}$ lb. fresh or tinned peas	6 cloves garlic
$\frac{1}{2}$ lb. runner beans	$\frac{1}{2}$ oz. fenugreek leaves
$\frac{1}{2}$ lb. carrots	$\frac{1}{4}$ oz. ground coriander

1 lb. potatoes	¼ oz. cummin
2 onions	1 tablespoon tomato paste or purée
1 oz. butter or cooking fat	½ teaspoon chilli powder
1 5-oz. bottle yogurt	1 teaspoon salt
½ oz. green ginger	

METHOD

Slice runner beans, chop carrots into ½-inch pieces, scrub potatoes (don't peel), and if new and small put them in whole. Put vegetables into a basin, mix, add salt and cover with boiling water for 10 minutes.

Mash garlic and green ginger with fork, or in a mortar, then slice onions finely and fry till golden brown. Add fenugreek leaves and when aroma rises put in the remainder of the spices, the yogurt and tomato, and fry for 10 minutes. Then place vegetables in a pan, add juice from garlic, ginger, fried onions, etc. and cook till vegetables are soft. Bring to the boil and simmer over a low flame.

Enough for three or four

ARVI BHAJJI (Artichoke Curry)

INGREDIENTS

1 lb. artichokes (Jerusalem)	½ teaspoon ground turmeric
1 large onion, finely sliced	½ teaspoon ground chilli
2 oz. butter	1 dessertspoon cummin seed
6 cloves garlic	4 tomatoes or 1 tablespoon tomato purée
6 cloves	1 teaspoon salt
6 cardamoms	½ oz. ground coriander
½ oz. fenugreek seed	1 5-oz. bottle yogurt
½ teaspoon ground ginger	

METHOD

Scrub artichokes thoroughly with stiff brush kept for scrubbing vegetables, and if large, cut into halves or quarters. If small, cook whole. Fry onion in butter till golden brown, then lowering the flame drop in fenugreek seed, cardamoms and cloves; and after 3 minutes, add spices and yogurt.

Mash garlic in mortar, mix into ¼ cupful of water and simmer for 5 minutes. Now add artichokes with enough water to form a gravy, and when this is done, rub in the cummin seed. If eaten in the Indian style this should be dry curry with little gravy, but if you like a thinner curry, add water or ½ cup coconut milk.

Enough for three

POTATO CHIP CURRY

INGREDIENTS

1½ lb. potatoes	1 oz. ground coriander
1 large onion	1 oz. ground turmeric
1 dessertspoon butter or fat	1 teaspoon salt
1 oz. fenugreek seed	1 oz. ground ginger
8 cloves garlic	1 teaspoon chilli powder
1 bottle yogurt	½ lb. fresh tomatoes

METHOD

Cut potatoes into slices and fry in deep dripping till golden. Put on one side. Heat butter and drop in fenugreek seed. When aroma rises, add sliced onion, and brown. Then add salt and spices. Mash garlic, cut tomatoes into quarters and mix with garlic. Add half cup of water over chips. Put into a pan and add browned onion, spices, etc. Simmer gently for 10 minutes. There is a tendency for potatoes to stick to the bottom, so stir from time to time and add a little water if necessary.

Enough for six

SABAT MOONG BHAJJI (Whole Moong Bhajji)

Whole 'moongs' are a variety of Indian lentils and may be bought at any shops specializing in curry spices.

INGREDIENTS

1 lb. whole moong soaked in water overnight	2 oz. fat
2 onions, finely chopped	1 teaspoon salt
2 tablespoons desiccated coconut	½ teaspoon ground chilli
2 green chillis	¼ teaspoon ground turmeric
A pinch of asafoetida	½ teaspoon whole mustard seed

METHOD

Wash and clean the moong and add to it all the spices except asafoetida and mustard seed. Warm the fat, then drop mustard seed and asafoetida into it. When they start popping, add moong, with all spices and salt. Pour in a cupful of water and mix well. Cook till moong is tender.

There is enough for 6 people and the cooking time is 45 minutes. The bhajji may also be made from other varieties of lentils, such as mussoor, kabuli, channa and black-eyes; but all must be soaked overnight.

ALOO BHAJJI

INGREDIENTS

1½ lb. potatoes, peeled and cut into small pieces	Squeeze of lemon juice
4 green chillis cut lengthwise	1 teaspoon salt
¼ teaspoon ground turmeric	½ teaspoon whole mustard seed
A pinch of asafoetida	2 tablespoons desiccated coconut

METHOD

Heat fat in a frying pan. Drop in mustard seed, green chillis and asafoetida and continue to heat till they pop. Add potatoes, coconut, lemon juice and salt with half cup of water. Cook over a low flame for 30 minutes when potatoes should be soft.

Enough for six

KHUMBI SAG

INGREDIENTS

½ lb. mushrooms	½ teaspoon ground chilli
2 oz. fat	½ teaspoon ground coriander
1 teaspoon salt	½ teaspoon ground cummin
2 large potatoes, finely chopped	¼ teaspoon ground turmeric
2 tomatoes, finely chopped	2 large onions

METHOD

Brown onions well and add tomatoes, then brown for 5 minutes more. Peel and cut mushrooms into halves and cut potatoes into small pieces. Add the mushrooms, spices and salt to onions, together with a cupful of water. Cook for 10 minutes more, then add potatoes, and when potatoes are cooked, the dish is ready for serving. Total cooking time about 40 minutes.

Enough for four

Peas may be used in this recipe instead of potatoes.

MUTTER CURRY (Pea Curry)

INGREDIENTS

2 lb. fresh peas	2 large tomatoes, cut into pieces
2 large onions, finely chopped	½ teaspoon ground cummin
2 oz. fat	¼ teaspoon ground turmeric
2 teaspoons salt	2 green chillis
½ teaspoon ground chilli	2 large potatoes, diced
½ teaspoon ground coriander	

METHOD

Fry onions to a golden brown, then add tomatoes; then continue to fry till brown. Now add shelled peas and all spices, including salt. Put in ½ cup of water and cook for 15 minutes. Then add potatoes and chillis. Cook this dish over a slow fire, and when potatoes and peas are soft, the dish is ready.

Enough for six

KOBI CHANNA DHALL CURRY (Cauliflower and Lentil Curry)

INGREDIENTS

1 fresh cauliflower cut into small pieces	½ teaspoon ground chilli
2 oz. fat	¼ teaspoon ground turmeric
1 teaspoon salt	½ teaspoon curry powder
½ cup of channa dhall, parboiled	2 tablespoons desiccated coconut
2 onions, finely chopped	Juice of a lemon

METHOD

Fry onions for 4–5 minutes. Add cauliflower, channa dhall (variety of lentil) and all spices, including desiccated coconut and salt. Put in a cup of water and cook on low flame till cauliflower is soft, then add lemon juice. Total cooking time about 30 minutes.

Enough for six

INDIAN BREAD AND SAVOURIES

UNTIL the advent of the British, bread made with yeast was virtually unknown in India. Unleavened bread was eaten, and is still eaten by the greater part of the population. Provided one has sound teeth (or well designed dentures), this type of bread is better for one than the puffed-up loaf.

Britons, who have made its acquaintance in India, like it, but it is rarely seen in English homes, for English wives seem to think that some mystery surrounds the making of it. It is much easier to make than British bread. I once read in the *Guardian* the story of an old Somerset labourer who for reasons of economy bought a hundredweight sack of wheat for 7s. 6d., ground it to flour in a stone hand-mill, then mixed a little with water, made it into round, flat cakes and took them to the baker, who baked them for 2d. Each 'loaf' lasted a week, and to that day this ancient preferred his home-made bread to baker's bread.

'D'have yeast in'n, what d'make 'ee zwell out. Ah,' he said, 'I d'like me own bread, and I d'still have teeth to bite droo'n.'

Indian bread is satisfying, but it doesn't swell one out. Try it, and you'll like it.

CHAPPATTIS

INGREDIENTS

One lb. wholemeal flour   1 cup water (approx.)

METHOD

Mix the flour with water and a pinch of salt to a fairly stiff dough. Knead it well. Pinch pieces off the dough and mould them into balls the size of a walnut. Roll each ball in flour and sprinkle flour on the bread board or table. Then roll each ball out to the thickness of a pancake. Place a large frying pan, *un*greased, on the fire and heat it. Then place the chappatti (the rolled-out cake) in the pan and fry for 2 minutes on each side. Remove it, apply a little melted butter on each side and fry to a light brown colour. Eat while hot, either plain or with curry.

[N.B. See note at end of following recipe.]

POOREES

METHOD

Knead wholemeal flour as explained in the previous recipe, but in this case the dough should be a little harder, i.e. use less water. Pinch off little pieces and roll into balls the size of a marble. Then roll into little flat cakes about 4 inches in diameter.

Put a frying pan with oil, margarine or butter on the stove and heat it. The tastiest poorees are, of course, made in butter. Drop each little cake into the boiling fat and then turn it after a few seconds. Cook each side till it is light brown, then remove and drain. Poorees must be eaten piping hot. If left, they turn leathery.

NOTE. In both the previous recipes it is as well after kneading, to cover the dough and let it stand in a warm place for half an hour before rolling out.

STUFFED PARRATTAS

METHOD

Roll out little flat cakes as in the previous recipe. Butter the surface of each cake (margarine may be used). Put a little cooked, mashed potato on it, and gather the edges of the pooree into the centre, making a bag. Or you can slit the dough from the centre to the edge and fold over. It matters little which method you adopt, so long as the potato is completely encased. Then roll out again, gently, into a round cake. Put it into a hot frying pan and cook each side for two or three minutes—or less—till light brown. *The pan must not be greased*, and the parratta should be eaten hot.

BRINJAL BHURTA

INGREDIENTS

2 large aubergines	$\frac{1}{2}$ teaspoon salt
1 onion, finely chopped	1 tablespoon desiccated coconut
1 green chilli cut into small pieces	1 bottle yogurt

METHOD

Paint a little olive oil over the aubergines and bake them in the oven till soft. Then remove the skins and mash the pulp well. Add to it the onion, chilli, salt, coconut and yogurt. Mix thoroughly. When cold, eat with plain boiled rice and dhall.

Enough for four

ONION KOCHUMBER

INGREDIENTS

1 large onion, finely cut lengthwise and soaked in cold water for $\frac{1}{2}$ hour	1 large tomato cut into small pieces
	Squeeze of lemon
1 green chilli cut into small pieces, or a pinch of ground chilli	$\frac{1}{2}$ teaspoon salt

METHOD

Strain the onion thoroughly, and add to it tomato, chilli, salt and a squeeze of lemon. This kochumber is usually eaten with birianee.

Enough for four

POTATO BHURTA

INGREDIENTS

1 lb. potatoes

4 oz. butter

2 large onions

2 oz. green coriander leaves (or mint or parsley)

1 green chilli

4 cloves

4 cardamoms

½ teaspoon chilli powder

The juice of a lemon

1 teaspoon salt

METHOD

Skin and cook potatoes till soft. Chop onions very finely. Mix half the onions with finely chopped green chilli, chopped coriander leaves (or parsley or mint), shelled cardamoms, cloves, chilli powder, salt and the potatoes, which must be mashed.

Fry the remainder of the onions in butter, add the potato mixture and cook for 10–15 minutes over a low flame. Serve with a sprinkling of lemon juice. This bhurta, too, is eaten with plain boiled rice and dhall.

An alternative is to mix all the ingredients together, except cloves and cardamoms, sprinkle with lemon juice and eat without cooking.

Enough for six

THOSE ALARMING SIDE DISHES

THE guest at an Indian or Pakistani home, club or restaurant finds himself confronted by an array of little dishes that mystify and alarm him. Some mystify because he doesn't know what they contain and wishes to find out; he is alarmed because he feels that if he omits to take a little of each, his host will consider him ignorant.

He need have no fear on that score, for he had only to ask to be told.

On one plate will probably be a mound of crisp pancakes of wafer thinness. These are poppadams, which can be eaten without the accompaniment of any other food; crumbled over rice, or eaten with rice and curry. They are so tasty and easy to eat that one can, without realizing it, consume a dozen. They *must* be served and eaten *hot*.

Poppadams may be bought at all shops selling Indian spices, and are packed in packets of 25, 50 and 100. They may be fried in fat, have a little butter spread on them and grilled, or grilled without any fat whatsoever. Women with a tendency to put on weight should adopt this last method.

Then there are chappattis, parrattas and poorees (pp. 44–5). All resemble pancakes. Chappattis and parrattas are about the size of a dinner plate; chappattis being made of wholemeal flour with the minimum of fat; parrattas often of white flour, with more fat. Poorees are usually somewhat smaller than a quarter plate, are cooked in fat or butter and usually contain a filling.

Chappattis and parrattas are eaten with curries or bhajjis, but not with rice. In parts of Northern India and Pakistan there are millions who eat very little rice. Chappattis or parrattas always appear with curries or bhajjis. In Bengal and in the South rice is the staple food and chappattis and parrattas were introduced from the northern wheat-growing areas.

Then there is Bombay duck, a species of cured fish, which when uncooked has a powerful offensive odour. Cooking transforms it. It may be cooked in fat or baked in the oven till crisp, when it is crumbled over rice or munched with curry or bhajji. Bombay duck could with advantage be introduced into English cookery and would add to the flavour of many insipid, boiled dishes. Don't be put off by the smell of uncooked Bombay duck.

On the table you will also find tiny dishes containing sambals: red or green chillis, gherkins, paprika, sweet capsicums, pickled onions, sweet chutneys, pickled fish, mango, lime, tamarind, brinjal or other pickles and chutneys.

They are all meant to garnish the main dish and give it an added relish. You are not bound to try any of them, though if your host knows you are a stranger to Indian food, he will be disappointed if you don't sample the lot.

There may also be a dish of yogurt and a dish of dhall on the table, and you are at liberty to help yourself to both. Both are eaten with rice or Indian bread. For my part, a good curry

47

needs no garnishing, but there is little doubt that some of these side dishes lend a piquancy to food.

Try them all and if you don't know what they are, ask! It will give your friends pleasure to tell you. And be sure to ask whether they are very hot, or not; and even if your friends say, 'Oh, no!' remember that what is normal to them may produce a fire on your palate. So, as far as pickles are concerned, walk warily; and don't help yourself to an entire chilli. Try a quarter, and nip off small sections and eat them.

If you find them too hot, don't reach for a glass of water. Eat rice, chappattis or parrattas to damp down the flames. At first you may wonder why any human being eats chillis, but before long you, too, may learn to enjoy them in small—very small, doses. In the East chillis cause one to perspire profusely and even to cry, and it is not uncommon to see a diner with beads of sweat starting from his brow and tears of enjoyment running down his cheeks, for it is not only the English who take their pleasures sadly!

In passing, it might be mentioned that in India the distinction between a chutney and a pickle is that a chutney may contain sweet ingredients such as treacle, molasses, sugar and raisins, and that the ingredients may be pounded or finely minced, whereas no sweet ingredients are used in a pickle, and the fruit or vegetables from which it is made are included whole, or cut or sliced in large pieces. In India mustard oil forms the base of many pickles but finds no place in a chutney.

There are dozens of different kinds of chutneys and pickles; the names of some of the most common are given below:

Chutneys: apple, tomato, coconut, mashed potato, plantain (a species of banana), cucumber, brinjal, green ginger and tamarind, green mango, til seed, dried mango, tomato and tamarind, tomato and tiparee (Cape Gooseberry), lime aloobokhara (cough plum— so called because the consumption of too many such plums gives one a very sore throat), sultana, sweet mango, hot mango.

Pickles: cabbage, red cauliflower, red cabbage, onions, mangoes, dried mango, nasturtium seed, beetroot, walnut, bamboo, cucumber, green ginger, jujube (narkelikul), coconut, lemon, brinjal, artichoke, mushroom, beans, eggs, amla (*emblica officinalis*), norephal (*glauca disticha*), jalpai or wild olive (*elaegnus conferta*), amra or hog plum (*spondias magnifera*).

If you dine at the homes of Indians and Pakistanis you may see small dishes containing pounded green herbs tinged with sugar, vinegar and other essences. These are known as 'sāgs' (pronounced 'saags') and are eaten to counteract the effect of too-oily or greasy foods and to purify the blood. There are also compounds known as 'bhurtas', made usually with mashed potato as a base, and including fresh herbs, chopped onion, garlic and other fresh but piquant vegetables.

In Britain it is rare to find more than half a dozen of these side dishes at any meal, but at a big Indian dinner or banquet so many appear that it is impossible to sample all without making a second meal of side dishes alone, especially as delicious but extremely rich and sickly sweets are to follow.

In the best circles in Old India, it was customary for guests to stuff themselves in order to show their appreciation, after which they would belch loudly to prove how full of good fare and enjoyment they were. This very natural picturesque custom has fallen into desuetude as far as public functions are concerned, but the writer has been at dinners where the satisfaction has been so great that guests have expressed themselves with veritable rolls of thunder.

It was also customary among certain of the rich commercial classes (banias, etc., who normally ate one large meal only, just before retiring) to tie a thin thread round the stomach and eat and eat until the distending stomach burst the thread, which was the signal to stop. They would then rub their stomachs with mustard oil. In such circles the words 'fat' and 'rich' were synonymous. An enormous paunch was not always a badge of shame, as it now is; for did not St Thomas Aquinas carry so much before him that a semi-circular piece had to be sliced out of the refectory table in order that he could sit down? And there were few more pious or learned characters than Thomas.

History does not record that he ever visited India, but had he done so his record as a trencherman would indeed have been impressive.

THE SECOND BOOK
OF CURRIES

SOME IDLE THOUGHTS ON FOOD
—ESPECIALLY CURRIES

GENERALLY speaking, the English don't make good cooks. Not because the culinary art is beyond them, for when the English turn their hands to anything, there are few of any race who excel them. Except, perhaps, the Scots.

Indeed, if works such as the *Forme of Cury,* the oldest of all English books on cookery, are to be believed, once in the distant past Englishmen were magnificent trenchermen and paid greater attention to their stomachs than any nation in Europe.

If one compares *The Apician Art of Cookery* with the *Forme of Cury,* innumerable points of resemblance may be seen between the Roman and British schools of cookery. Roman cuisine was influenced by that of the East, for at the zenith of Roman power the finest cooks from India and the Near East were inveigled to Rome by fat rewards to prepare the fashionable Lucullan banquets.

The Romans brought many of their recipes with them when they came to Britain and the natives of this island grew to be discriminating cooks. Many of the concoctions must have contained spices from the Orient and may even have resembled curries. Most of their dishes were based on vegetables, as in Eastern cookery, and meat and meat juices were employed sparingly. Only when the Romans left the shores of Britain for good, and the rarer spices were no longer easily obtainable, did English cookery begin to develop along its own lines.

The great feasts of mediaeval England were enormous, and lasted days. Cooking was indeed a noble art at that time and a mediaeval manuscript states that the compilers were 'the *chef* maister cokes of Kyng Richard', whose literary work was done 'by assent and argument of maisters of phisik and philosophie that dwellid in his court'. But great eaters and doers seldom go hand in hand.

When the English, cut off from the Continent by prolonged wars, lost the art of cooking and eating, they became Empire Builders. If life is bereft of enjoyment, one almost certainly goes round making trouble for others! The Thin Red Line were famous for their reckless bravery. On their rations, so would you be.

The Romans, Chinese, French, Italians, Spanish, Portuguese and Greeks fell for the lure of the table, became soft and pleasure-loving, and their possessions melted away. Heroic deeds call for heroic food.

Until comparatively recently there have been few among the English like Dr Samuel Johnson; he it was who said, 'Some people have a foolish way of not minding, or pretending not to mind, what they eat. For my own part, I mind my belly very studiously and very carefully: for I look upon it, that he who does not mind his belly will hardly mind anything else'.

During the past fifty years or so British eating habits have changed, albeit very gradually.

It was at the turn of the century that Britain's supremacy began to wane, and the British character was slowly undermined!

Exotic dishes now appear—rather diffidently—on the most unexpected tables. Holiday-makers return from their travels clutching recipes of rare dishes, and concoct them in their kitchens—plain evidence that the Empire is crumbling! Britain's position as a dominant power has been usurped by the Americans and the Russians, neither of whom are renowned for the subtlety or imaginativeness of their fare.

The Puritans have much to answer for—in England and in America, where their influence is still felt. My paternal grandfather was of that ilk; in his eyes food was meant for nourishment, not enjoyment. No wonder one of my uncles became a Trappist monk—and I a complete hedonist, detesting anything that is 'good for me'!

That a good curry causes the salivary glands to work and the gastric juices to do whatever is necessary, is incidental. Our prime motive in offering you these recipes is to enable you to enjoy curry.

Don't imagine that I exaggerate. I can hear the tolerant chuckle of the native. 'These foreigners: they don't understand us. Plain English fare is the best in the world—there's nothing like it'.

We agree. Nothing. But where can you get it? Williamson's in Bow Lane; Simpson's in the Strand; Rule's in Maiden Lane; a few old chop-houses, one or two clubs, and in the homes of those who revere good food.

Even Englishmen once removed are apt to raise their eyebrows. A Newfoundlander spoke thus on the air not long ago: 'I have come to the conclusion that in England it is not what you eat, but how you eat it that matters. The approach is everything.' Another critic wrote to the *Manchester Guardian* from a safe aerie in Switzerland: 'British catering is run mainly by people who are ignorant about food, careless about cleanliness, and con-temptuous about their customers . . . Our cafés and restaurants enjoy every advantage, yet most provide meals that are either cheap and nasty, or dear and nasty . . .'

English cooking has been so bad because the English have been too preoccupied to attend to it. And yet, as the French chef, Eustache Ude, asserted: 'Cookery in England, when well done is superior to that of any country in the world.' True, he hadn't been to the East!

All is not lost. Here and there one finds men who love their food and proclaim it by their generous figures; men like G. K. Chesterton, James Robertson Justice and Philip Harben who are walking advertisements of the creed that good food makes for contented bodies.

Well-prepared food announces its tastiness by its appetizing smell. 'Ah,' you say, with a few preliminary sniffs, 'fried onions!' And the salivary juices start to flow in anticipation. Walk down any street where coffee is being roasted. Doesn't the very aroma tempt you to stop and idle away a few minutes sipping a cup of the brew that stimulates conversation?

Take garlic—the queen of all herbs.

Raw garlic must never be eaten, except as in Italy, where everyone else eats it and the birds and the bees and the trees can't protest. But garlic cooked, in almost any dish, helps to make it. It is one of the pillars upon which a successful curry stands. And when well cooked, garlic leaves no obnoxious odour on the breath.

Onions, garlic and the spices of the East—cummin, coriander and the rest—give curry

Salmon with Spinach
(*See recipe page 29*)

its delightful, appetizing odour. When this assails the nostrils the phenomenon known as hunger is aroused.

Some years ago the famous naturalist and gardener, Luther Burbank, managed to produce an onion without either smell or pungency. He claimed that it could be peeled and chopped without causing a single tear, but was otherwise exactly the same as the ordinary variety. However, housewives everywhere rejected it, for when cooked it failed to give out that delicious aroma we invariably associate with fried onions.

Onions, garlic, bay leaf, spices and herbs used in various ways and quantities, bring out the flavours of fish, flesh and vegetables. Fruit, too, for some, like plantains (bananas) and *papayas* (paw-paws), can be made into excellent curries.

But cooking, like gardening, needs 'green fingers'. Two people can follow the same instructions, and yet achieve different results. My wife and I make curries with identical quantities of the same ingredients; but the results are not the same.

This, I believe, is a common experience in all types of cookery. So if the curries, savouries and sweets you concoct do not titillate your palate as you anticipated, don't hurl this book into the fire!

Boiled rice, for instance, is the easiest dish in the world to cook. When ready, with the water drained away, it should be white and fluffy, each grain separate from the others. Yet one woman I know failed to produce perfectly boiled rice for 18 years, although I showed her time and again how it was done. Either it was too hard or it came out in a revolting, glutinous mass. One day, however, by pure chance she succeeded, and ever since then her rice has been just right.

Curry spices are not in themselves pungent. The 'kick' is supplied by either chilli powder or black pepper. It is advisable always to use less chilli powder than recommended at first, increasing this next time if the flavour is not hot enough. Eat plenty of rice with curries. Observe this advice and you should enjoy Indian food.

This book is not complete in the manner of the traditional Indian cookery books. They were indeed comprehensive, including invaluable hints on such matters as Diarrhoea in Cows; Condition Powder for Horses; To Keep Posts From Decay; To Judge the Height of a Tree by Trigonometry; Mother Shipton's Prophecy; and how to buy food—'Coffee should be bought by bushels; salt should be bought by maunds (80 lb.); and coriander, mustard seed, cummin seed and fenugreek should be fresh and new and free from weevils.' As we hope they are.

If such titbits are not included, don't blame us; we point to the price of printing and the impatience of our publisher!

CHEMICAL ANALYSIS OF CURRY SPICES

The idea that curry spices are harmful to health is quite mistaken. Health may be injured only if too-pungent curries are eaten too often and if too much fat is used in cooking; then the membranes of the stomach and intestines are unduly irritated and the digestion impaired. In actual fact curry spices are antiseptic and preservative and have a high content of vitamins D and C. A table of the properties of curry spices, analysed by Professor J. L. Rosedale, is given below.

Spices	Water %	Mineral parts/ thousand	Protein %	Fat %	Fibre %	Carbo- hydrate %
Cardamom	17·9	5·8	10·0	3·4	22·1	40·8
Aniseed	12·8	7·8	10·67	0·55	39·71	28·43
Chillis	14·2	5·0	12·8	4·5	25·6	37·9
Cinnamon	13·1	2·2	3·31	2·4	11·3	67·69
Clove	23·6	4·7	5·75	15·8	10·0	40·15
Coriander	9·64	10·73	11·1	0·33	12·5	55·7
Garlic	58·7	1·3	4·3	0·1	0·8	26·6
Ginger	91·1	0·54	2·1	0·86	1·7	3·7
Onion	82·8	0·5	1·23	0·1	0·6	15·37
Pepper	16·06	4·6	10·63	9·4	12·1	53·21
Tamarind	26·2	1·5	2·86	0·44	8·1	60·9
Turmeric	14·34	5·1	0·48	4·9	3·2	71·98
Fenugreek	15·9	5·1	25·25	4·1	10·5	39·15
Coriander leaf	91·19	0·7	2·3	0·03	0·59	5·19
Curry leaf	60·2	3·8	9·7	1·7	10·3	14·3

MEAT AND GAME CURRIES

KABABS, KAWABS or KABOBS

THE *Kabab*, or Kabob, is a dish popular from Morocco to Malay and has, therefore, many variations.

SEIK KABAB

This is rarely eaten with rice, the usual accompaniment being either *chappattis* or *parrattas*, or slices of the ordinary baker's loaf, preferably without butter.

The tastiest *kabab*—or so it seems to me—is that made over a charcoal fire in a crude stall in some bazaar where the only illumination is a naphtha flare. Here, at night, amid all the bazaar noises; of friends roaring at each other from a yard away; of cow bells and conchs; of some minstrel droning away in a monotonous voice while he twangs a one-stringed instrument; here sits the *kabab*-maker cross-legged in front of his glowing fire, grilling mutton or beef on skewers or *seiks*, and flicking his dough adroitly from one hand to the other, as the flaccid mass fans out into round, white elephant's ears.

If your *kabab* can't vie with his, remember, he has inherited the tradition of a thousand years. You will need:

INGREDIENTS

2 lb. beef, mutton or veal	¼ teaspoon ground garlic
2 tablespoons mustard oil	1 teaspoon ground turmeric or saffron
4 teaspoons ground onions	½ teaspoon salt
¼ teaspoon ground chillis	1 five-oz. bottle of yogurt
¼ teaspoon ground ginger	Juice of one lemon
¼ teaspoon ground coriander seed	Ghee, butter or other fat

METHOD

Remove all bone, then chop the meat into pieces about 1½–2 inches square.

Now mix together all the condiments and spices, including mustard oil, yogurt and lemon juice and thoroughly steep the chopped meat in the mixture, turning occasionally till most of the liquid is absorbed. This will take an hour or two.

Then take a thin metal skewer or *seik*, and pass it through the middle of each piece of meat. This done, hold over the grill and cook, basting the whole time with the ghee, or fat. Keep on turning the skewer so that the meat does not burn and cook it to a deep, rich brown. Then remove it from the skewer and serve hot.

Enough for four

The grilling may be carried out *under* the grill, and the meat removed from time to time to be rubbed with the fat.

Real experts say that there is nothing to beat a charcoal fire, but charcoal fires are difficult to get in Britain. Incidentally, *kabab* can be made over the blazing coke of a night watchman's fire—if only you can make friends with one.

TICK-KEEAH KABAB

INGREDIENTS

2 lb. fat beef or mutton	¼ teaspoon ground ginger
1 teaspoon ground onion	½ teaspoon ground hot spices (*garam massala*)
¼ teaspoon ground turmeric	1 tablespoon yogurt
⅛ teaspoon ground garlic	Ghee, butter or other fat for grilling
¼ teaspoon ground chilli	½ teaspoon salt
½ teaspoon ground peppercorns	1 egg

METHOD

Wash the meat, cut it into very small pieces, pound it into a pulp, remove all fibres and bones and mix it thoroughly with the spices and yogurt.

Now beat the white of an egg till stiff, add the yolk and beat further and mix in ½ teaspoon of salt; mix well with the meat. This prevents the meat from breaking up.

Make the meat and spices into balls of equal size, flatten each slightly and rub lightly with ghee, butter or other fat. Pass a metal skewer about 18 inches long through the middle of each and press each *tick-keeah* along till it almost presses against the next, and grill in the same way as the *seik kabab*, though *tick-keeahs* cook faster.

In India these are usually wrapped in a plantain leaf before cooking, which imparts a slight flavour to the meat.

To be eaten with *chappattis, parrattas* or the ordinary baker's loaf.

Enough for four

HUSSAINEE BEEF CURRY or BEEF CURRY ON STICKS

INGREDIENTS

2 lb. beef	¼ teaspoon ground garlic
1½ oz. ghee or butter	½ teaspoon chilli powder
½ teaspoon salt	1½ inches sliced green ginger
4 teaspoons ground onions	2 or 3 small onions, finely sliced
1 teaspoon turmeric	1 five-oz. bottle of yogurt
½ teaspoon ground ginger	6 metal or wooden skewers, each 6 inches long
½ cup of water	

METHOD

Cut the beef into pieces about an inch square and pass a skewer through the middle of each piece, then a piece of ginger, another bit of beef, and an onion; and so on, alternately, until all six skewers are filled.

Put the ghee into a pan and heat it, then add the spices and half-cup of water and cook, stirring the while, till they take on a brown colour. Put in the six skewers; add the yogurt and pour the mixture of yogurt, spices and water over the meat again and again till it is thoroughly impregnated.

Clap on a tight lid and simmer on a very low heat for two hours. Then, make sure that the meat is soft and serve in a large warmed dish *without* removing the sticks.

This dish is best eaten with *parrattas* or *chappattis*.

Hussainee curry can be made with mutton, veal, udder, liver or game. With mutton the simmering time is about 30 minutes; veal 1 hour; udder and liver about $1\frac{1}{2}$ hours; game 1 hour.

Enough for four

VINDALOO or BINDALOO—A Portuguese Dish

Some call this dish—which as far as one can discover was first concocted by Portuguese settlers in India, and now brought to perfection by their descendants the Goanese— *Vindaloo*; others, *Bindaloo*. But, call it what you will, it should taste delicious if the instructions are carried out to the letter.

INGREDIENTS

2 lb. pork, beef or a duck	2 or 3 bay leaves
6 oz. ghee, lard, dripping, or mustard oil	12 peppercorns
1 tablespoon garlic cloves, mashed	6 cloves—ground
1 tablespoon ground ginger	5 cardamoms, ground
1 teaspoon ground chilli	6 small sticks of cinnamon (2 inches each), ground
1 teaspoon ground coriander	4 oz. malt vinegar
$\frac{1}{4}$ teaspoon ground cummin	$\frac{1}{2}$ teaspoon salt

METHOD

NB—The tastiest *vindaloo* is cooked in mustard oil. Cut beef or pork into large cubes, or the duck into pieces as for curry. Mix vinegar, all the ground condiments and half a teaspoon of salt thoroughly and steep the meat or duck in this concoction for 18–24 hours. This impregnates the flesh, which can then be kept for two or three days without the slightest danger or sign of putrefaction.

Heat the fat in a thick pan, toss in the meat, condiments and vinegar, add peppercorns and bay leaves, simmer gently over a slow heat for two hours until the meat is tender; then turn out and serve up hot.

Enough for six to eight

MADRAS MEAT CURRY

INGREDIENTS

½ lb. sliced *cold* mutton or beef (previously cooked)   ½ teaspoon salt

1 lb. mashed potatoes   ½ teacup stock mixed with 2 tablespoons vinegar

2 oz. ghee, butter or mustard oil   ½ teaspoon ground red chilli

3 onions, sliced   6 cloves garlic

METHOD

Put the ghee, butter or mustard oil into a thick pan and heat till blue smoke rises. Drop in the onion and fry till light brown; then add chilli and garlic and fry for five minutes over a brisk flame, stirring all the time. Add meat and stock, mix thoroughly and simmer for ten minutes.

The potatoes must be boiled, mashed, mixed with parsley and mint and moulded into a circular wall, inside which the curry is poured. Serve hot.

Enough for four

KURMANASH

INGREDIENTS

2 lb. beef, sliced as for steaks   1 pint water

1½ inches green ginger, chopped   ¼ lb. ghee, butter or mustard oil

2 green chillis—chopped   1 tablespoon vinegar

2 onions—chopped   ½ teaspoon salt

METHOD

Mix ginger, chillis, onions and salt and place a layer on each slice of meat. Put the water, fat, vinegar and beef into a thick pan, clap on a tight-fitting lid and bring to the boil. Simmer till the water has evaporated, stir the meat gently and fry for five minutes. Then turn out into a dish. Cooked to a turn, *Kurmanash* is a very tasty dish. There should be no gravy.

Enough for six

BUFFADO

INGREDIENTS

1 plump duck   1 tablespoon of butter, ghee or mustard oil

1 cabbage cut into four   3 green chillis slit lengthwise

1 teaspoon ground saffron or turmeric   6 cloves garlic, chopped

1 pint water   1½ inches green ginger, sliced finely

1½ teaspoons salt   4 oz. (about ½ cup) vinegar

6 large onions cut into halves

METHOD

Use a large, deep saucepan. Place the cabbage on the bottom, and if you wish, cut it into smaller pieces. Now put in the duck, whole. Mix the saffron (or turmeric) and salt into the water and pour it over the duck. Then onions, chillis, green ginger and garlic—and finally the fat.

Bring to the boil and let it boil for an hour. Then open the lid, make sure that the duck is cooked; if not simmer till the flesh is tender. Five minutes before serving, add vinegar—and serve hot.

Enough for eight

VINTHALEAUX CURRY

INGREDIENTS

1 lb. mutton cut into small pieces	½ teaspoon ground red chillis
1 tablespoon of ghee, butter or mustard oil	¾ cup of stock
1 large sliced onion	½ teaspoon salt
2 cloves garlic, chopped	1 teaspoon sugar (brown)
2 teaspoons ground cummin seed	1 dessertspoon vinegar
1 teaspoon ground mustard seed	¾ teaspoon ground saffron or turmeric

METHOD

Fry onion to golden brown in the fat; add garlic and spices, and fry; then mutton, and fry further. Now add ¾ of a cup of stock, salt and sugar. Cover and boil for 25 minutes, and before serving, mix in a dessertspoon of vinegar. Serve hot.

Enough for four

CHICKEN MALAY GRAVY CURRY WITH WHITE PUMPKIN

INGREDIENTS

1 chicken	½ teaspoon ground ginger
¼ of a medium-sized pumpkin	¼ teaspoon ground garlic
2 oz. ghee or butter	1 cup coconut cream, or the milk of a large coconut
½ teaspoon salt	2 blades of lemon grass
4 teaspoons ground onions	4 cloves, ground
1 teaspoon ground turmeric	4 cardamoms, shelled and ground
½ teaspoon ground chillis	4 sticks cinnamon—1 inch each—ground

METHOD

Peel off the skin of the pumpkin, remove the portion containing the seeds, cut up into about sixteen segments or squares, and steep in water for fifteen minutes.

Fry all the ground ingredients in the fat and when brown, put in the chicken and salt. Fry till the chicken is light brown, then add the pumpkin, having allowed the water to drain away. Pour in the coconut milk and lemon grass and simmer for half an hour, or more if the chicken is still tough.

Before serving the curry, take out the lemon grass.

NB—On no account should coriander or cummin seed be used.

Enough for six

BRAIN CURRY

INGREDIENTS

Three lambs' brains	½ teaspoon turmeric
1 large chopped onion	½ teaspoon coriander—ground
2 large tomatoes, cut up	½ teaspoon cummin—ground
1 teaspoon chilli powder	¼ lb. margarine
1 teaspoon curry powder	Salt to taste (about a teaspoon)

METHOD

Wash the brains in cold water, then cover with cold water and boil with the turmeric for ten minutes. Remove and cut into halves. Fry onions to a golden brown in the margarine and add tomatoes, salt and the other spices. Then put in a cup of water, bring to the boil and add the brains. Cook for ten minutes over a low heat. Eat with rice, *chappattis* or baker's bread.

Enough for six

CURRIED BRAINS WITH SPINACH

METHOD

Use the same recipe, but when the tomatoes, spices and cup of water have been added, put in 1 lb. spinach and cook for ten minutes. Then fold in the brains, and cook for ten minutes more. Alternatively nettles may be used.

BRAIN BHAJIAS (*See* Cauliflower Bhajias—*under* Savouries)

Pieces of brain dipped in batter and made into *bhajias* make an excellent relish

LIVER AND UDDER KOAFTAH CURRY

INGREDIENTS

1 lb. liver	½ teaspoon ground ginger
1 lb. udder	½ teaspoon ground peppercorn
4 oz. lard, ghee or mustard oil	3 cloves of garlic—ground
6 oz. water or stock	1 dessertspoon finely chopped garden herbs
1 oz. ground onions	3 tablespoons breadcrumbs
1 teaspoon ground chilli	1 egg
¼ tablespoon ground turmeric	1 teaspoon salt

METHOD

Mince liver and udder very finely so that they can be moulded into balls. Mix with pepper, salt, herbs, breadcrumbs and egg and make into balls, about 1½ inches in diameter. Add a little of the stock if necessary.

Melt the fat, then put in the onions, garlic, and curry spices, and fry till brown. Then put in the remainder of the stock, bring to the boil, add the *koaftahs* (or meat balls), and simmer for about two hours. Serve hot, with rice.

Enough for eight

CHICKEN KORMA

INGREDIENTS

1 chicken cut into pieces	½ teaspoon ground ginger
5 oz. ghee or butter	2 cloves of garlic—ground
2 five-oz. bottles yogurt	10 peppercorns
1 teaspoon ground chillis	5 cloves
4 teaspoons ground onions	6 cardamoms—ground
1 teaspoon coriander seed	3 bay leaves
6 small sticks cinnamon (about an inch long), ground	½ pint water or stock
3 blades of lemon grass	Juice of a lemon
1 teaspoon salt	12 large onions cut lengthwise into slices

METHOD

Warm the ghee or butter, fry the sliced onions to a golden brown and set them aside. Then fry all the condiments including the ground spices and garlic, and when brown, throw in the pieces of chicken, and salt, and cook till brown. Then add the yogurt, bay leaves, lemon grass, stock and fried onions; bring to the boil, put on a close-fitting lid and simmer for 1½–2 hours, till the chicken is tender.

Take off the stove, pour in the lemon juice, mix, remove the lemon grass, and serve rice, *chappattis* or *parrattas*.

Enough for six

CHICKEN CURRY

INGREDIENTS

1 chicken	1 teaspoon ground turmeric
2 oz. ghee, butter or cooking oil	½ teaspoon ground chillis
1 pint of stock, or water	½ teaspoon ground ginger
¼ teaspoon salt	¼ teaspoon ground garlic
4 teaspoons ground onions	½ teaspoon ground coriander

METHOD

Take a medium-sized chicken; divide it into sixteen pieces. Melt the ghee, butter or oil, and the moment it starts to bubble, throw in the ground onion and cook till golden. Then add the remainder of the ground condiments and stir till brown. Now put in the pieces of chicken and salt and cook to a light brown colour. Add stock or water, clap on a tight fitting lid and simmer till the water is reduced by half. This should take from half to three quarters of an hour, by which time the dish is ready to be served.

Enough for six

PISH-PASH

INGREDIENTS

½ lb. *bassmuttee* or fine rice   ½ teaspoon *garam massala*—or hot spices

1 chicken   1 teaspoon salt

1½-inch stick of ginger—sliced   2 oz. butter or ghee

1 large onion—sliced   3 or 4 bay leaves

12 peppercorns

METHOD

This is a tasty dish, often given to invalids in India!

Thoroughly wash the rice. Clean and cut the chicken into pieces. Then cook the onions in the butter or ghee to a golden brown, and add all together, the chicken and other ingredients. Put in enough water to cover the contents—but no more. Simmer slowly till the chicken is tender. The water from the rice will be completely absorbed, but it will be more pappy than the normally cooked rice, where every grain is firm and separate. Serve and eat while hot.

Enough for four

FISH CURRIES

A SIMPLE FISH CURRY

INGREDIENTS

4 cod or other fish cutlets	Salt
2 dessertspoons butter, ghee or mustard oil	6 onions, sliced finely
1 cup of coconut milk	2 tablespoons thick tamarind juice
1 tablespoon *garam massala*	

METHOD

Sprinkle the fish finely on both sides with salt, fry in half the fat and set aside.

Put the coconut milk in a thick pan, add to it a dessertspoon of the remaining fat, the *garam massala* and the sliced onions. Mix well, then add the fish and bring to the boil. Simmer gently for 15 minutes, add the tamarind juice, simmer for two minutes and serve.

Enough for four

PRAWN KOAFTAH CURRY

INGREDIENTS

30–40 prawns	1 dessertspoon finely chopped garden herbs
4 oz. of lard, ghee or other fat	¼ teaspoon ground garlic
1 cup stock or water	½–1 teaspoon salt
1 oz. ground onions	3 tablespoons fine breadcrumbs
1 teaspoon ground chillis	1 egg
1 tablespoon ground turmeric	3 bay leaves
½ teaspoon ground ginger (optional)	3 blades lemon grass
¼ teaspoon ground peppercorns	

METHOD

Remove heads and shells and wash the prawns in salt water. Pound them to a pulp and mix with salt, pepper, garden herbs and 2 tablespoons of breadcrumbs. Add a little stock or milk, and mix well.

Beat the egg-white stiff, fold in the yolk, add it to the mixture and mould into balls the size of large walnuts and roll in the remaining breadcrumbs.

Put the fat into a pan and bring it to the boil. Put in the onions, garlic and ground spices, sprinkle with cold water, and fry till brown. Then add the *Koaftahs* or balls and fry them for five minutes. Pour in the remainder of the stock (or water), lower the heat, put on a tight-fitting lid, and simmer gently till cooked through, first adding the bay leaves and lemon grass, which can be removed before serving.

Enough for four

PRAWN PILAU

INGREDIENTS

1 large cupful of prawns—heads and tails removed	Salt
½ cup coconut cream	4 cardamoms—the seeds only
6 onions, sliced lengthwise	4 small sticks cinnamon (1 inch)
4 oz. butter or other fat	2 blades mace
½ lb. fine 'pilau' rice	6 peppercorns
½ dozen cloves	

METHOD

Thoroughly wash the rice. Fry the onions in the fat till they are golden brown and set them aside. Then fry the rice in the remainder of the butter and throw in the spices; and prawns.

When the rice is light golden, mix in the coconut cream and add sufficient water to just cover the contents in the pan. Lower the heat till the contents simmer gently, put on a tight-fitting lid and cook till the water has been absorbed and the *pilau* is quite dry. Turn out into a warm dish and strew with fried onions.

Sometimes, in addition to the fried onions, hard-boiled eggs cut either into halves or sections may be added.

There are many variations of *pilau*, which was originally an Arab dish and may be made with chicken, mutton or beef; and sultanas, pistachios and cashew nuts may be mixed in with the rice.

Enough for four

FISH CURRY

Of every kind of curry there are many varieties. This is a popular one from Ceylon.

INGREDIENTS

2 half-pound slices of fish, such as cod, hake or haddock	Salt to flavour
15 dry chillis, ground	A pinch of saffron or turmeric—about ½ teaspoon
3 dessertspoons sliced red onions	1 teaspoon sweet cummin, slightly roasted
2 slices green ginger—about one inch each	and ground
2 cloves of garlic, chopped	One tamarind bean, soaked and squeezed, and
One 2-inch piece of cinnamon	mixed into a cup of thick coconut milk
One 2-inch piece of rampa	¼ teaspoon fenugreek
A sprig of curry leaves	In addition, 1½ cups of thick coconut milk

METHOD

Wash and cut the fish into pieces and put them into a deep pan. Mix the coconut milk with all the dry ingredients, pour over fish, bring to the boil and simmer over a low heat till a thick gravy forms. Shake the pan so that the ingredients do not stick, but avoid stirring because this causes the fish to break into small pieces and become part of the gravy.

This should be eaten with rice and a little acid pickle, such as lime or mango (not sweet mango).

Miss G. L. Bhadrane de Silva   *Enough for two*
Waesnagiri
Degoda Lane
Amcalangoda
Ceylon

EEL STEW

INGREDIENTS

2 medium size eels	9 green chillis
6 inch-pieces of green ginger	½ cup coconut milk
1 teaspoon flour	1 teaspoon saffron or turmeric
¼ teaspoon pepper	1 dessertspoon mint
A small piece of mace	1 dessertspoon coriander
2 tablespoons sliced onion	6 leaves chopped spinach
A handful of meat bones	½ teaspoon sugar
1 dessertspoon butter	Juice of one lemon
1 dessertspoon Worcester sauce	Peel of one lemon
1¼ teacups of water	Salt, to taste
8 cloves	

METHOD

Put the bones, lemon peel, mace, spinach, mint, coriander, sugar, salt, half the pepper, half the butter, half the onions and a quarter cup of water into a pan and simmer for 15 minutes, stirring so that none of the ingredients stick; then add a cup of water and boil for a further 15 minutes. Skin the eels, cut them into three-inch pieces and slit them down the middle. Grind the chillis, saffron (or turmeric) and a little salt and rub this mixture into slit portions of the fish. Split the green chillis down the middle.

Place the eel pieces in a stewing pan, add the chillis, ginger, pepper, cloves and coconut milk. Strain the bone broth and pour over the fish and spices. Simmer for half an hour, then remove the fish and place it in a dish.

Put the remainder of the butter and the flour in a clean pan and fry for 2 minutes. Then pour the gravy in which the fish was cooked, over it, and boil for 2 minutes. Now add lemon juice, Worcester sauce, lemon peel and coconut milk, bring to the boil and pour over the fish. Serve hot with rice. Cooking time should be just over an hour.

Enough for four

CHALLUM

This is a South Indian dish.

INGREDIENTS

1 breakfast cup prawns	2 tablespoons coconut oil (or other cooking fat)
1 breakfast cup grated coconut	3 cloves garlic
3 red chillis, chopped finely	½ teaspoon ground turmeric
¼ teaspoon ground cummin	Salt to taste

METHOD

Boil the prawns till soft, then grind them into a paste. Add chillis, cummin, garlic and turmeric and mix well with the prawn paste. Add the grated coconut and salt and mix again.

Shape into round cutlets and fry in coconut oil. Most people who are not accustomed to it, dislike food cooked in coconut oil. I am one, and find butter, ghee, mustard oil, or cooking oil preferable. In South India, however, coconut oil is always used.

Enough for two

FISH MOLEE

INGREDIENTS

1 lb. white fish cut into squares	1 sliced green chilli
1 tablespoon ghee, or other fat	1 inch of finely sliced green ginger
1 breakfast cup of coconut milk	2 small onions, chopped
1 onion, sliced	1 tablespoon vinegar or tamarind juice
1 teaspoon ground turmeric	1 teaspoon salt

METHOD

Heat half the fat in a frying-pan, put in the sliced onion and turmeric and fry till the smell disappears. Then add the coconut milk, green chilli, ginger and chopped onions. Cook and stir for three minutes, and pour into saucepan.

With the other half of the fat, fry the fish (sprinkled with salt) and add it to the contents of the saucepan. Keep the pan uncovered, and when the fish is quite tender, pour in a tablespoon of vinegar, or better still, tamarind juice. Turn out at once into an earthenware casserole.

Enough for two

FISH CURRY (One of many kinds)

INGREDIENTS

1 lb. white fish	6 cloves of garlic, minced
The milk of one coconut	1 teaspoon finely sliced ginger

68

1 teaspoon rice flour

1 teaspoon mustard seed

1 teaspoon ground turmeric

1 sliced onion

2 green chillis, sliced lengthwise

1 tablespoon tamarind juice

½ teaspoon salt

METHOD

Mix rice flour, mustard seed, turmeric and coconut milk. Add onion, garlic, ginger and chillis. Stir mixture in a thick pan on moderate heat till it thickens. Then put in the fish and when tender, add salt, and just before serving, a tablespoon of tamarind juice.

Enough for two

PRAWN CURRY (1)

INGREDIENTS

1 lb. prawns (weight after removing heads and tails)

1 breakfast cup of coconut milk

2 *tablespoons* ground coriander

1 inch of turmeric

¼ teaspoon cummin seed—ground

2 red chillis

1 inch green ginger

6 cloves of garlic

2 oz. ghee or other fat

1 onion, sliced

1 tablespoon tamarind juice

½–1 teaspoon salt

METHOD

Fry onion in fat and when golden in colour put in the prawns and brown them. Then sprinkle with a little salt and add the spices, which must be ground or crushed and mixed. Dilute half the coconut milk with an equal amount of water and pour over the prawns. Simmer till tender, put in one tablespoon of tamarind juice and the remainder of the coconut milk. Serve hot.

Half a pound of white pumpkin, potato and carrot, diced, may be added with the diluted coconut milk and simmered till tender. This is optional.

Enough for four

PRAWN CURRY (2)

INGREDIENTS

1 lb. prawns (shelled and tailed)

¼ cup desiccated coconut

¼ teaspoon turmeric

1 teaspoon mustard seed

1 teaspoon chilli powder

2 tablespoons yogurt (about 1 five-oz. bottle)

1 large chopped onion

5 cloves of garlic, mashed

¼ teaspoon fenugreek (*maythi*)

2 tablespoons ground-nut oil

Salt to taste

½ fresh lemon

69

METHOD

Fry the onion in oil and when golden brown add all the ingredients, together with a cup of water. Cook for ten minutes. Then put in the prawns and squeeze the juice from half a lemon into the pot. Cook for another ten minutes and serve.

Enough for four

PRAWN BAFAT (A favourite Bengali dish)

INGREDIENTS

1 lb. prawns (weight after removing heads and tails)	2 tablespoons vinegar
1 teaspoon cummin seed—ground	1 dessertspoon ground coriander
1½ teaspoons turmeric—ground	1 breakfast cup of coconut milk
¼ teaspoon ginger—ground	1½ oz. ghee or other fat
6 cloves of garlic, mashed	1 onion, finely sliced
½ teaspoon ground chillis	½–1 teaspoon salt

METHOD

Fry onion in the fat till brown. Put in the prawns and when they turn red, add salt and spices. Fry till the raw smell vanishes (about 5 minutes); then add coconut milk, simmer for ten minutes, and before serving, put in the vinegar.

Enough for four

FISH CURRY (Another way)

INGREDIENTS

1 lb. white fish, cut into pieces	½ teaspoon ground ginger
The juice or pulp of six tamarind pods	6 cloves of garlic, mashed
1 breakfast cup of coconut milk	2 red chillis or ½ teaspoon ground chillis
½ teaspoon ground cummin	½ teaspoon fenugreek (ask for *maythi*)
6 peppercorns	1 tablespoon ground coriander
2 tablespoons ghee or butter,	1½ teaspoons ground turmeric
or 4 oz. mustard oil or other fat	½–1 teaspoon salt

METHOD

Heat the fat, throw in the fenugreek and fry for 3 minutes. Add the salt, garlic and spices and brown, then put in the fish with half a breakfast cup of water. Simmer for ten minutes, add tamarind pulp; and just before serving, mix in coconut milk.

Enough for four

SALMON CURRY

INGREDIENTS

1 large tin salmon	1 teaspoon ground poppy seed
½ teaspoon chilli powder	1 tablespoon ground coriander
6 cloves of garlic, mashed	¼ teaspoon ground ginger
1 onion, cut up finely and mashed	½ teaspoon ground cummin
2 teaspoons ground turmeric	½ teaspoon salt

METHOD

Bring the fat to the boil and drop in the seasonings and spices.

Pour the liquid from the tin of salmon, into a cup. Remove the fish without breaking it more than can be helped.

When the spices are brown, stir in the salmon, add the liquid from the tin and simmer for ten minutes. If you wish, put in two tablespoons of vinegar before serving.

Enough for two

VEGETABLE CURRIES

Legumes

UNTIL a few years ago legumes were used in Britain mainly for making pease pudding, and the most popular species were lentils and green split peas. For the past thirty years all sorts of legumes have been on show in the windows of Soho grocers, but the average Englishman will pass a shop twice a day for half a lifetime without entering and asking for some article with which he is unfamiliar!

During the war some hundreds of thousands of servicemen found themselves abroad, and a few discriminating souls broke through the food barrier, returning to Britain with the knowledge that tasty, exotic and satisfying meals could be cooked by foreigners. 'The things they do with lentils,' a repatriate informed me, 'were staggering. I had no idea that so insipid a food could be made into so many delicious dishes.'

These pulse foods are eaten throughout India and Pakistan—and Asia in general—cooked in a variety of ways. Imagination is one of the essentials of good cooking. In China, for instance, a banquet, from soup to sweet, can be served, entirely of soya bean, and the diner will believe he is tasting fish, flesh, fowl and sweet!

The reasons for so many lentil and bean dishes in the Indian cuisine are (1) India is largely vegetarian; (2) she is poor, and pulse foods are cheap, easily grown in a tropical climate, and do not need much manuring; (3) they are extremely sustaining; and (4) they can be eaten alone or as an accompaniment, and can be made into sweets!

The lentil is, therefore, an all-purpose food and gives more nourishment for a smaller outlay of cash than any other comestible. Indeed, of all the foods known to man, pulses have the highest protein value—even surpassing meat, in many cases. Because of this concentrated protein content legumes should be eaten sparingly, and to avoid indigestion no more than a quarter of a pound (dry weight) should be consumed in one day.

Salt must be added to all the following dishes, the amount varying according to taste, so no specific quantity is given.

CHANNA DHALL

INGREDIENTS

1 cup *channa dhall*	½ teaspoon *garam massala*
1 large onion—chopped	Salt to taste
2 tablespoons desiccated coconut	¼ teaspoon mustard seed
½ teaspoon ground turmeric	¼ teaspoon cummin seed
½ teaspoon chilli powder	2 tablespoons ground-nut oil

72

METHOD

Thoroughly wash the *channa dhall* and pour it into three cups of boiling water. When it has boiled for four or five minutes, add onions, coconut, turmeric, chilli powder and salt. Continue to boil till the *channa dhall* is soft, then mix in the *garam massala*.

Now heat two tablespoons of ground-nut oil and when hot put into it the mustard and cummin seed. When the seed begins to pop, mix into the pan with the *channa dhall*. Cook and stir for a minute or two: then serve.

Enough for four

CHANNA DHALL WITH CAULIFLOWER

INGREDIENTS

½ cup *channa dhall*	½ teaspoon mustard seed
1 cauliflower	½ teaspoon cummin seed
3 tablespoons of desiccated coconut	1 teaspoon tamarind
3 green chillis chopped lengthwise (optional)	2 tablespoons ground-nut oil
½ teaspoon ground turmeric	3 curry leaves
1 teaspoon chilli powder	Salt to taste
1 teaspoon sugar	

METHOD

Soak the *channa dhall* overnight. Boil till it is tender. Cut the cauliflower into small pieces and wash them; then boil with two cups of water. When semi-cooked, add the *channa dhall*, coconut, chillis, chilli powder, turmeric, sugar and a little salt. Cook till the cauliflower is tender. Now make a paste with the tamarind and two tablespoons of hot water. Add this to the mixture in the pan and cook for five minutes.

Heat the oil in a frying-pan and toss in mustard seed, cummin seed and curry leaves, till the seed begins to pop. Then add to the mixture, cook and stir for a minute or two.

This dish goes excellently with *chappattis* or *parrattas*.

Enough for six

LOBIA or BLACK-EYED BEANS

INGREDIENTS

2 cups *lobia*, soaked overnight	1 teaspoon sugar
2 large onions—chopped	½ teaspoon cummin seed
2 tablespoons desiccated coconut	2 tablespoons ground-nut oil
3 green chillis chopped up lengthwise	Salt to taste
½ teaspoon turmeric—ground	

METHOD
Soak the *lobia* overnight. Mix together *lobia*, onions, chillis, coconut, turmeric, sugar and a little salt.

Heat the oil in a pan and toss in cummin seed. Cook till the seed pops then add two cups of water to the mixture. Cook on a slow fire till the beans are tender, when the dish will be ready.

Enough for six

MUSSOOR or CONTINENTAL LENTILS

INGREDIENTS

1 cup *mussoor dhall*, washed and cleaned	½ teaspoon ground turmeric
1 large chopped onion	½ teaspoon chilli powder
2 tablespoons desiccated coconut	½ teaspoon *garam massala*
Salt to taste	

In addition you will need 2 tablespoons of frying oil and 3 or 4 cloves of garlic.

METHOD
Bring 3 cups of water to the boil and then toss in the *mussoor dhall*. If the water is already boiling the *mussoor* breaks up easily. If not, it takes longer to cook.

When semi-boiled, add the ingredients given above with the exception of the oil and garlic, and cook till the *mussoor* is soft but not soggy.

Now heat the oil in a frying-pan and after chopping the garlic into pieces, drop it in, cook till golden brown, then add to the *mussoor* and other ingredients.

New or diced potatoes, or prawns may be added: and the dish is best eaten with boiled rice.

Enough for four

MUSSOOR DHALL CHUR-CHURREE

INGREDIENTS

1 doz. onions of medium size	½ teaspoon ground turmeric
2 teaspoons butter	1 teaspoon ground chillis
1 cupful *mussoor dhall*	½ teaspoon ground ginger
2 cloves of garlic, mashed	Salt to taste

METHOD
Soak the *mussoor dhall* for an hour, then drain in a colander. Slice the onions finely lengthwise and fry till golden brown, in one teaspoon of the butter. Put the *dhall* into a deep pan with the garlic, salt and spices, add the remainder of the butter and fry till light brown. When this is done, add just enough water to cover the *dhall* and simmer for 15 minutes till soft. By this time all the water will have evaporated; but take care not to allow the *dhall* to stick to the pan. Serve strewn with the fried onions.

If *channa dhall* is used, soak it for at least twice as long before cooking, as *channa* is much harder.

Enough for four

URAD (or URD) DHALL

INGREDIENTS

1 cup *urad dhall*

1 large onion—chopped

½ teaspoon ground turmeric

½ teaspoon chilli powder

¼ lb. butter or cooking fat

Salt to taste

METHOD

Bring three cups of water to the boil and add the *urad dhall*. Let it boil for four minutes then add turmeric, chilli powder and salt. Fry the onions till they are brown, and when the *dhall* is soft, mix them in. This is a simple, quickly made dish very popular in the Punjab, where it is eaten with *parrattas*.

Enough for four

KABULI CHANNA or CHICK PEAS

INGREDIENTS

2 cups *kabuli channa*

2 finely chopped onions

3 medium-sized tomatoes—cut up

½ teaspoon turmeric

¼ teaspoon chilli powder

½ teaspoon ground cummin seed

1 teaspoon ground coriander seed

¼ packet margarine or cooking fat

Salt to taste

METHOD

Soak the *kabuli channa* overnight. Fry onions in the fat till brown. Add tomatoes and fry again for five minutes, then mix in the salt, spices and *channa* with half a cup of water. Cook for 20 minutes.

Enough for four

MOONG or SPROUTING BEANS

INGREDIENTS

2 cups of *moong* (bean sprouts)

2 onions—chopped

2 tablespoons of desiccated coconut

2 green chillis, chopped

¼ teaspoon turmeric—ground

½ teaspoon chilli powder

½ teaspoon whole mustard seed

Pinch of *hing* (asafoetida)

2 tablespoons of ground-nut oil

Salt to taste

75

METHOD

Soak the *moong* overnight. Mix onions, coconut, chillis, spices, *moong* and a little salt together; but not the mustard seed or the *hing*.

Heat ground-nut oil in a pan, then add the mustard seed and *hing* and cook till the seeds begin to pop. Now pour in a cup of water and continue to cook till the *moong* is soft. This dish should be very dry.

Enough for four

DHALL CURRY

INGREDIENTS

2 breakfast cups *channa dhall*	One half-inch stick of cinnamon
2 medium size red onions	1 cup of thin coconut milk
1 heaped teaspoon mustard seed	1 cup of thick coconut milk
1 teaspoon powdered fish (this can be bought)	A sprig of curry leaves
3 green chillis	1 teaspoon saffron or turmeric
The juice of half a lemon or lime (preferably lime)	An inch-piece of rampe
1 dessertspoon coconut oil, *ghee*, cooking fat or butter	Salt to flavour

METHOD

Wash the dhall till all trace of froth disappears.

Pour the thin coconut milk into a deep pan, bring it to the boil and slip in the dhall. Stir well to prevent catching as dhall sticks easily. After three minutes pour in the thick milk and add the salt. Cook for another five minutes, remove from heat and pour over it the lemon or lime juice.

Into another pan put the fat and when it is just about to bubble, stir in the onions, curry leaves, rampe and mustard seed. Cook and stir till the onions are golden-brown; then add the dhall, clamp on a tight cover and simmer for two minutes. Serve with rice and sour pickle.

Miss G. L. Bhadrane de Silva
Waesnagiri
Degoda Lane
Amcalangoda, Ceylon

Enough for four

CAULIFLOWER CURRY

In few Indian restaurants in Britain does one see curried cauliflower, and customers must wonder why. The reason, perhaps, is that the cauliflower is a delicate vegetable, the florets break up easily, and it isn't the ideal vegetable for cooking done on a large scale.

INGREDIENTS

1 large cauliflower	1 teaspoon turmeric
1 lb. tomatoes (or a 1 lb. can)	½ teaspoon cummin
1 lb. potatoes (preferably new)	¼ teaspoon ginger
1 lb. carrots	½ teaspoon chilli powder
1 breakfast cup broad beans or 1 can of broad beans	1 large lemon
3 or 4 sprigs of parsley	2 medium sized onions
2 oz. butter or mustard oil or cooking oil	Salt
1½ teaspoons coriander	

METHOD

Make a paste of the coriander, turmeric, cummin, ginger and chilli powder and a tablespoon of cold water. Then gradually add boiling water and keep mixing till you have one breakfast cup full.

Chop onions finely and fry till brown in whatever fat you are using.

Cut away the cauliflower heads and stems from the main stalk, place them in a colander (or cullender) and spray gently with running water. Set aside.

Put the fried onions and fat into a deep saucepan, add the curry spices and tomatoes, and bring to the boil. When they reach boiling point, and not before, put in the beans, though if canned beans are used they can be added with the other vegetables.

Chop the carrots and potatoes into cubes and add them. When they are half-cooked, put in the cauliflower and cover with water. Quarter the lemon and add that; bring to the boil, then simmer till cauliflower is tender, but firm. Don't stir, but shake the pan gently to prevent sticking. Garnish with parsley and serve with rice and pickle.

Enough for four

MASAK LEMAK (Malay Dish)

INGREDIENTS

1 large onion	2 cloves garlic
5 red chillis	1 cup coconut milk
1 tablespoon dried shrimps	1 teaspoon bally chow or balachong
1 cabbage—small	

METHOD

Pound the dried shrimps in a mortar or bowl and mix with the bally chow. Make sure that there are no pieces of shell attached to the shrimps.

Wash and chop the cabbage, onion and garlic, and slit the chillis down the middle. If you don't want the dish to be too pungent, remove the chilli seeds.

Put the coconut milk and one cup of water into a pan, then shrimps, onion and garlic and bring to the boil. When boiling hard, add the cabbage and cook fast for 10 minutes when the cabbage should be tender, but crisp. Serve with curried fish.

Enough for four

BANANA-SKIN CURRY

INGREDIENTS

2 breakfast cups of green banana skin	1 green chilli, chopped
2 tablespoons grated coconut	1 dessertspoon ghee
3 onions	½ teaspoon mustard seed
1 teaspoon ground cummin	2 or 3 curry leaves
1 teaspoon saffron or turmeric	Salt to taste

METHOD

Wash the unripe bananas and with a sharp knife peel off the top green skin. Chop two cups of the skin, cover with water and boil with a little salt. Add all the ingredients except the mustard and curry leaves. Mix well, clap the lid on the pan and allow to simmer for ten minutes.

Place the ghee in a frying-pan and add the mustard seed and curry leaves. As soon as the mustard starts to pop, put in the banana skin and cooked spices. (The water, incidentally, should be absorbed.) Fry for two or three minutes, turn out and serve while hot.

The bananas will not, of course, be wasted. They will ripen in the normal way and be fit for consumption within a few days.

Enough for four

BRINJAL BAKE or BYGAN BAKE

INGREDIENTS

4 large *brinjals* (aubergines)	Pinch of salt
4 eggs	Breadcrumbs
6 medium-sized potatoes	The whites of 2 eggs
4 medium-sized onions	6 small onions
3 green chillis, chopped	1 breakfast cup of boiled prawns
Pinch of black pepper	Ghee or cooking fat

METHOD

Wash and halve each *brinjal*, retaining a portion of the stalk. Cover with water, add salt and boil. When parboiled, scoop out the soft middle pulp and set the skins aside.

If the potatoes are new, merely scrub them; if not, thinly peel. Cut the 4 medium-sized onions into small pieces. *Hard*-boil the eggs and cut them too into small pieces. Chop the prawns up small.

Put a tablespoon of fat in a pan and heat. Slice the small onions and put them in. When brown put in the potatoes, diced, and the chopped onions. Fry for five minutes.

Then add the *brinjal* pulp, eggs, green chillis, pepper and salt. Then the chopped prawns. Mix all this with sufficient breadcrumbs to fill the *brinjal* skins, and fry well in the fat.

Now fill the skins with the stuffing, brush them over with white of egg and sprinkle with breadcrumbs. Put into the oven (medium heat) and bake till brown.

Enough for four

KHUTTAH CURRY or ACID VEGETABLE CURRY

Take small quantities of vegetables in season.

INGREDIENTS

1 lb. potatoes	½ teaspoon chilli powder
¼ lb. artichokes	2 cloves of garlic
¼ lb. sweet potatoes	1 teaspoon ground coriander seed
¼ lb. carrots	2 oz. mustard oil
½ lb. red or white pumpkin	½ oz. tamarind
½ lb. tomatoes	1 dessertspoon 'foot' sugar or Demerara sugar
1 onion cut up small	1 teaspoon onion seed or *colinga*
1 teaspoon ground turmeric	Salt to taste

METHOD

Mash the tamarind and mix it into a paste with a little water. Then add water to make two breakfast cupsful. Mix in the 'foot' sugar. Add the spices and garlic. Cut the vegetables into fairly large pieces and add them to this liquid and bring to the boil.

In a separate pan heat the mustard oil and when the oil bubbles, throw into it the *colinga*. When the seeds start to pop, pour the oil and seeds over the boiled vegetables. Then place a tight lid on the pot and simmer for 20 minutes. It is better eaten cold than hot.

Enough for four

ALOO DUM (Potato Curry)

INGREDIENTS

1 lb. new potatoes—fairly small	3 cassia leaves
½ teaspoon *garam massala*	2 oz. sour milk
½ teaspoon ground turmeric	4 oz. ghee or butter, or other fat
½ teaspoon ground coriander	½ teaspoon cummin seed—ground
¼ teaspoon each of red and black pepper	A pinch of aniseed
Pinch of dried ginger	Salt to taste

METHOD

Put turmeric, coriander, pepper and ginger into a bowl, add a little water and work into a paste.

Scrub potatoes and boil them till they are done but *firm*. Mix the spice-paste into the sour milk and smear it over the potatoes.

Melt the fat in a saucepan, put in the cassia leaves, aniseed, cummin and *garam massala*. Add the potatoes, cook for a minute, add two tablespoons of water, allow to simmer for five minutes and then when nearly dry, remove.

Enough for two

BHOONEE KHICHIRI (Khedgeree)

INGREDIENTS

½ lb. of fine rice

¼ lb. lentils

6 onions sliced lengthwise

4 oz. butter or other fat

1½-inch stick of green ginger

12 peppercorns

Salt to taste

½ dozen cloves

The seeds of 2 cardamoms

4 bay leaves

4 small sticks of cinnamon

METHOD

Melt the fat, and when bubbling throw in the sliced onions. Cook them until reddish brown in colour, then remove and set them aside.

The lentils must be soaked for an hour before cooking, and the rice washed. Drain both, toss them into the pan and fry till the fat has been completely absorbed. Then add the green ginger (sliced) and all the other ingredients. Mix well together and just cover the contents with water.

Use a stout pan with a well-fitting lid. Put on the lid and simmer gently till all the water is absorbed. Do not stir after the first mixing, but gently shake the pot from time to time to prevent the contents from sticking.

When the water has been absorbed and the rice is dry, turn the contents into a warm dish, garnish with the fried onions and serve.

Enough for four

Note—There are many kinds of *Khichiri*, and the dish may be made with *mussoor* or red *dhall*; *moong* or small-grained yellow *dhall*; gram or *channa dhall* (a very large variety); or green peas.

In many families it is customary to make *jurrud* or yellow-tinted *khichiri*, which is done by sprinkling a teaspoon or more of saffron or turmeric over the rice and lentils while frying them. It gives the dish a slightly more delicate flavour and renders it more attractive to the eye.

Bhoonee means crisp; but there is yet another kind known as *geela* or soft *khichiri*. In this, *moong dhall* is used and little or no butter. The onions are boiled along with the rice, *dhall* and spices. It is less tasty than *bhoonee khichiri*, but more suitable for invalids.

INDIAN SWEETS

THE average Englishman never acquired a real liking for Indian sweets, largely because their delicate flavour is killed by the alcoholic beverages favoured by Europeans. Moreover, the bon-bons are inclined to be greasy or sticky, while the desserts are usually large, soft and syrupy—rather cloying, to the masculine palate, although women generally enjoy them.

However, many Indian sweet dishes are made from milk curd, and are therefore very sustaining; they are foods in the best sense of the word, and do not merely give one temporary energy. Wrestlers and strong men often eat *rasgullas, rab-ri* and *saundaesh* as part of their training diet.

HULVAS

Hulva is a traditional dessert all over Northern India, and a segment of *hulva* will enable one to miss a meal quite happily.

Carrot, green ginger, saffron, marrow and even semolina are used, and really delicious sweets may be produced with all. If you feel that the recipe contains too much fat, cut it down to suit your palate.

All *hulvas* may be made with or without saffron, turmeric or rosewater. Experiment and decide for yourself.

GAJAR-KA HULVA

INGREDIENTS

2 lb. carrots (young if possible)	1 quart of milk
½ lb. sugar	½ oz. saffron or turmeric
¼ lb. butter	2 oz. sultanas
2 oz. mixed nuts—ground	1 dessertspoon rose-water

METHOD

Scrub and grate the carrots, put them into a thick saucepan with the milk, bring to the boil; then lower the heat and simmer for *two hours*, stirring occasionally with a wooden spoon to ensure that they do not stick. When the carrots and milk have coagulated into a thick pulp, put in the butter and sugar, cook on a fairly high flame for 15 minutes—stirring the while— then add the ground nuts and sultanas. Mix the saffron or turmeric in a tablespoon of boiling water; remove the pan from the stove, stand for a few minutes and mix in the saffron or turmeric. Cook over a high flame for a couple of minutes, stirring; then remove, pour into a dish and cool. Sprinkle with rose-water. Should set firmly.

MARROW HULVA

INGREDIENTS

1 lb. ripe marrow or squash

½ lb. butter

¼ lb. sugar

½ oz. saffron or turmeric

1 teaspoon rose-water

METHOD

Peel marrow, cut into sections and gouge out the seeds. Place pieces in a saucepan, just cover with water and cook to a thick pulp. Now strain the pulp through a fine sieve or butter muslin and fry in butter till brown.

Make a syrup with the sugar and a pint of water and boil till it thickens. Add this to the marrow and cook for 15 minutes till stiff. Mix saffron or turmeric with a little boiling water and add. Stir well, remove from the flame and allow to cool. Sprinkle with rosewater.

A similar *hulva* may be made with ripe pumpkin instead, but owing to the coarser flesh more sugar must be used.

SOOJEE HULVA

INGREDIENTS

½ lb. semolina

½ lb. butter

½ lb. sugar (Demerara)

1 teaspoon ground cinnamon

4 oz. blanched almonds

4 oz. sultanas

10 cardamoms (seeds only)

1 pint water

METHOD

Add sugar to water and bring to the boil, then set aside. Melt butter, add semolina and cook till golden brown. *Very slowly*, add the syrup and cook, mixing the while, till water is completely absorbed. Add sultanas, almonds, cardamom seeds and cinnamon and stir for a minute. Put into a flat dish and pat down till level. Eat either cold or warm.

JALABEE (*pronounced* Ja-lay bee)

This is a favourite Indian sweet, and unique in my experience. *Jalabees* can be made either very badly, or very well. At their best, they are succulent morsels fit to grace the Lord Mayor's Banquet.

INGREDIENTS

½ lb. plain flour

2 lb. sugar

1½ lb. butter, mustard oil or other fat

½ oz. yeast

1 teaspoon of saffron or turmeric (*essential*)

A wide-mouthed pouring funnel

METHOD

Place yeast, flour and sufficient water into a bowl to work into a batter thick enough for pancakes. Or mix the yeast with three dessertspoons of warm water and a teaspoon of flour; then cover and put in a warm place to rise. When risen, mix in the flour.

Meanwhile melt the sugar with a little water and make into a thick syrup. Place on a hotplate.

Mix saffron or turmeric with one tablespoon of boiling water, add to syrup and mix well.

Melt butter or oil in a wide, shallow pan and heat till bubbles are seen. Then turn down heat to maintain that temperature. Now fill the funnel with the batter and place a finger over the aperture at the bottom to keep it in.

Then hold the funnel over the pan of hot fat or oil, remove the finger and make a circle about four inches in diameter. Then, inside it, a smaller one, and end up with a blob of batter in the middle. Cover the end of the funnel with your finger immediately.

Cook the *jalabee* till it turns golden, and with a slice turn it to cook on the other side. Take out and drain, and then slip it into the pan of warm syrup. The batter, being porous, instantly absorbs syrup. If cooked just right, it should be crisp, juicy and succulent.

Make as many *jalabees* as you require; the rest of the batter and syrup will keep for a while.

JALABEES WITH EGG CUSTARD

Any jalabees left over may be put into a buttered dish, with a pint of milk into which two eggs have been beaten poured over them. Sprinkle with a little grated nutmeg, and bake for hour in a slow oven until a custard forms. Can be eaten hot or cold.

RASGULLAS (*literally* Balls of Juice)

INGREDIENTS

1 quart of milk	1 dessertspoon rose-water
1 large lemon	1 lb. sugar

METHOD

Make the sugar into a thick syrup with a little water. Heat the milk to about 200°F. and add to it the juice of the lemon. The milk will crack at once and separate into curd and whey. Strain the milk through a piece of butter muslin and the whey will run off. Gather the ends of the muslin and squeeze the contents till all the liquid has run off. Let it cool; then mould the curd into balls of about 1½ inches in diameter.

Place the balls in the boiling syrup and cook them gently till they are golden brown all over. Then place them on a grid and allow them to drip. When cool, sprinkle with rose-water or any other flavouring you prefer. Properly cooked, the *rasgullas* will be spongy and juicy.

SEMOLINA LUDDOO

INGREDIENTS

1 lb. medium semolina	4 oz. chopped almonds
1 lb. sugar	4 oz. sultanas
½ lb. butter	4 oz. mixed nuts—chopped
1 oz. pine kernels	½ oz. cardamoms—shelled

METHOD

For the first time, it may be advisable to use half the quantity of cardamoms, as they have a strong flavour. Add more on the next occasion.

Melt the butter in a thick saucepan, fold in the semolina, add the cardamoms and cook over a high flame, stirring all the while.

When the semolina is a golden brown, add the other ingredients and simmer for 15 minutes. Remove from the stove, cool, and mould into 1½-inch balls.

GOOLAB JAMOON

INGREDIENTS

1 lb. self-raising flour	1 tablespoon rose water
3 oz. butter or margarine	6 cardamoms
1 large tin full-cream condensed milk	2 or 3 sticks cinnamon
1½ lb. sugar	Fat for deep frying

METHOD

Make a thin syrup with 1½ pints of water, the sugar, the seeds of the cardamoms and the sticks of cinnamon. Boil well and when cool add the rose-water and set aside. Rub the butter (or margarine) into the flour, then add the condensed milk and knead into a soft, smooth dough, which must not crumble or crack. If too stiff, add a little milk—about a tablespoonful. Roll the dough into cigar shapes about three or four inches long and as thick as the normal adult's finger.

Bring the fat to the boil, then lower the heat till it just simmers. Pop the fingers into the fat and cook until they are *dark* brown. When cold, drop into the syrup and *soak well*. Goolab Jamoons should have a charred-looking skin. This effect, though not a charred taste, is obtained by mixing a pinch of bicarbonate of soda into the dough.

SAVOURIES

INDIANS love savouries which are always served at Indian restaurants in Britain, along with curries and rice; or curries and *parrattas* or *chappattis*. They range from *bhurtas*, which are composed mainly of raw herbs, tomatoes, potatoes and other vegetables, to chutneys, pickles and relishes, such as Tamarind Fish and *Ballychow*; and of course, *dahi* or yogurt.

In writing for the British public one's choice is restricted, because some of the tastiest chutneys and pickles are made from mangoes, and both the price and quality of mangoes in Britain put them outside our range. The recipes given, however, offer a fairly wide choice with indigenous materials. In making *bhurtas*, note that they will not keep, so make only enough for one or two meals.

DAHI (Sour Milk or Yogurt)

Boil a pint of milk. When it is still tepid (about 110°F.) mix in a 'starter': lime or lemon juice; tamarind juice; a tablespoon of whey, or a dessertspoon of yogurt or sour milk. Mix thoroughly, put in a warm place, such as an airing cupboard, and wrap entirely in flannel or straw. If you have a haybox, put the jug in that. It should be ready in from 10 to 16 hours and can be eaten alone; with sugar, honey or fruit; with salt and pepper; or with curries and rice. It is an all-purpose health food, good for digestive troubles, contains plenty of protein and is non-fattening.

GOOJIAS or MINCE PUFFS

INGREDIENTS

1 lb. cold beef or mutton previously cooked	12 oz. self-raising flour
1 teaspoon salt	1 green chilli, cut into small pieces
1½ inches of green ginger, sliced	2 cloves of garlic, chopped
2 onions, finely shredded	6 oz. butter, ghee or other cooking fat

METHOD

Put the meat through a mincer, and then into a thick saucepan together with all the ingredients *except* flour and 4 oz. of butter or ghee. Cook for 15 minutes, adding a little water and stirring to prevent burning.

Rub the 4 oz. of fat into the flour and work into a stiff dough. Roll out dough to a thickness of about ⅛ inch, and cut into squares measuring 4 inches by 4 inches. Place a little of the cooked mince on each square, and bring each corner of dough over to form an

85

envelope. Press down and seal the edges, put into an oven at about 350°F. (Regulo 4), and bake for 20 to 30 minutes. Remove when golden brown.

BHAJIAS or SPICED VEGETABLE SAVOURY BALLS

INGREDIENTS

1 teaspoon ground coriander	½ teaspoon chilli powder
4 tablespoons *basoon* flour	1 onion, chopped
4 teaspoons ground cummin	2 cloves of garlic, chopped
1 lb. butter, ghee or vegetable cooking fat; or	Salt to taste

alternatively, a pint of mustard, olive or other cooking oil.

METHOD

Make a pancake-type batter of the *basoon* and cold water. Mix in the salt, spices, garlic and onion.

Put the fat or oil into a thick pan and heat till almost at the boil. Then, taking a full teaspoon at a time of the batter and spices, drop it into the oil or fat. Instantly the fat will start to bubble and sizzle. Cook for about a minute till the outside of the batter is golden brown; then remove. In a large pan three or four spoonfuls of batter can be dropped in one after the other and cooked together. (Use a wire basket.)

Bhajias can be made even tastier if two tablespoons of cooked diced potato, or carrot, or cabbage, or a mixture of all three, are added to the batter. Or, alternatively, the same quantity of chopped cold beef or mutton.

From start to finish this savoury does not take more than 15 minutes to make. Bhajias should be eaten hot, or they become leathery.

BRINJAL SAMBAL

INGREDIENTS

1 dessertspoon minced onion	1 green chilli, minced
1 dessertspoon thick tamarind juice	¼ teaspoon salt
1 dessertspoon skinned tomatoes with seeds removed—mashed	¼ oz. ghee or mustard oil

2 dessertspoons *brinjals* (aubergines) roasted, skinned and mashed

METHOD

Mash and mix in the other ingredients, except the ghee or oil, with the *brinjals*. Warm the ghee or oil, put in the other ingredients and fry till all the fat is absorbed. Serve either hot or cold. To be eaten either as a savoury or with curries and rice or/and *chappattis* or *parrattas*.

Prawn Curry, Parsee Style
(See recipe Kolbi Patia page 30)

LOOCHEES

Loochees, as they are known in Bengal; or *poorees* elsewhere in North and Central India, are usually served for supper, and at ceremonial gatherings. They would go down very well at cocktail parties.

INGREDIENTS

½ lb. self-raising flour   ½ lb. ghee or butter

METHOD

Place the flour in a bowl and work in ¼ oz. of butter or ghee. Add enough water to knead into a fairly soft dough; then divide the mass into about 18 balls.

Take each ball in the greased palms of the hands and press into an oval shape. This done, smear it with a little flour and flatten it till it is about four inches across, by means of a rolling pin.

Now melt the remaining ghee or butter in a large thick frying-pan or a very shallow saucepan, and when blue smoke rises put the oval cake in and press gently with a flat ladle; preferably one with perforations in its surface. The side of the *loochee* in contact with the hot surface of the pan will swell. At this point turn the *loochee* and cook the other side; but *don't repeat the operation.*

Loochees should be eaten hot from the pan and with the addition only of a little salt. They are excellent on their own or with fried potatoes, or with *Aloo Dum.*

DHALL POOREES

INGREDIENTS

½ lb. *channa dhall*   1 oz. mustard oil

1 lb. flour   ½ lb. ghee or butter

1 teaspoon each of red and black pepper, ground

    ginger and asafoetida

METHOD

Steep the *channa dhall* in water overnight, and next day grate into a pulpy mass. Put the mustard oil into a pan and fry the *channa* to a golden brown, together with the spices.

Remove when the mass is doughy, and when cool knead into balls the size of large marbles.

Next, knead the flour with a little fat, as in the case of *loochees*; divide the dough and make into as many balls as the *channa*. Make each into a cup form, and mould round a *channa dhall* marble, ensuring that the dough encases the *channa* evenly; then roll into a flat circular cake, with a greased roller on a greased surface. Fry gently till the under surface is a golden brown; then turn and fry the other side. Put only a smear of grease in the pan at a time.

Alternatively these may be filled with a *chur-churree* mixture (see page 74). They make a particularly good accompaniment for *Aloo Dum.*

KACHOWREES

INGREDIENTS

½ lb. green *kalai* or any other cereal, or lentils   Salt to taste

1 lb. flour   1 lb. of butter, ghee or other fat

1 teaspoon each of ground ginger, asafoetida, and   1 oz. mustard oil
  cummin

METHOD

Steep the green *kalai* or lentils in water overnight. Next day grate them finely and mash them into a doughy mass.

Mix the spices and a little salt, put into a pan with the very hot mustard oil, and singe. Then cool. Knead and roll out the flour, as for pastry, with a little butter or ghee; cut into cases, fill with dollops of *kalai* or lentil, fold over and fry in a panful of ghee, butter or cooking fat.

Kachowrees are usually eaten with hot pickle.

BOONDI (1)

INGREDIENTS

2 cups *basoon* flour   1 teaspoon chilli powder

Salt to taste   2 cups ground-nut oil

METHOD

Add water gradually to the *basoon* to produce a batter thick enough to trickle through the holes of a perforated ladle. Add salt and the chilli powder and beat till the batter is smooth and light. Bring the oil to the boil and gently pour the batter into the perforated ladle so that it drops through the holes into the hot oil. As soon as the batter turns golden brown, lift the cakes from the oil with a wire strainer and place on clean white paper which soaks up the superfluous oil. Can be eaten either hot or cold; preferably hot.

BOONDI (2)

Soak two dessertspoons of *boondi* in cold water for half an hour. Drain away water and mix it into a cupful of yogurt that has been well beaten.

CAULIFLOWER BHAJIAS

INGREDIENTS

1 cup water   1 teaspoon chilli powder

1 medium-sized cauliflower   ½ teaspoon ground cummin

1 cup *basoon* flour   ½ teaspoon ground turmeric

Salt to taste   Enough ground-nut oil for deep frying

1 teaspoon baking-powder

METHOD

Make a batter of *basoon* and cold water and mix into it the baking-powder, chilli powder, cummin, turmeric and salt. Cut the cauliflower into small pieces.

Bring the oil to the boil; dip pieces of cauliflower into the batter and drop into the oil. When they turn golden brown, lift them out, and eat, if possible, when warm. A wire basket should be used, for quickness.

Bhajias can be made with all kinds of vegetables: potatoes, carrots, aubergines, bits of cabbage, spinach—and even hard-boiled eggs. If you like the savoury a trifle more pungent, add pieces of chopped-up green chilli.

SALTED POOREES

INGREDIENTS

2 cups plain or self-raising flour

2 tablespoons ghee or ¼ lb. butter or cooking fat

A pinch of baking-powder if plain flour is used

½ teaspoon cummin seed (black)

Sufficient water to make dough

Fat or oil for frying

Salt to taste

METHOD

Rub the butter or ghee into the flour, salt and cummin seed, slowly add water to make a dough of medium stiffness. Knead well and set aside for 30 minutes. Make ten balls of equal size, roll each out into a pancake and fry them in deep oil, fat or ghee.

May be eaten hot or cold, and will keep for *weeks—if* any are left!

SHANKER PALI

INGREDIENTS

1 cup wholemeal flour

1 tablespoon ghee or butter

2 tablespoons sugar

½ cup of water

Fat or oil for frying

METHOD

Mix the sugar and water thoroughly and add gradually to the flour till you get a hard dough. Knead well, and set aside for 30 minutes. Divide dough into four and roll out like thin pancakes. Cut each pancake into small squares and fry in deep oil or fat. Remove when golden brown and eat, preferably when hot.

BASOON OMELETTE

INGREDIENTS

½ cup *basoon* flour

1 egg

Salt to taste

¼ teaspoon chilli powder

1 green chilli, chopped (optional)

½ onion, finely chopped

METHOD

Make a batter with *basoon* and cold water. Beat the egg and mix in with the batter and again beat well. Add chilli, salt and onion and fry in a little fat as you would an omelette.

BHAJIA CURRY

INGREDIENTS

½ cup *basoon* flour

Salt to taste

¼ teaspoon chilli powder

¼ teaspoon baking-powder

1 large onion

½ teaspoon turmeric—ground

½ teaspoon coriander—ground

½ teaspoon cummin—ground

1 teaspoon curry powder

2 tablespoons ground-nut oil

Deep fat or oil for frying

METHOD

Make a batter with *basoon* and cold water. Mix in the salt and chilli, then the baking-powder. Heat the frying oil or fat and drop teaspoonsful of batter into it. Cook till golden brown, remove and place in *cold water*.

Chop onion finely; fry to a golden brown in ground-nut oil and add a cup of water. Now lift the *bhajias* from the water, squeeze the liquid out of them and drop them into the onions and ground-nut oil.

Add the turmeric, coriander, cummin and curry powder and boil for ten minutes. To be eaten with boiled rice, *chappattis* or baker's bread.

DOSAI (A Madrassi Dish)

This dish can be made only if one has a grinding stone, or food grinder.

INGREDIENTS

2 cups rice

¼ cup *urad dhall*

Salt to taste

½ teaspoon baking-powder

1 tablespoon ground-nut oil

METHOD

Soak the *dhall* overnight and grind them while wet. Add the salt and baking-powder and make into a thin batter. Keep the batter for 8–10 hours.

Bring a tablespoonful of ground-nut oil to the boil in a frying-pan and make pancakes, using a tablespoonful of batter each time. Fry on both sides to a golden brown. These may be eaten hot with either chutney (preferably) or curries; syrup or jam.

INDIAN FRIED POTATOES (Tooka)

INGREDIENTS

2 large potatoes

½ cup of ground-nut oil

Salt to taste

¼ teaspoon chilli powder

½ teaspoon ground coriander

½ teaspoon ground cummin

Pan of deep fat

METHOD

Peel and slice the potatoes into rounds, about ½ inch thick. Fry in deep fat. When half-fried, remove and press each slice, on a board, to half its thickness. Return these pressed slices to the pan of fat, add salt, chilli, coriander and cummin and fry till golden brown. Eat hot.

DHALL FRITTERS

INGREDIENTS

½ lb. *channa dhall*

¼ teaspoon salt

¼ tablespoon yogurt

1 egg

3 sliced onions

1 red chilli—ground

2 green chillis—sliced

½ teaspoon ground turmeric

1 cup of mustard oil

METHOD

Soak the *channa dhall* overnight in just enough water to cover it. Next morning pour it into a sieve and drain away the water. Then grind the *dhall*, which will be soft, into a paste, and add to it the salt, yogurt, egg (beaten), onions, chillis and turmeric. Mix thoroughly, and then with the addition of a little cold water, make into a thick batter.

Heat the mustard oil till a wisp of blue smoke rises from the surface; then drop the batter—a dessertspoonful at a time—into the oil and fry till brown.

Should be eaten hot.

BYGAN BHAJJI

Bhajjis are fried dishes made of vegetables, and one of the best vegetables for making *bhajjis* is the *bygan* or *brinjal* or aubergine. And the best oil for frying vegetables is mustard oil.

INGREDIENTS

2 very large or 3 medium-sized aubergines

4 oz. mustard oil

1 teaspoon ground turmeric

1 teaspoon ground coriander

½ teaspoon ground cummin

½ teaspoon ground chillis

Salt to taste

METHOD
Wash the aubergines thoroughly and cut them into slices about ⅛ inch thick. Fry them in oil till light brown in colour. Drain away the oil and place the fried slices on a hot plate.

Mix the spices into a paste with one tablespoon of boiling water, add to the oil and cook for three minutes.

Put the slices back into the pan, pour the spices and oil over them and simmer for ten minutes till well browned. Serve hot, with rice and a little chutney or pickle.

GOOLGOOLAS

INGREDIENTS

1 lb. *basoon* or self-raising flour	4 oz. raisins
6 oz. brown sugar	1 lb. ghee, butter or mustard oil

METHOD
First mix the *basoon* or flour and sugar thoroughly. Then, by adding cold water, little by little, make a thick batter. Now add the raisins and mix again. Bring the fat to the boil and drop in three or four dessertspoonfuls of batter separately. Cook till they are dark brown, remove and allow to drip. Eat while warm, and cook only as much as you need. The batter will keep.

FOOLOWRIES

INGREDIENTS

1 lb. *basoon*	2 green chillis
1 teaspoon salt	1 doz. fresh mint leaves
2 onions	1 lb. ghee, butter or mustard oil

METHOD
Mince onions, chillis and mint very finely. Put them into a bowl, add the *basoon* and salt, and mix. Add water gradually, to make a thick batter.

Heat the fat, and drop in three or four dessertspoonfuls of the batter, separately. Cook till brown, remove, drain and eat while hot.

BHURTAS AND OTHER RELISHES

BHURTAS or mashes of vegetables and spices are accompaniments to almost every Indian meal. They are easily compounded, extremely tasty and lend a tang that pickles and chutneys do not possess.

POTATO BHURTA

INGREDIENTS

1 moderate-sized onion	Salt to taste
2 green chillis	1 teaspoon mustard oil
8–10 medium-sized potatoes	Juice of one lemon or lime

METHOD

Boil the potatoes well so that they can be mashed easily. Chop the onion and chillis into small pieces and squeeze over them the lemon or lime juice. Then mix with mustard oil, adding salt to taste. Add this to the mashed potato and mix and beat thoroughly. Mustard oil has a distinctive flavour; if you dislike it, substitute a teaspoon of butter.

BRINJAL BHURTA

INGREDIENTS

1 medium-sized onion	2 large *brinjals* or aubergines
2 green chillis	1 teaspoon mustard oil
Juice of one lime or lemon	Salt to taste

METHOD

Prepare the onion, lime or lemon juice and mustard oil as for the potato *bhurta*. Bake the *brinjals* till the inside is soft and palatable. (The best way, which brings out the flavour more than any other, is to roast them in the ashes of a wood or coal fire.) When thoroughly cooked, scoop out the insides and mix with the onion, chillis, lemon juice, salt and mustard oil.

TOMATO BHURTA

INGREDIENTS

6 large tomatoes

½ teaspoon (or less) ground chilli

Pinch of ground ginger

½ teaspoon mustard oil

1 onion

Lemon juice

Salt to taste

METHOD

Bake the tomatoes till the skins crack; then mash them and mix with the chillis, ginger, mustard oil, lemon juice, onion and salt. Rather less lemon juice will be necessary for this *bhurta* as the tomatoes have their own oxalic acid.

HERRING BHURTA

This is perhaps the tastiest of all *bhurtas*.

INGREDIENTS

1 large herring

1 onion

2 green or 3 red chillis

1 lemon or lime

1 large potato—optional

Salt to taste

METHOD

Grill the herring and bone it. The skin adds to the flavour, but it may be removed, if you wish.

Chop the onion and chillis into tiny pieces. Boil the potato till soft, then mash and mix it with chillis and onion, salt and lemon juice. Then mash the herring with a fork and mix it with the other ingredients, adding the oil that dripped out of the herring as it cooked, unless you find it too rich—although this will be absorbed and neutralized by the potato.

BALLYCHOW or BALLACHONG

This is a breakfast relish, and has many local variations.

One version

INGREDIENTS

1 lb. dried prawns—shelled and cleaned

1 dessertspoon dried chillis—ground

6 oz. mustard oil or ghee
(mustard oil is much better)

½ cup of tamarind juice

4 curry leaves

1 dessertspoon green ginger,
shredded very finely

METHOD

Mash or pound the prawns and thoroughly mix with the dried chillis, green ginger and tamarind juice.

Bring the oil to the boil, drop in the curry leaves and then stir in the other ingredients. Keep stirring and cook for ten minutes. Bottle when cool. The level of the oil should be about half an inch above the other ingredients, and it is this oil that enables one to keep the *ballychow* indefintely

And another

INGREDIENTS

1 lb. boned salted fish	1 tablespoon *ghee*, butter or mustard oil
10 oz. minced onions	3 lb. tomatoes
2 oz. garlic	$\frac{1}{2}$ teaspoon salt
4 oz. green chillis	1 teaspoon ground saffron or turmeric
4 oz. green ginger	$\frac{3}{4}$ pint vinegar
$\frac{3}{4}$ lb. tamarind—seeded and shredded	

METHOD

Soak the fish and tomatoes in hot water, and skin tomatoes. Skin the fish. Mince all ingredients and mix together, except tamarind and saffron. Soak the tamarind in the vinegar.

Bring oil or fat to the boil and fry the fish and saffron till brown. Add the remainder of the ingredients and boil till thick. When cold, put into jars. Should make about $5\frac{1}{2}$ lb.

TAMARIND FISH

This is another relish, to be eaten with curries.

INGREDIENTS

3 lb. white fish cut into $\frac{1}{2}$-inch thick slices	$\frac{1}{2}$ oz. cummin seed—ground
2 lb. tamarind pulp	$1\frac{1}{4}$ oz. turmeric—ground
$1\frac{1}{2}$ oz. red chillis	Salt
$\frac{1}{2}$ oz. garlic	1 pint vinegar
4 oz. green ginger	1 large jar or bottle with wide mouth

METHOD

Clean, wash and dry the fish thoroughly on a cloth. Sprinkle it with salt, spread the pieces on a large dish and turn at intervals of half an hour.

Place the tamarind in a bowl, just cover it with vinegar and soak for 12 hours. Then strain through a coarse muslin. Before soaking, all stones and fibre must be removed.

Slice ginger, garlic and chillies very finely and add enough vinegar to the cummin and turmeric to make a thick paste. Mix in the ginger, garlic and chillies, and if necessary add a little more vinegar.

After the fish has been steeped in salt for 12 hours, wipe it dry. Then place some of the curry paste in the jar and on it slices of the fish. Cover with curry paste and a layer of tamarind pulp; then again fish, paste and pulp. Any ingredients over after the last piece of fish is in should be placed on top, and the whole covered with vinegar. Fit with an air-tight stopper, keep for a fortnight, then fry as much as you need for each meal in ghee or mustard oil.

CHUTNEYS AND PICKLES

GOOSEBERRY CHUTNEY

In India Cape Gooseberries are used, but this chutney can be made with the English fruit.

INGREDIENTS

4 lb. gooseberries	2 oz. garlic
3 lb. brown sugar	2 oz. red chillis
1 lb. cleaned, chopped raisins	1 oz. salt
$\frac{1}{4}$ oz. finely sliced green ginger	1 pint malt vinegar

METHOD

Boil fruit and sugar to the consistency of jam. Add raisins and ginger. Mash the garlic and red chillis in vinegar, mix in the salt and pour over the gooseberries, raisins and ginger. Simmer on a low flame till the concoction thickens. Then cool and bottle in an air-tight jar.

FRESH BENGAL CHUTNEY

INGREDIENTS

2 pods fresh tamarind	Pinch of chilli powder
1 teaspoon brown sugar	$\frac{1}{2}$ inch of green ginger—ground
1 dessertspoon chopped raisins	1 dessertspoon vinegar
2 cloves of garlic	Salt to taste
1 dessertspoon blanched and finely sliced almonds	

METHOD

Grind the tamarind in vinegar. Mash the raisins and green ginger; then mix these and all the other ingredients with the tamarind. This chutney should be made and eaten on the same day, for one should never keep either garlic or onions that have not been thoroughly cooked or heavily pickled in vinegar.

TOMATO CHUTNEY

INGREDIENTS

10 large tomatoes	3 cloves of garlic
3 red chillis	3 small onions
$\frac{1}{2}$ teaspoon cummin—ground	1 teaspoon lemon or tamarind juice
1 dessertspoon ghee, butter, or mustard oil	$\frac{1}{2}$ teaspoon salt

METHOD

Pour boiling water over the tomatoes, drain away the water, and peel them. Cut them into halves and place them in a pan.

Grind the other ingredients, except the onions, to a paste and mix with tomatoes. Pour in a little water and bring to the boil, and when the tomatoes are soft, mash them with a fork. There should be so little water that the mixture forms a thick paste. Add the sliced onions. Then mix in the ghee, butter or oil, cook for five minutes and add the lemon juice or tamarind. Should be eaten cold, with curry and rice.

BRINJAL CHUTNEY

INGREDIENTS

6 lb. ripe aubergines	$\frac{1}{2}$ oz. dried chillis—ground
$\frac{1}{4}$ oz. saffron or turmeric—ground	1 pint mustard oil
$\frac{3}{8}$ oz. mustard—ground	$\frac{1}{4}$ pint vinegar
$\frac{3}{8}$ oz. cummin—ground	6 oz. brown sugar
$1\frac{1}{4}$ oz. garlic—mashed	1 teaspoon salt
1 teaspoon fenugreek (*maythi*) ground	

METHOD

Cut off the stalks and slice *brinjals* finely. Spread with ground saffron (or turmeric) and set aside.

Mix mustard, cummin, fenugreek, garlic and dried chillis in the vinegar. Fry the *brinjal* slices in the mustard oil till brown, then drain and place in a dish. Now throw the salt, ground spices and vinegar into the oil and cook for ten minutes. Toss in the fried *brinjals*, add the sugar and boil for 15 minutes more. Allow to cool and bottle next day. Will keep for weeks.

MINT CHUTNEY

INGREDIENTS

$2\frac{1}{2}$ oz. green mint leaves	$1\frac{1}{2}$ oz. onions
$2\frac{1}{2}$ oz. green chillis	$5\frac{1}{2}$ oz. tamarind
1 oz. salt	$\frac{1}{4}$ breakfast cup vinegar
$\frac{1}{2}$ oz. garlic	

Wash and dry the mint leaves, and grind with the vinegar into a thick paste. Remove any fibre and seeds from the tamarind and mix with the remaining ingredients, all chopped. Add this to the mint and vinegar and mix again. Bottle and store for a few days in air-tight bottle. These quantities should make about 1 lb. of chutney.

TAMARIND CHUTNEY

INGREDIENTS

1 lb. ripe tamarind, stoned	½ oz. ground cinnamon
1 oz. ground chilli	2 oz. currants
1 oz. ground ginger	2 oz. raisins
1 oz. garlic, chopped	½ lb. brown sugar
½ pint vinegar	1 oz. salt

METHOD

Put the ingredients into a preserving pan (glazed earthenware). Make the sugar and vinegar into a syrup and pour into the pan only as much as will cover the mixture. Simmer until the liquid is absorbed and the chutney thickens. Then add the remainder of the syrup and simmer again until thick. Stir the whole time to prevent sticking. When cool, bottle in air-tight jars.

COCONUT CHUTNEY

INGREDIENTS

½ cup desiccated coconut	1 tablespoon ghee or ground-nut oil
½ cup yogurt	½ teaspoon mustard seed
2 green chillis or ½ teaspoon chilli powder	1 teaspoon curry leaves
Salt to taste	

METHOD

Grind or mash the coconut, chillis and salt. Heat the oil in a frying-pan and drop in the mustard seed and curry leaves. When the seed starts to pop, fold in the coconut, chillis and salt. Cook and mix for two minutes, remove from the flame and when cool, add the yogurt and stir. To be eaten with curries.

SWEET LIME CHUTNEY

There are many kinds of lime chutney; this one may be compounded either from limes or lemons.

INGREDIENTS

25 limes or lemons	1 oz. green ginger—finely sliced
2 oz. salt	1 oz. garlic—finely chopped
½ pint vinegar	½ oz. dried red chillis
¼ lb. raisins	½ oz. mustard seed
¼ lb. chopped dates	4 oz. brown sugar

METHOD

Divide the limes (or lemons) into quarters but do not separate the pieces. Rub the flesh with salt and expose the fruit to the sun for three days, turning daily, or put in a warm oven until dried off. Remove the seeds, grind the fruit in the vinegar and other ingredients, bring to the boil and simmer for half an hour. Allow to cool and bottle. Can be used at any time.

DRIED FRUIT PICKLE

INGREDIENTS

1 lb. dates—stoned and cut into rings	1 quart French vinegar
1 lb. apricots—stoned and quartered	¼ lb. sugar
1 lb. damsons—stoned and cut into pieces	1 oz. cinnamon (sticks)
1 lb. prunes—stoned and cut into pieces	1 oz. peppercorns
1 lb. apples—eaters; preferably hard,	½ oz. salt
crisp and sweet	1 oz. green ginger, finely shredded

METHOD

Make a thick syrup of the sugar and vinegar. Quarter the apples and arrange them, together with the other dried fruit, in wide-mouthed bottles. After each layer of fruit, sprinkle some ginger, cinnamon, peppercorns and salt. Pour over the whole as much vinegar syrup as will cover the fruit, then clamp on air-tight stoppers and keep for a month.

GREEN TOMATO PICKLE

INGREDIENTS

1 lb. green tomatoes	1 dessertspoon mustard
2 tablespoons sliced onions	16 green chillis
1 teaspoon cloves	½ pint vinegar
2 six-inch sticks of cinnamon	1 oz. salt

METHOD

Cut the tomatoes into thin slices, sprinkle with salt and allow to stand for two days. Then pack them, with the salt and spices, in alternate layers, into an earthenware or enamelled saucepan, cover with vinegar and simmer till the tomatoes start to break up. When cold, bottle.

BRINJAL PICKLE

INGREDIENTS

3 lb. aubergines, ripe and tender	½ oz. green ginger, finely sliced
1½ oz. green chillis	6 currypillay leaves
1 dessertspoon fenugreek (*maythi*)	2 tablespoons salt
1 dessertspoon cummin seed	½ pint mustard oil
In addition, the following ingredients must be ground:	2 pints vinegar
2 oz. dried chillis	1 oz. saffron
5 oz. garlic	1 oz. green ginger
1 teaspoon mustard seed	

METHOD

Stalk the green chillis and slit each half-way down. Lop off the *brinjal* stalks and slit each into quarters, but do not separate.

Pour the oil into a thick enamelled pickling pan and add the spices in the first list, except ginger and green chillis. Then add the garlic, and when this turns reddish brown, put in the other ground spices and cook on a medium heat for three minutes. Now add the vinegar and salt and mix well. Then the *brinjals,* ginger and chillis. Bring to the boil and simmer for 20 minutes. Bottle when cool.

OLIVE PICKLE

INGREDIENTS

4 lb. olives (either green or black)	4 oz. green ginger, finely sliced
1¾ oz. dried chillis—well pounded	½ oz. cummin seed—ground
1¾ oz. mustard seed—pounded or ground	¼ oz. fenugreek (*maythi*)—ground
1 oz. saffron or turmeric—ground	12 whole peppercorns
4 oz. garlic—chopped fine	½ pint mustard oil
3½ oz. green chillis—slit	1 lb. salt
¾ pint of vinegar	(use less if you think this will be too much)

METHOD

Halve and stone the olives. (This will be much easier with the black variety.) Sprinkle with salt, and let them soak for three days. Drain them, keep the liquid and put the olives in the sun for five or six days, till quite dry; or in a warm oven. Then put them back into the brine, which will be absorbed.

Fry garlic in oil till golden brown; add the ginger and fry that; then the other ingredients —and mix well. Now put in the olives, stir and simmer for 15 minutes. Put into wide-mouthed bottles and cover with vinegar. Cap with air-tight stoppers.

STUFFED CAPSICUM PICKLE

INGREDIENTS

1 dozen capsicums	¼ oz. turmeric
¼ teacup of mustard seed	1 ripe *papaya* or paw-paw
6 red chillis	Vinegar
¼ oz. garlic	½ teaspoon salt
¼ oz. green ginger	

METHOD

Wash and wipe the capsicums, remove the stalks, slit each one half-way and remove the seeds.

Grind the mustard seed, chillis, garlic and ginger in a little vinegar to make a thick paste. Add the turmeric and a little more vinegar and mix again.

Now take a ripe *papaya*, cut it in half, and remove the little black seeds. Then scoop out the inside, mash it with half a teaspoon of salt and place it in a dish. The salt and juice will form liquid, which must be drained off.

Mix the fruit pulp with half the ground spices and stuff the capsicums with this; then add vinegar to the rest of the ground spices and pour it over the capsicums. Bottle in wide-mouthed, air-tight jars.

SEA-FISH PICKLE

INGREDIENTS

3 lb. cod	½ teaspoon mustard seed, ground
1¼ oz. chilli powder	1 teaspoon ground cummin
3½ oz. garlic, chopped	6 dried curry leaves
⅜ oz. ground turmeric or saffron	¾ pint mustard oil
¾ oz. green ginger, finely shredded	½ pint good vinegar
1 oz. green chillis, slit	½ pint crude vinegar
½ teaspoon fenugreek (*maythi*), ground	1 teaspoon salt

METHOD

Wash fish in the crude vinegar and drain it off, then fry in oil, remove skin and bones and cut it into small pieces.

Heat the oil again, add the curry leaves, salt and spices and when brown and cooked through, put in the fish and fry for ten minutes. Then add the good vinegar and let it simmer for 10 minutes. Bottle next day.

NASTURTIUM SEED PICKLE

INGREDIENTS

¾ lb. nasturtium seeds

1 pint white wine vinegar

2 oz. sliced onions

⅛ oz. cloves

⅛ oz. ground mace

¼ oz. sliced green chillis

Salt

METHOD

Gather the seed pods while they are still green and soak them for four days in brine, changing the salt and water daily.

Boil the spices, onions and chillis in vinegar for 15 minutes; then fill one or two glass jars with the salted pods. Put some of the spices, chillis and onions into each jar and cover with vinegar. Keep for three months before using.

RED CAULIFLOWER PICKLE

INGREDIENTS

2 large fresh cauliflowers

6 cloves of garlic

½ oz. green ginger, sliced

3 green chillis cut into small pieces

1 quart vinegar

1 lb. sugar

3 cinnamon sticks (1-inch)

1 large boiled beet

12 peppercorns

Salt

METHOD

Cut off the sprigs of cauliflower, rub gently with salt and set aside for 12 hours. Drain away any water that collects. Dry for two days, then put into a large, wide bottle with the peppercorns, garlic, ginger and chillis.

Put sugar and vinegar into a pan and boil into a syrup. Drop in the cinnamon. Then bruise and pound the beet and squeeze out the juice. Add this to the vinegar.

Drop the cauliflower sprigs into wide-mouthed bottles, cover with the vinegar-beet syrup, and screw on air-tight stoppers. Keep for three months before using.

HOT MIXED VEGETABLE PICKLE

INGREDIENTS

1 lb. beans—runner beans will do

1 lb. cauliflower heads or sprigs

1 lb. onions

1 lb. gherkins

Salt

METHOD
Soak the vegetables for two days in brine, then drain and dry.

INGREDIENTS

12 oz. mustard (powder)	1 oz. mustard seed
4 quarts vinegar	1 oz. red chillis
1 oz. peppercorns	1 oz. ground turmeric
1 oz. cloves	1 oz. ground ginger

METHOD

Mix the 12 oz. mustard with the vinegar into a smooth paste; then by adding more vinegar, into liquid form. Put this, together with all the other ingredients, into a pan and bring to the boil; then simmer for two hours, stirring the while to ensure that no lumps form. When cool bottle in air-tight jars and keep for three months before using.

TOMATO KASOUNDI

INGREDIENTS

8 lb. tomatoes	2 oz. salt (or to taste)
2 oz. red chillis	¾ lb. brown sugar
2 oz. garlic	1 pint mustard oil
2 oz. mustard seed	1 pint vinegar
2 oz. tamarind	1 oz. saffron or turmeric

METHOD

Cut the tomatoes into quarters; if large, into smaller pieces. Grind the spices in vinegar. Mix the salt, spices, vinegar and oil together. Bring to the boil and drop in tomatoes; simmer for two hours. When cool, bottle. Keep for a week, then use.

THE THIRD BOOK
OF CURRIES

'A LITTLE OF WOT YER FANCY'

'How a poor woman makes palatable Mince Pyes of stinking Meat.'

None of the recipes in this book deals with the problem. They have no need to. But in the eighteenth century, before the advent of refrigeration, meat often went bad, especially in the homes of the poor who eked out their supplies over weeks; and in his delightful little book, *Meet Mr Ellis*, Vicars Bell gives extracts, supplemented by comments, of life in Little Gaddesden, Herts, two centuries ago.

According to Mr Ellis, a prosperous farmer, 'This is a poor industrious Woman that rents a little Tenement by me of Twenty Shillings a Year, who for the Sake of her Poverty is Every Week relieved, with many others, by the most noble Lord of Gaddesden Manour; who killing a Bullock almost every week for his large Family, he has the Offald meat dressed, and is so good as to have it given to the poorest People in the Neighbourhood. But as it sometimes happes, through the Negligence of careless Servants, that this charitable meat is apt to stink in hot Weather, for want of its due cleaning, boiling, and laying in a cool Place. However, the Poor are very glad of this Dole, as it does their Families considerable Service.

'And to recover such tainted Meat, this Woman, after boiling and cleansing it well, chops and minces it very small, and when mixed with some Pepper, Salt, chop'd Sage, Thyme, and Onion, she bakes it: This for a savoury Pye. At another Time she makes a sweet Pye of this flesh, by mixing a few Currants and Plumbs with it. But in either Form the Taint is so lessened that it is hardly to be perceived.'

People in the Far East, however, were never forced to eat tainted food, as tribes in more temperate climates were, for the spices in which they prepared meat, fish and vegetables preserved such comestibles for days, if not weeks, and where mustard oil was used, for months!

Incidentally, according to C. C. Furnas, Associate Professor of Chemical Engineering, Yale University, and S. M. Furnas, formerly Instructor in Nutrition, University of Minnesota, putrefying food is not necessarily harmful and, indeed, many highly civilized peoples like certain dishes rather 'high'. 'The organisms,' say these gentlemen, 'which cause it [putrefaction] are for the most part not harmful to man and the eating of rotten meat is a relatively safe practice provided there has been no contamination *of man's own making*. Many primitive peoples in small communities thrive on it.'

Apparently it's only the uncultured who, knowing nothing about gastronomy, like their food fresh. The gourmet rarely touches a medlar till it is soft and half rotten. To him jugged hare is a delicacy, and in the 'best' clubs and restaurants grouse is hung till infested with maggots.

In his fascinating autobiography, *A Pinch of Pound Notes*, John Dingle, a famous chef, describes how, when he was at the Junior Constitutional Club, one of his chores was to take down and salvage grouse past the peak of their 'prime'.

One evening two portions of cold grouse were ordered: 'A toast *canapé* was made with a slice of toast loaded with *pâté de foie gras* paste prepared from the hearts and livers of the birds. On this were mounted the half bird, small cornets of ham filled with aspic jelly and gherkins. Beetroot salad with bouquets of cress comprised the garnish, with a few game chips.'

Later, a waiter descended to the kitchen and remarked, 'I've never served grouse risotto cold before'.

'What do you mean?' asked Dingle.

'That's what it was, wasn't it?'

'No; it was simply cold, roast grouse.'

'Well,' retorted the waiter, 'I carved them at table; I served the breast and half a *canapé* with salad to each guest, and I could have sworn the carcass was stuffed with risotto.'

Dingle jumped to his feet and rummaged in the waste bin till he found the carcasses, and sure enough they were packed tight with what appeared to be risotto but, in fact, was roast maggots! To his relief, when they had eaten, the diners sent a message down to the chef to say they had seldom tasted grouse more delicious!

People who know nothing about cheeses reel away from Camembert, Roquefort and Stilton because the plebeian proboscis is not equipped to differentiate between the sordid and the sublime.

Delectable as provender that is 'high' or 'ripe' may be, however, there is no need for those who eat curry to sample it—and curry dishes can be even more mouth-watering. Their first appeal is to the nose so that, unlike the dishes already mentioned, one does not have to steel oneself before tasting.

Curry spices were never meant to camouflage tainted flesh or vegetables, but to preserve their freshness in climates where food deteriorates rapidly.

Professor A. G. Winter of Cologne University has done some research on mustard oil, horse-radish and other spices and has discovered that they kill harmful bacteria in the intestines; and when pigs and chickens kept on a diet short of proteins had these spices added to their food they improved in health.

Do they contain some principle which we are not as yet aware of? Dr Barbara Moore proved recently by taking three long walks of 110, 373 and 1000 miles respectively, in rain, sleet and snow, that one can maintain both health and vigour without the traditional bread and meat, for her sole sustenance was honey and water, an egg, carrots, lettuce and tomatoes! Moreover, many in the East live on what we would term a starvation diet, but they don't die; what is more, they keep their health and agility. Is it because of the mustard oil and spices they eat?

Mustard oil contains a little vitamin B_{12} which is known to prevent anaemia, and when this is rubbed on Indian children, some of the vitamin is absorbed through the skin. Their food, when cooked in mustard oil, must also provide the vitamin.

Almost all curries are eaten to the accompaniment of pickles made with mustard oil, chillies and fresh vegetables or fruit. Often only the oil is heated, and the fruit is raw, thus retaining its vitamin C.

Curries are not only eaten in India and Pakistan but in every country where spices are cheap and plentiful. Obviously, they were provided by Nature for man's use and enjoyment, and herbs and spices such as aloe, anise, dill, balm, bay, hyssop, marjoram, cinnamon, coriander, cummin, caper, gall, onion, garlic, leek, mint, mustard, rue, and saffron have Biblical sanction.

In this little book we give you recipes from countries as far west as Turkey and Persia, and as far east as Malaya and Indonesia, embracing more than a quarter of the world's population. They have eaten spiced foods and traded in spices for more than 4000 years, and where there exists a variety of spiced foods and no over-indulgence men live as long as in any other part of the world: sound testimony that such foods are good for you.

There are few surer guides to health than the eye, nose, palate and digestion. When all four are in agreement, then only is that dear old philosopher and physician, Marie Lloyd, vindicated—for did she not trill nightly in music-halls throughout Britain, in terms that even the most unsophisticated could understand, 'A little of wot yer fancy does yer good!'

DISHES OF BURMA

NGA-BAUNG-DOKE

INGREDIENTS

1 lb. cod or other white fish	1—2 dried red chillies
1 tablespoon salt	1 tablespoon sessamum, mustard or
½ teaspoon powdered turmeric	other good cooking oil
1-inch piece of fresh ginger, or 1 teaspoon	1 tablespoon flour
ground ginger	1 tablespoon thick coconut milk
8 medium-sized onions	4 cloves garlic
15–20 pieces of cabbage leaf—in Burma	Toothpicks for pinning leaves
banana leaves are used	

METHOD

Clean the fish and rub thoroughly with half the mixed salt and turmeric; then cut into pieces 3 inches by 1½ inches.

Pound the chillies, garlic, ginger and 3 onions and add them to a paste made of the flour, coconut milk, oil and the remainder of the salt and turmeric. Slice the remainder of the onions very finely and mix into this.

Cut the cabbage leaves into 6-inch squares and on each square put a spoonful of paste, then a piece or two of fish; then some more paste and one or two pieces of fish. Fold the ends of the cabbage leaf and secure with a toothpick. Steam in a double boiler for 15–20 minutes.

An alternative method is to place the paste and fish on a nasturtium leaf and cover with another nasturtium leaf; and finally place the lot in a cabbage leaf and pin together with a toothpick.

In Burma banana leaves are used for the outer casing but any durable leaf which is edible may be used.

Enough for four

SHA-NGA-BOUNG

INGREDIENTS

1 lb. cod or other white fish	1 tablespoon rice flour or cornflour
4 red chillies	1 teaspoon ground ginger or powdered ginger
6 cloves garlic	1 cup mustard, olive, sessamum or other good cooking oil

110

1 small stalk lemon grass (the white part)

The milk of 1 coconut, or the equivalent made from
   desiccated coconut—about ½ pint

3 onions, ground

Salt to taste

METHOD

Wash the fish, then bone and mince it.

Slice the chillies, remove the seeds, and soak in a tablespoon of water.

Now pound the chillies with the salt and other seasoning (leaving 1 onion) and mix with the fish and flour. The fish will now be in a thick paste, so mould it into cutlets.

Slice the remaining onion and fry it till light brown in the oil. Set it aside for garnish.

Then fry the fish cutlets till they are golden brown and cut them into slices.

Finally, pour the coconut milk into a pan, bring to the boil and put in the slices of fish. Put on a tight cover, lower the heat till the contents just simmer, and cook for 15 minutes.

Serve with rounds of fried onions on top and, if you wish, with some raw onions as well.

Enough for four

FISH CURRY

In Burma this curry is usually made with *hilsa*—sable fish, a delicious fresh-water variety full of small bones, but as *hilsa* is not obtainable in Europe, any variety will do.

INGREDIENTS

2–3 lb. fish

3 medium-sized onions

2 heads (*not* cloves) of garlic

½ inch (square) of root ginger

2–3 green chillies

1 cup vinegar

2 teaspoons salt

1 teaspoon powdered turmeric

¾ cup mustard oil

METHOD

Clean the fish and rub thoroughly first with salt and then turmeric; then cut lengthwise in slices 1 inch wide and ¾ inch deep, and steep in vinegar for 12 hours.

Pound the onions, garlic and ginger into a paste. Boil the mustard oil, add the pounded ingredients and the whole chillies, stir well, put in the fish and cover with water. Simmer gently and feel from time to time with a fork or sharp knife, till the bones are soft.

Enough for six

STEAMED FISH

INGREDIENTS

1 lb. white fish

¼ coconut i.e. a coconut divided into 4

6 medium-sized onions

1 head of garlic

9 squares of cabbage leaves

1 small bunch of lemon grass

1 small green chilli

Toothpicks

Salt to taste

111

Clean and mince the raw fish. Extract 1 cup of milk from the coconut (directions on page 211). Chop the onions, garlic, lemon grass and chilli into small pieces and pound together.

Now mix the coconut milk, minced fish and seasoning and mould into finger-shaped rolls. Then wrap them in the cabbage-leaf squares, fasten each with a toothpick and steam for 15 minutes.

Enough for four

SMOKED FISH

INGREDIENTS

2½ lb. fine-textured fish	2½ tablespoons malt vinegar
4 large onions	1 tablespoon saffron powder
1½ oz. root ginger	1 tablespoon tomato sauce
1½ oz. garlic	14 oz. sessamum or mustard oil
1 tablespoon salt	10 long green chillies

METHOD

Mix the salt and saffron powder and rub thoroughly into the cleaned fish. Cut the fish lengthwise into slices ¾ inch wide, and fry in the boiling oil. When done, drain and place the fish in a dish.

Slice the onions and fry till light brown. Drain and put them in another dish. Crush the ginger and garlic, drain off the juice and pour it on to the fish, together with the vinegar and tomato sauce. Mix gently, taking care not to break the fish.

Now place the fish in layers, sticking the chillies between the layers, and cover with fried onions; pour over this the fried oil. Cover and steam gently for 3–4 *hours*.

Enough for six

BALACHAUNG

INGREDIENTS

7 oz. dried prawns	1 onion
11 oz. sessamum or mustard oil	10 cloves garlic
1½ oz. shrimp paste (uncooked)	1 inch of fresh root ginger
1 level teaspoon turmeric	Salt to taste

METHOD

Pick and wash the prawns and pound them in a mortar. After peeling slice the garlic, onion and ginger finely. Heat the oil till smoke rises from it and then fry separately the garlic, onion and ginger. Remove and place them in a dish. If added pungency is desired, grind 3 chillies and add them to the prawns.

Now mix the prawns with powdered turmeric and fry till crisp. Strain off oil. Stir the shrimp paste into such oil as clings to the pan and cook for 2 minutes. Then mix the prawns and cooked shrimp paste; add salt, garnish with the fried garlic, onion and ginger and serve with curry and rice.

The ingredients given should fill a 1-lb. bottle, and will keep for weeks, if not months.

PRAWN AND TOMATO CURRY

INGREDIENTS

3–4 green chillies	2 tablespoons best Tavoy fish sauce (optional)
14 oz. prawns	½ oz. coriander leaves
1 large onion	3 tomatoes, halved
4 cloves garlic	1 cup water
1 teaspoon turmeric	Salt and pepper to taste
4 tablespoons mustard or other cooking oil	

METHOD

Grind the onion and garlic to a paste, and bring the oil to the boil. (Either ground-nut or mustard are the best oils for this dish.)

Fry the ground ingredients, turmeric, salt and pepper in the oil, and after cleaning the prawns, add them, together with the fish sauce (if used), coriander leaves, green chillies and tomatoes.

Now add the water and simmer till the prawns are cooked and the water has been absorbed, leaving a thick, rich gravy.

Enough for three

CHICKEN KAUKSWE

INGREDIENTS

A 3–4-lb. chicken	½ cup vegetable oil
4 pints water	1 coconut from which 3 cups of milk should be extracted
1 teaspoon ground saffron	1 tablespoon *dhall* flour (gram)
4 cloves garlic	3½ lb. spaghetti
2 teaspoons powdered ginger or 2 slices of fresh ginger	10 onions
4 chillies (optional)	Salt to taste

METHOD

Quarter the chicken and rub the pieces thoroughly with saffron. Place in a pan with 4 pints of water and salt to taste, and bring the water to the boil. Then simmer till the flesh is tender.

Remove the chicken, strip the flesh from the bones and put it aside. Crack the bones and add them to the still simmering stock.

Now pound 9 onions, the garlic, ginger and chillies (if used) together and rub this mixture into the chicken meat. (The ingredients may be pounded in a mortar, ground on a *seel* [flat stone], or minced).

Heat the oil in a 2-quart saucepan till smoke rises, slice the remaining onion and brown it in the oil. Add the chicken and brown it also; then the stock, and simmer. Make a paste of the *dhall* flour and 1 cup of water, add it to the stock and simmer for 15 minutes; finally pour in the coconut milk and simmer for 10 minutes.

Boil the spaghetti in salt water till soft; drain away the water, put the spaghetti in a dish and pour the chicken over it. Serve with hard-boiled eggs cut into quarters, green (or 'spring') onions and sliced raw onions.

Enough for eight to ten

ROAST DUCK

INGREDIENTS

1 duck of about 3–4 lb.	2 teaspoons salt
14 oz. pork	1 oz. dried mushrooms
2 eggs	5 large stalks of celery
3 oz. Chinese soy sauce	1 cup vegetable oil
1 oz. Chinese black sauce	1 length of sugar-cane, 12 inches long
7 medium-sized onions	(optional)
15 cloves garlic	1 teaspoon pepper

METHOD

Clean the duck thoroughly, then drain and dry it. Mix $\frac{1}{2}$ teaspoon salt, $\frac{1}{2}$ oz. Chinese black sauce and 1 oz. soy sauce and rub mixture over the duck, inside and out.

Mince the pork; chop the onions and 10 cloves of garlic; soak the mushrooms in hot water and then chop them. Chop the celery into 1-inch pieces.

Mix the above ingredients with the two eggs and add the remainder of the black sauce, soy sauce, salt, half the pepper and $\frac{1}{2}$ cup of oil. This is the stuffing for the duck.

Stuff the duck and sew it. Then mash the remainder of the garlic, and mix in the rest of the pepper. Bring the remainder of the oil to the boil, add the garlic and pepper, remove from the stove, mix thoroughly and when still hot pour over the sugar-cane, which has been arranged at the bottom of a large dish. Sugar-cane is usually unobtainable in Britain, however; so merely pour the mixture into the dish, place the duck on top and roast for $1\frac{1}{2}$ hours.

Enough for eight

DUCK CURRY

INGREDIENTS

1 duck of about 3–4 lb.	15 cloves garlic
1 teaspoon powdered saffron	2–3 curry leaves or bay leaves
1 tablespoon salt	10 dried chillies—or less (this is optional)
3 tablespoons Chinese soy sauce	5 peppercorns
10 medium-sized onions	1 cup vegetable or mustard oil
1 inch of fresh ginger or 1 teaspoon ground ginger	

Clean the duck and cut it into 8 pieces. Rub thoroughly with salt, saffron and soy sauce and put it aside for an hour.

Grind or pound 5 of the onions with the ginger, about half the garlic and the chillies (if used).

Heat the oil till smoke rises and toss in the peppercorns, curry leaves and ground ingredients. Add the duck. Brown and simmer for 5 minutes. Then add sufficient water to cover the duck and no more. Simmer for 2 hours.

Slice the remaining onions and garlic and garnish the duck with them about half an hour before serving.

Serve hot.

Enough for eight

COCONUT RICE

INGREDIENTS

2½ cups rice (about 1¼ lb.)	½ teaspoon sugar
1 coconut	¼ teaspoon salt
2 teaspoons vegetable oil	1 onion

METHOD

Grate the flesh of the coconut; soak in a cup of boiling water, and then squeeze the milk through thin muslin.

Wash the rice and place it in a pan with a thick bottom. Add the coconut milk to the rice till it is ¾ inch above it. Additional water might be needed.

Peel and quarter the onion and add to the rice; then put in the oil, sugar and salt. Mix well, then simmer till the liquid has evaporated and the rice is tender. Take out a grain or two and feel from time to time between finger and thumb.

Enough for four

These recipes were kindly supplied by

MRS D. F. BYRNE
45 LANGLEY AVENUE
WORCESTER PARK
SURREY

DISHES OF CEYLON

EGG STEW

4 eggs	1-inch piece of ginger
4 medium-sized potatoes, sliced	1-inch stick of cinnamon
2 medium-sized onions, chopped	3 cups water
1 tablespoon green chillies, sliced thinly	1 clove garlic
$\frac{2}{3}$ teaspoon powdered turmeric or saffron	1 tablespoon flour
2 tablespoons pickling onions, sliced thinly	2 cloves
2 sprigs *karapincha* (curry leaves)	5 cardamoms
4 1-inch pieces of *rampe* (or screw-pine) or lemon grass	25 peppercorns
3 tablespoons Maldive fish, powdered (Bombay duck	Salt to taste
will do)	3 tablespoons coconut oil or butter
1 tablespoon vinegar	

METHOD

Grind the cloves, cardamoms and peppercorns together. Whisk the eggs and add 1 table-spoon sliced pickling onions, 1 tablespoon sliced green chillies, pinch of salt, 1 tablespoon powdered fish and half of the ground cloves, cardamoms and pepper. Mix well, pour into a pudding basin and steam for 30 minutes, then cut into 4 or 6 pieces and set aside.

Place the sliced potatoes in a bowl and add 3 cups of water, 1 tablespoon flour, 1 tablespoon vinegar, $\frac{2}{3}$ teaspoon turmeric (or saffron), 1 tablespoon sliced pickling onions, 2 pieces of *rampe* (screw-pine) or lemon grass, 1 sprig of curry leaves, 2 tablespoons ground fish, the cinnamon, garlic, ginger, remainder of the ground seasoning, and salt.

Heat the coconut oil (or butter) in a thick pan and in it fry the medium-sized chopped onions, 2 pieces of lemon grass (or *rampe,* etc.) and a sprig of curry leaves for 2 minutes. Add the potato mixture to the fried ingredients and cover the pan. When cooked, put in pieces of the steamed egg mixture, simmer for 5 minutes and remove from the stove and serve.

Enough for four

MISS ESTHER APONSO
WINIFRED ESTATE
DIVULAPITIYA
CEYLON

BRINJAL POHIE

INGREDIENTS

4 medium-sized *brinjals* (aubergines)

1 tablespoon ground mustard seed

¼ stem lemon grass

1 small sprig curry leaves

1 tablespoon pounded Maldive fish (Bombay
    duck will do)

4 cloves garlic, chopped

3 red chillies, sliced

2-inch stick of cinnamon

2-inch piece of *rampe**

20 dried chillies, pounded (start with 2!)

1 tablespoon sugar

1 tablespoon coriander seed

1½ teaspoons ground white cummin mixed with ½
teaspoon sweet cummin seed

1 tablespoon vinegar

1½ oz. tamarind squeezed in a tablespoon of salt water

3 tablespoons coconut† or other
    oil for frying, or margarine

½ teacup thick coconut milk

About 1 teaspoon each of ground saffron and salt

1 tablespoon sliced red onions

METHOD

Slice the *brinjals,* rub the insides with the salt and saffron and fry in oil or margarine.
Mix all the ground spices with the vinegar and tamarind in salt water.

Heat 2 tablespoons of oil or fat in a pan and when very hot put in the ground spices and
other ingredients except the coconut milk and sugar. Cook for 2–3 minutes, then add the
brinjals, and finally the coconut milk and sugar.

Bring to the boil and then simmer on a slow heat for 15–20 minutes, stirring gently, so
as not to break up the *brinjals.*

Enough for four

* *Rampe* or *rampa* is another name for screw-pine.

† Coconut oil is frequently used for cooking in Ceylon, Malaya, West Africa and elsewhere, but it
may not agree with Britons.

MISS BHADRANE DE SILVA
WAESNAGIRI
DEGODA LANE, AMCALANGODA
CEYLON

STUFFED CHILLI CURRY

INGREDIENTS

6 large green capsicum chillies (these are not pungent)

¼ lb. red onions

2 oz. Maldive fish, pounded; or Bombay duck

¼ teaspoon chilli powder

Salt to taste

2 tablespoons coconut oil, frying fat or unsalted
    margarine

1 dessertspoon lime juice

METHOD

Slit the chillies lengthwise about 2 inches from the tips. Remove pulp and seeds. Slice the
red onions finely, mix with the rest of the ingredients, stuff the chillies with this mixture as
well as the pulp and seeds that have been removed and fry in very hot oil or fat till brown.

Ingredients for the curry

1 cup thick coconut milk, or cow's milk	1 sprig curry leaves
1 teaspoon ground chilli	A pinch of saffron
1 teaspoon Maldive fish or Bombay duck	2 teaspoons lemon juice
4 red onions	Salt to taste

METHOD

Slice the red onions, mix with the other ingredients and pour into a saucepan. Then add the stuffed chillies. Place pan on the stove, bring to the boil and then simmer for 10–15 minutes.

In Ceylon a little curry powder is sprinkled over the dish just before it is removed from the stove, but this is not recommended, as the treatment makes it somewhat too harsh for European palates.

Enough for three

MRS H. A. PERARA
EXCISE BUNGALOW
MATARA
CEYLON

FRIED POTATOES

This dish bears no resemblance to chipped potatoes or fried potatoes done in the English way.

INGREDIENTS

3 large potatoes	2 teaspoons chilli powder
1 large Spanish onion	1 tablespoon dripping
1 sprig curry leaves or bay leaves	Salt to taste
2 teaspoons powdered Maldive fish or Bombay duck	

METHOD

Boil the potatoes in their jackets after first scrubbing them well. Peel and cut them into small pieces. Add to them half the chilli powder and some salt and set on one side.

Cut the large onion into thin slices; add the remaining chilli powder and salt to these and mix well.

Now heat the dripping in a frying-pan and add the sliced onion and curry leaves. Fry till the onion is soft; then add potatoes and fry all together, stirring all the time. Just before removing from the stove, add the powdered fish.

The entire operation should not take more than 20–25 minutes.

Enough for four

MRS DAVID THOMPSON
ROBGILL GROUP
BOGAWANTALAWA
CEYLON

Birianee
(See recipe page 34)

CHICKEN CURRY

INGREDIENTS

1 large chicken	1 green chilli, sliced
2 teaspoons chilli powder	2 slices of green ginger
1 teaspoon curry powder	1½ cups thin coconut milk
3 cloves garlic	½ cup thick coconut milk
2-inch stick of cinnamon	1 dessertspoon pickling onions, sliced
1 sprig celery	1 dessertspoon dripping or any cooking fat
8 cloves	½ teaspoon fenugreek
1-inch piece of *rampa* (optional)	Salt to taste
1 large sprig curry leaves (or bay leaves)	Juice of 2 limes or lemons

METHOD

Cut the chicken into neat joints and season with salt, curry powder and chilli powder. Heat the dripping in a large saucepan and when it is very hot crush 2 cloves of garlic and toss them in. Fry till brown. Now add half the fenugreek and also fry till brown; after which add the sliced onions, *rampa* (if used), green chilli, celery (cut into large bits), cinnamon, curry leaves (or bay), and fry till the onions are golden brown. At this stage, put in the chicken and fry, stirring all the time. When the pieces of chicken are brown, add the thin coconut milk and cloves, the green ginger and the remaining fenugreek and garlic, cut into tiny pieces.

Stir well, cover the pan with a snugly fitting lid and simmer gently till the chicken is tender, after which add the thick coconut milk and lime (or lemon) juice. Stir well and simmer slowly till the gravy thickens, but be sure NOT to cover the pan after adding the thick coconut milk.

Enough for four

MRS DAVID THOMPSON

HOT STEW WITH RICE

INGREDIENTS

2 lb. mutton	1 teaspoon curry powder
1 lb. fine-grained rice, such as Patna, Burma or Kashmir	¼ lb. raisins
6 gills water or stock	¼ lb. chopped cashew nuts
4 tablespoons ghee, margarine, or equivalent cooking fat or oil	¼ lb. cooked green peas
	½ teacup thick coconut milk
2 oz. red onions	A pinch of ground garlic
2 teaspoons powdered black pepper	A pinch of powdered ginger
¼ teaspoon mixed powdered spices— cloves, cardamoms, cinnamon	1-inch piece of *rampe* (optional)
	Salt to taste

Wash the rice well in warm water and place it in a thick pan with stock or water, and salt to taste. Stock may be made by boiling the mutton in 6 gills of water. Boil rice.

When the rice is soft, but with each grain firm and separate from the others, press it into a rice mould in the form of a ring that has been greased with ghee or margarine. Then turn it into a large fireproof dish or casserole.

Heat the fat or ghee in a frying-pan; slice the onions and brown them, together with the *rampe*, if used. Put in the mutton, cut up in cubes, and braise.

Now stir the ground ingredients into the coconut milk, add this to the mutton, bring to the boil and simmer for 5 minutes, or until soft.

Remove the *rampe*, then place the cooked mutton in the centre of the rice ring. Make a little gravy with flour, egg and seasoning and pour it over the meat. Sprinkle the rice with the raisins, cashew nuts and peas and put the dish in a slow oven for 20 minutes.

Enough for six to eight

MRS J. J. EVIJESEKERA
MONROVIA GROUP
DODANDUWA
CEYLON

MOLOGOTHANNIE

INGREDIENTS

1 lb. beef	1 sprig curry leaves
10 peppercorns	A pinch of saffron or turmeric
2-inch stick of cinnamon	3 cloves garlic
1 large onion	1 inch of ginger
1 large, ripe tomato	1 teacup milk
1 piece of *rampe* leaf	½ dessertspoon white cinnamon
½ dessertspoon ground coriander	8 red onions, sliced
6–8 cups water	½ dessertspoon ground chillies
½ dessertspoon ghee or dripping	2 teaspoons curry powder
1 piece of *sera* leaf (or bay can be used)	

METHOD

Boil the beef with the peppercorns, cinnamon, tomato, large onion, coriander, *rampe*, *sera* and curry leaves, garlic, ginger, 4 red onions and 2 quarts water.

When meat is tender, add saffron (or turmeric) and ground chillies, mixed into a paste with the milk. Boil for 5 minutes, then simmer.

Slice the remainder of the red onions finely, fry in ghee (or dripping) and mix in, stirring thoroughly. Simmer gently for 10 minutes, strain and eat with rice and chutney or lime pickle.

Half a dessertspoon of ground chilli will make this dish much too pungent for European palates; so half a TEAspoonful is advised at first. If you like it hotter, add more the next time.

Enough for four

MISS PEARL DE SILVA
'MARYLANDS'
MORUPOLA ESTATE
GAMPAHA, WP, CEYLON

SATHE CURRY

Seasoning and Spices

INGREDIENTS

1 *rounded* teaspoon raw curry powder   A pinch of *powdered* ginger (sweet)

½ level teaspoon powdered pepper   1 level teaspoon *ground** ginger

¼ level teaspoon chilli powder   1 level teaspoon garlic (crushed)

¼ level teaspoon powdered cinnamon   1 dessertspoon vinegar

⅛ level teaspoon powdered cloves   Salt to taste

⅛ level teaspoon powdered cardamom

Also:

INGREDIENTS

1 lb. beef, roasted or boiled and cut into 16 1-inch cubes   12 red onions

5 tablespoons coconut oil, salad oil, butter or margarine   Salt to taste

24 whole, small red onions   ⅛ level teaspoon turmeric powder

1½ cups coconut milk, fresh cow's milk or   3 green chillies, sliced

unsweetened tinned milk   1 sprig curry, bay or marjoram leaves

1 *rounded* teaspoon cornflour or rice flour   Juice of 1 large lime or lemon

2-inch piece of *rampe*   Metal or thin wooden skewers for threading beef, etc.

METHOD

Mix the beef thoroughly with the seasoning ingredients and spices, and allow to marinade for 1 hour. Skewer beef and red onions alternately: 4 cubes of beef and 3 onions.

Heat 3 tablespoons of fat in a heavy, shallow pan and braise beef for 20–30 minutes, and when well browned remove from the pan and arrange on a flat meat dish.

Pour the remainder of the fat into another pan and when hot add curry leaves, *rampe*, the remaining 12 red onions and green chillies. When the onions are golden, add the cornflour, coconut milk and turmeric powder. Stir well, add salt and lime or lemon juice, and when the sauce has cooked thoroughly, remove *rampe* and curry leaves and pour over beef.

Sathé Curry may be garnished by cutting 4 ripe, red chillies lengthwise from tip to

* Ground ginger is stick or root ginger which has been pounded or ground, and it contains some juice. Powdered ginger is the dried root ground into powder and has no juice in it.

stalk. Retain the stems but remove seeds and inner pith. Drop the chillies into iced water and chill for 2 hours, when the chillies will open into lovely flowers. Arrange them on the dish with a few sprigs of parsley or other herbs.

Enough for four

MISS IRIS MUNASINGHE
15 APONSO AVENUE
DEHIWELA
CEYLON

BEEF CURRY

INGREDIENTS

2 lb. beef	20 dried chillies
¼ lb. onions	2 teaspoons coriander seed
1 clove garlic	10 cardamoms
1-inch piece of greenginger	1-inch stick of cinnamon
2-inch piece of *rampe* or bay leaf	Salt and vinegar to taste
2-inch piece of *sera* or curry leaf	2 tablespoons vegetable oil
Milk from ½ coconut, about ½ pint	

METHOD

Cut the beef into 1-inch cubes, put into a bowl and mix with the salt, vinegar and curry powder.

Curry powder: this is made by pounding 20 dried chillies, 2 teaspoons coriander, 10 cardamoms, 1-inch stick of cinnamon, and then roasting them till they give off a strong odour.

Let the beef and spices marinade for half an hour. Then heat the oil and fry the sliced onions, garlic and ginger till brown. Put in the meat and spices in the liquid and brown. Add *rampe* and *sera* leaves and cook till the liquid is absorbed. Then put in the coconut milk and cook again till the beef is tender and the gravy thick.

Enough for four

MRS VYVETTE LOOS
'KINGSTON'
NEGOMBO
CEYLON

OX-HEART BLACK CURRY

Clean, slice and soak the heart in about ½ pint vinegar while you get together the following ingredients:

INGREDIENTS

2 cloves garlic, sliced	12 dried red chillies
4 1-inch slices of ginger	1 dessertspoon fat, ghee, butter or cooking oil
10 onions, finely sliced	1 piece of lemon grass
2 cloves, powdered	1 piece of *rampe* leaf
1-inch stick of cinnamon	1 teaspoon fennel
6 cardamoms, powdered	1 tablespoon small onions
1 cup grated coconut	Juice of 1½ limes or lemons
1 tablespoon coriander seed	2 cups water
6 curry leaves	1 teaspoon sugar
1 teaspoon white cummin seed	Salt to taste
½ teaspoon sweet cummin seed	

METHOD

Add the cloves, garlic, ginger, sliced onions, cinnamon and cardamoms to the vinegar in which the heart is soaking.

Roast till dark brown the grated coconut; then grind the coriander seed, curry leaves, white cummin, sweet cummin, and 12 red chillies together and add to the roasted coconut. Mix well.

Put 1 dessertspoon of fat into a thick pan, add the lemon grass, *rampe* leaf, fennel and the tablespoon of small onions. When brown, add the sliced meat, etc., salt, browned coconut and other ingredients. Mix well, add 2 cups of water and the juice of the lemons or limes, bring to the boil and simmer till the heart is quite soft.

Before removing from the stove, mix in 1 teaspoon of sugar.

Enough for at least four

MRS VYVETTE LOOS

SPICY CEYLONESE PORK CURRY

INGREDIENTS

1 liver (pig's)	8 peppercorns
1½ lb. pork (lean and fat mixed)	½-inch piece of turmeric
2 large onions	2-inch stick of cinnamon
12 red chillies	6 cloves
6 cloves garlic	1 tablespoon sweet oil
1 inch of ginger	Vinegar
1 teaspoon white cummin seed	

METHOD

Parboil pork and liver and cut both into tiny cubes. Grind all the spices in a little strong vinegar.

Put the oil into a frying-pan and fry pork and liver till brown. Some of the fat from the pork will melt. Drain this away into a receptacle, leaving only a trace in the pan. Chop the onions and fry in this remaining fat, and when cooked, add them to the pork and liver.

Now wash the pan, add the ground spices and salt to the meat, etc., return to the pan and mix thoroughly.

Simmer over a low flame till tender. Add a tablespoon of vinegar, 3 chillies and a stalk of curry leaves as garnish.

Enough for six to eight

MRS VYVETTE LOOS

VERY YOUNG MILK SHARK CURRY

This exotic-sounding dish was once beyond the reach of people in Britain, but now that sharks are caught off Cornish waters, some of the luckier ones may indulge in this concoction. If you can't get hold of shark, cod will do. If shark is used, skin it.

INGREDIENTS

1 baby shark, 12–15 inches long, or cod

For every 2 lb. fish use:

4 cloves garlic, chopped	1 sprig curry leaves
3 slices of green ginger, chopped	1-inch stick of cinnamon
2-inch piece of *rampe* leaf	1 tablespoon coriander seed
½-inch stem lemon grass	1 teaspoon white cummin seed
	½ teaspoon sweet cummin seed

Roast and powder these ingredients. You will also need:

2 cloves garlic	2 1-inch pieces of turmeric
2 1-inch slices of ginger	½ teaspoon chopped fennel leaves
1-inch stick of cinnamon	Milk of 1 coconut
5–6 curry leaves	½ teaspoon ground saffron
10 cardamoms, powdered	20 dried chillies (roasted dark and ground)
Juice of 2 limes or lemons	1 dessertspoon tamarind juice
1 dessertspoon ghee or cooking oil	Salt to taste

METHOD

Place the first batch of ingredients into a thick pan and fry in a little fat till dark brown.

Mix the second batch—except the tamarind juice—with the fish, and cook in the fat. When fried, add the first batch of ingredients, mix thoroughly, simmer with the added tamarind juice and salt to taste.

Do not boil. Simmer and remove from the pan when the fish is soft and flaky.

When the fish is done, one should add a spoon of arrack. As arrack is not generally available in Europe, however, use rum; but this last stage is optional.

If shark, enough for six. If cod, enough for four

MRS VYVETTE LOOS

FISH CURRY

INGREDIENTS

2 lb. fish	Vinegar and salt to taste
1 dessertspoon mustard oil or cooking oil	1 dessertspoon ground mustard
1 piece of *rampe* leaf, *sera* leaf or 2–3 curry leaves	$\frac{1}{2}$ teaspoon saffron
4 cloves garlic, sliced	2–3 fennel leaves, chopped
4 1-inch slices of ginger	$\frac{1}{2}$ teaspoon ground or powdered chilli
10 onions, sliced	1 dessertspoon jaggery,* 'foot' sugar, or 'pieces'

METHOD

Skin, wash and cut the fish into pieces. Put it into a pan, add a little water, vinegar and salt to taste. Boil for 5 minutes, remove from the stove.

Heat the oil and brown the sliced onions, garlic, ginger, and *rampe, sera* or curry leaves.

Add the remainder of the spices, fish and the liquor (water and vinegar) and boil for 10 minutes without covering. Just before removing, add the jaggery or sugar. This gives it a distinctive tang.

This fish curry should be served with lime pickle.

MRS VYVETTE LOOS   *Enough for four*

CRAB CURRY

INGREDIENTS

5 large crabs	Salt to taste
3 cups thin coconut milk	6 green chillies
2 cups thick coconut milk	2 dessertspoons ground chillies
2 handfuls *murunga* leaves	(try *tea*spoons first!)
6 red onions	1 sprig curry leaves
Juice of 1 lemon	1 dessertspoon coconut oil, ghee, butter or margarine

METHOD

Wash the crabs well and place the edible portions in a thick saucepan. Slice the onions and brown them in the oil or fat. Add them with the coconut milk and the other ingredients to the crab, bring to the boil and simmer till the crab meat is tender. Cook till the gravy is reduced to no less than 4 cups.

If the crabs are very large and the hard shell has to be split, salvage the juice that runs out, and use it in the cooking.

Enough for six

MRS N. REGINALD
HARROW ESTATE
PUNDULAYA
CEYLON

* Jaggery is palm sugar, made from the sap or juice of the palm. If it can't be obtained, ask your grocer for 'foot' sugar, which is very black and has a rich, treacly smell, or for 'pieces' (Barbadoes sugar).

125

DISHES OF INDIA AND PAKISTAN

THE cuisine of India and Pakistan has been very fully dealt with in the *First* and *Second Books* and therefore only a few recipes have been included here.

INDIA

VEGETABLE PILAU

INGREDIENTS

1 breakfast cup fine rice—Patna, Kashmiri or Burma

4 medium-sized carrots, peeled and sliced

½ breakfast cup cauliflower heads

¾ cup fresh shelled peas

2 large onions, sliced

5 tablespoons seedless raisins or sultanas

4–6 bay leaves

1 teaspoon salt

2 tablespoons butter, ghee or margarine

¾ cup peanuts, almonds, pine kernels, cashew nuts

METHOD

Wash the rice and soak it for an hour.

Place the peas, carrots and cauliflower in 4 breakfast cups of water in a thick saucepan, put on the lid and boil till tender but *not soft*; then strain off the water and keep for stock.

Heat the fat and fry half the sliced onions as well as the nuts till golden brown, then remove them from the pan.

Put the cooked vegetables into the remainder of the hot fat, mix them well but take care not to break them up. Do not brown them. After they have been mixed with the fat, remove them and set them aside.

Now put the rice, that has been drained, into the pan with the hot ghee or fat, add the raisins or sultanas, simmer and stir for a couple of minutes, then pour in the stock, add salt and the bay leaves.

Bring to the boil, then turn down the heat and simmer till the rice is done and the stock absorbed.

Mix the rice and cooked vegetables together, empty into a serving dish and garnish with remainder of onions, fried crisply, and nuts.

Other vegetables, in season, may be used.

Enough for four

SERPATHALA

INGREDIENTS

1 pint pig's blood	1 oz. tamarind
1 pig's heart and liver and ¼ lb. pork	½ teaspoon salt
4 oz. ghee or mustard oil	½ teaspoon ground saffron or turmeric
6 dried chillies, ground	8–10 small onions
½ teaspoon ground black pepper	5 oz. best malt vinegar
½–1 teaspoon ground cummin	6 green chillies
¼–½ teaspoon ground cinnamon	¼ teaspoon ground ginger
12 cloves, ground	6 cloves garlic

METHOD

Place the tamarind in a bowl, cover with boiling water and soak for an hour, then put it into a cheese-cloth or fine muslin and squeeze out the juice.

Boil the pig's blood till it turns black; then boil the pig's heart, liver and pork, with the salt; then cut them up and fry them in 2 oz. fat or oil, together with the saffron or turmeric.

Now slice the onions finely and brown them in 2 oz. of fat. Drain off the fat and in it fry the dried chillies, pepper, cummin, 3 cloves of garlic (mashed), cloves and cinnamon. Add these to the onions.

Put these spices and onions into a thick pan, pour in the vinegar and tamarind juice; add the fried liver, etc., blood, the remainder of the garlic, ginger and green chillies chopped into small pieces. Cover the vessel and simmer for an hour, or until such time as the gravy is thick. To be eaten with rice.

Enough for four

MOONG DHALL

INGREDIENTS

½ lb. *moong dhall* (these lentils may be bought at any shop which sells Indian spices)	½ teaspoon ground ginger
	¼ teaspoon ground garlic
¼ lb. ghee or butter	1 teaspoon salt (more, if needed, to be added after cooking)
4 teaspoons ground onions	
1 teaspoon ground chillies	6 onions, finely sliced
½ teaspoon ground turmeric	

METHOD

Place the *dhall* in a thick pan and brown it, mixing the while with a wooden spoon. When slightly browned, put in salt and all the ground condiments and add enough water to rise 2 inches above them. If you have boiling water handy, use it, as this helps to break up the *dhall* quickly. Boil till the *dhall* is quite dissolved. Don't mix it with a spoon, but allow it to cake.

When the *dhall* is well dissolved, whisk it. In India this is done with a wooden instrument called a *ghootnee*, but a wire whisk will serve as well.

Warm the ghee or butter in a separate pan, put in the sliced onions and fry till dark

127

brown and then mix into the churned *dhall*; then pour *dhall* and onions into the remains of the melted ghee in which the onions were fried.

Mix well, place a well-fitting cover on the pan and simmer for 15 minutes. To be eaten with either rice, or rice and curry.

Enough for four

PAKISTAN

SHAMI KABAB or CABOB

INGREDIENTS

1 lb. mince (very fine)	4 cardamoms
2 small onions cut into pieces	8 black peppercorns
½ cup *channa dhall* or split peas	1 egg
4 cloves	Salt to taste

METHOD

This is a very simple but tasty dish.

Place all the ingredients except the egg in a thick-bottomed pan, cover with water and boil gently till the water has evaporated and the mixture is thick, and the meat tender.

Now mix in one raw, beaten egg, pass the mixture through a mincer and allow to cool. Finally, mould the mixture into small, flat cakes and fry on either side till brown.

Enough for four

Shami Kabab may be eaten with rice or bread, but it goes best with either *chappattis* or *parattas*, and should be accompanied with either chilli, tomato and beet pickle; lime pickle; or merely raw green chillies. The last, would, however, prove much too fiery for the average British palate and one is advised to treat raw green chillies with great respect until the palate is accustomed to them. The eating of food that is too pungent has put many an experimenter off curries for good.

CHICKEN KORMA

INGREDIENTS

1 roasting chicken, about 2 lb., cut into pieces	½ teaspoon mashed garlic
½ lb. butter or ghee	1 5 oz. bottle plain yogurt
1 medium-sized onion	1-inch piece of ginger, sliced
½ teaspoon ground saffron or turmeric	1 teaspoon each of cloves, black
3 teaspoons ground coriander seed	pepper and cummin seed, whole
½ teaspoon ground chilli	Salt to taste

METHOD

Slice the onion finely, brown in the butter and then place in a small dish. Put the ground spices into a breakfast cup of water, add to the fat in the pan and cook for 3 minutes, stirring the while. Now add the chicken, mix well, see that the meat is just covered by water and boil for 20 minutes with the lid on the pan.

When the liquid has almost evaporated, continue to cook, but stir the chicken till golden brown.

Crush the browned onion with a spoon and add it to the chicken with the yogurt, salt to taste and remainder of the spices. Add a cup of water, put on the lid and simmer gently till the chicken is tender. If the chicken is not quite done and the liquid has evaporated, add a little more water and cook for a further period.

The entire process should take about $1\frac{1}{2}$ hours.

Enough for six

SINGARAS

Singaras are a very tasty savoury and are often given to visitors as a form of light refreshment. They are also excellent as part of a supper meal, or for taking on picnics, for they pack easily.

INGREDIENTS

1 lb. potatoes	Spices, such as cummin, coriander, chilli powder,
1 lb. flour, either plain or self-raising	mustard seed and turmeric, or
ghee, butter, or cooking fat	1 or 2 teaspoons of **panch phora**

METHOD

Find by experiment which combinations you like best.

Boil the potatoes and when soft, but firm, peel and cut them into small cubes. If the potatoes are new, don't peel. Strew a teaspoon or two of mixed spices, or **panch phora** over the pieces and salt, according to taste.

Use one ounce of fat and work into the flour. Add a little water and make a dough; then divide the mass into 36 balls. Flatten each ball on an oily surface with an oily roller. In Bengal, where singaras are a favourite, a roller 7 inches by 3 inches, is used.

Roll the balls into ovals, and cut breadthwise. Moisten the borders by dipping a finger in water and running over them. Put a few potato pieces into one of the halves and cover with the other, forming a triangular-shaped pocket filled with potato. Moisten and stick down the edges and fry each in fat. They are best eaten while piping hot but are also quite palatable when cold.

TONGUE CURRY

INGREDIENTS

1 sheep's tongue	6 cloves
1 tablespoon curry powder	1 stick cinnamon
12 green chillis	8 curry leaves
8 cloves of garlic	2 tablespoons sliced onion
12 slices of green ginger	1 tablespoon **ghee**, butter or cooking fat
1 ounce tamarind	Salt

129

METHOD

Cover the tongue with water, add salt, and simmer till the tongue is tender enough to be pierced with a cocktail stick. When the tongue is tender, peel off the skin, which if boiled sufficiently will come away easily. Now cut it into inch cubes.

Put the cooking fat into a pan and fry the onions till golden brown. Slit the green chillis; then add chillis, garlic, curry leaves and other spices. Add the cubes of tongue and one breakfast cup of water in which it was boiled. The remainder will do as stock.

Simmer the tongue and curry spices till the gravy thickens. Mix the tamarind with a little of the stock and add this to the gravy, bring to the boil and serve with plain boiled rice.

Enough for four

FISH-ROE SAMBAL

INGREDIENTS

3 heaped dessertspoons of fish-roe

6 small onions, chopped

3 green chillis, chopped

2 oz. butter or cooking fat

3 tablespoons vinegar

The juice of 2 lemons

1 tablespoon Worcester sauce

METHOD

Fry the roe thoroughly in the cooking fat. Chop the onions and chillis finely and mix with the vinegar, lemon juice and Worcester sauce. Mix thoroughly with the hot fish-roe and serve with rice. Sambals are not complete dishes in themselves but are flavourings, or adjuncts, to a main dish. This sambal is eaten with any dish with plenty of rice.

CRUMB CHOPS (An Anglo-Indian dish)

INGREDIENTS

8 tender loin chops

4 green chillis

2 eggs

2 oz. butter

8 pickling onions

A sprinkling of black pepper

Bread crumbs

Mutton stock

Salt

METHOD

Cut the chops, in fine lines, on one side only.

Slice onions and green chillis finely, mix with pepper and salt, and rub the mixture into the cut side of the chops.

Brush with egg and cover liberally with bread crumbs. Heat the fat and fry each chop, first on the crumb side, then on the bare side, till brown. When the chops are nearly tender, cover them with mutton stock and simmer for five minutes. Serve with mashed potatoes, carrots and peas.

Enough for four

DISHES OF INDONESIA AND THAILAND

INDONESIA

THE main dishes in Indonesia consist usually of rice and fish, chicken, meat and vegetables. The Indonesian *consommé,* or *soto*, is very popular all over Java and Madura. Sometimes it is consumed as a main dish, with either boiled or steamed rice.

SOTO AJAM

INGREDIENTS

1 chicken	2 sticks celery
1 large onion, finely sliced	2 leeks, cooked
3 cloves garlic, finely sliced	2 medium-sized potatoes, peeled
½ teaspoon ground ginger	1 dessertspoon lemon juice, a pinch of red
1 large tablespoon mustard oil or cooking oil	pepper (optional)
2 eggs	Salt and pepper to taste
2 large carrots, cooked	4 meat cubes (optional)

METHOD

Cut the chicken into pieces. Fry the onion and garlic to a golden colour, then boil the chicken till tender, with the onion, garlic, ginger and salt and pepper, in enough water to cover it—about 1 quart.

Hard-boil the eggs, slice them and cut the slices into halves. Slice the peeled potatoes and fry them; chop the carrots into small cubes and slice the celery and leeks finely.

To serve, put into each *bouillon* cup or bowl a piece of chicken, a few pieces of egg, some fried potato, onion, garlic, carrot, celery and leek. Then pour hot chicken broth into each cup and serve at once. If added flavour is desired, make a sauce by dissolving 4 meat cubes in boiling water and flavouring with a dessertspoon of lemon juice and a pinch of red pepper.

Enough for four to six

M. JUSUF RONODIPURO
PRESS AND CULTURAL ATTACHÉ
KEDUTAAN BESAR REPUBLIK OF INDONESIA
38 GROSVENOR SQUARE
LONDON, W1

131

SATE AJAM—one version

INGREDIENTS

1 chicken	4 tablespoons peanut butter
Some metal skewers	1 meat cube dissolved in a little boiling water
1 teaspoon ground black pepper	Juice of 1 lemon
1 red chilli, steamed till tender	1 cup ketchup
3 cloves garlic, fried	Salt to taste

METHOD

Pound together the red chilli, garlic and peanut butter and mix into a sauce with the lemon juice and the meat cube dissolved in boiling water.

Cut the chicken into small pieces and thread these on to the skewers. Mix the black pepper, salt and ketchup and pour the mixture over the chicken, and steam till the chicken is tender. Then grill on the skewers and serve with the sauce. Add more lemon juice if needed.

Enough for four

M. JUSUF RONODIPURO

SATE AJAM—another version

INGREDIENTS

2-lb. chicken or 1 lb. mutton	1 large clove garlic
2 walnuts	Juice of 1 lemon or 1 teaspoon tamarind juice
1 onion	Salt
1-inch piece of ginger	

METHOD

Cut the chicken (boned) or mutton into 1-inch pieces. Mix the remainder of the ingredients together with a pinch of salt; then grind or crush them. Rub mixture thoroughly into the chicken or meat and allow it to stand for an hour.

INGREDIENTS

Sate or Sauce

½ cup roasted peanuts	Salt to taste
1 green chilli	1½ dessertspoons thick Japanese soy sauce
1 small onion	1 tablespoon cooking oil (coconut)
1 onion sliced finely	Juice of 1 lime or lemon

METHOD

Fry the sliced onion brown and put on one side. Remove the thin red skin from the peanuts and grind them. Grind the chilli and small onion together and fry them in hot coconut oil. After 3 minutes, add the peanuts and salt. The fried mixture will be thick, so add a little warm water and make into a smooth sauce.

132

Now remove from the stove, mix in the soy sauce and lemon juice and pour over the chicken. Sprinkle fried onion over the dish and serve.

Enough for four

AJAM PANGGANG

INGREDIENTS

1 chicken	3 green chillies
1-inch piece of ginger	Milk of 1 coconut, about ½ pint
1-inch piece of saffron or turmeric or ½ teaspoon	1 saffron leaf
ground saffron or ground turmeric	Small piece of lemon grass
1 large clove garlic	Salt to taste
2 medium-sized onions	

METHOD

Split the chicken along the line of the breast. Grind the ginger, garlic, onions, chillies, saffron or turmeric and mix thoroughly. Add the coconut milk and salt and mix again. Pour into a thick-bottomed pan, toss in the lemon grass and saffron leaf and bring to the boil.

Now put in the chicken and gently stir the liquid while turning the chicken, and simmer slowly till every drop of the milk evaporates.

Finally, remove the chicken from the pan and brown *very gently* under a grill for 1½ hours.

In Indonesia this operation is conducted over a charcoal fire which gives out a slow, steady heat, but as the normal housewife does not cook over charcoal, the grill will have to suffice.

Enough for four

OTAK-OTAK

INGREDIENTS

2 tablespoons olive oil	½ cup milk
2 trout (or other fresh-water fish)	4 tomatoes
¼ teaspoon coriander seeds, ground	1 small lettuce
1 large onion, chopped	1–2 strips of red pepper
4 cloves garlic, chopped	Pepper and salt to taste
1 egg	Some cabbage leaves

METHOD

Wash the fish and beat gently with the back of a heavy wooden spoon or a meat-beater to loosen the skin; then carefully remove the flesh with as little damage to the skin as possible. Remove all bones from the flesh, and chop it finely.

Mix the flesh with the coriander, chopped onion, garlic, egg, milk, pepper, and salt.

133

Fill both fish skins with this stuffing, secure, then wrap each fish in cabbage leaves and steam for 20 minutes.

Finally, fry the fish brown in olive oil and serve garnished with small pieces of red pepper, tomato and lettuce. Parsley may also be used for garnishing, or water cress.

Enough for four

M. JUSUF RONODIPURO

NASI KUNING (Yellow Rice)

INGREDIENTS

3 cups milk	A few celery leaves
1 teaspoon turmeric powder	2 red peppers
1 bay leaf	½ small cucumber
½ teaspoon salt	1 large onion
2 cups rice	2 eggs

METHOD

Add the turmeric, bay leaf and salt to the milk and bring it to the boil. Then remove the bay leaf. Wash rice and stir milk into it. Cook till the milk is absorbed, then steam till the rice is dry.

Cut the red peppers into flower shapes, the cucumber into slices, fry the onion in rings and make the eggs into an omelette, and cut into strips.

Turn the rice out into a large dish and garnish with the celery leaves, red peppers, cucumber, onion rings and strips of omelette.

Enough for two

M. JUSUF RONODIPURO

SERIKAYA

INGREDIENTS

3 eggs	1 cup milk
1 vanilla pod (or less), powdered	3 bananas
1 cup sugar	

METHOD

Beat the vanilla into the eggs, add the sugar and milk and stir the mixture well.

Now add the bananas, sliced, pour the mixture into a deep basin or dish and steam or bake gently for 20–30 minutes till set.

Enough for two

M. JUSUF RONODIPURO

THAILAND

RAMA'S BATH

INGREDIENTS

1 lb. beef	Soy sauce
1 lb. grated coconut	1 lump of palm sugar or 1 large teaspoon 'foot' or
7 dried red chillies (try 2 for a start!)	Barbados sugar
4 shallots	5 teaspoons roasted peanuts
4 large cloves garlic	2½ tablespoons flour
1½ inches of ginger	1 lb. spinach or the equivalent of spring greens
Small stalk lemon grass	Cream or yogurt
½ teaspoon salt	

METHOD

Wash the beef and slice it into strips. Boil the coconut in a pint of water, allow it to cool, strain the 'cream', and put aside.

Boil the beef in the remainder of the coconut milk, and when it comes to the boil, simmer it with a little soy sauce, sugar and peanuts ground or pounded coarsely.

Pound the shallots, chillies, garlic, ginger, lemon grass, and salt together and mix into a sauce with the 'cream' from the coconut milk. Add the boiled beef, sauce, sugar, etc.; make a thin paste of the flour with a little cold water, and pour over the concoction. Bring to the boil, stirring, put on a close-fitting lid, and simmer till the beef is tender.

The greens should be boiled very rapidly in a little salted water for not more than 8–10 minutes; then drain off the water, arrange the greens on a dish, place the beef on top and crown with 2 teaspoons of cream or a bottle of yogurt.

This should always be eaten with rice. (Don't throw away the water from the greens, but use it as stock.)

Enough for four

DOVE or WOOD-PIGEON

INGREDIENTS

1 large dove or wood-pigeon	1 dessertspoon sugar
1 small cucumber	A few crushed coriander leaves
1 small onion, sliced	1 dessertspoon flour
1 large clove garlic, sliced	1 tablespoon lard
3 green chillies	2 dessertspoons Chinese soy sauce
1 tablespoon best wine vinegar or ¼ pint cider	Salt to taste

METHOD

Dismember the pigeon, and slice the cucumber, preferably without peeling it. The best cucumbers are NOT the thick ones, but those that are thin and very dark green. These are succulent, whereas the large, light-green or yellowish cucumbers are tough and packed with seeds.

Slice the green chillies, remove the seeds, and cut them into diamond shapes.

Mix together the vinegar (or cider), salt, sugar, soy sauce and flour.

Fry the garlic till golden brown, add the bird and stir for 2 minutes. Then put in the other ingredients (except chillies and coriander) and the blended liquid and stir again. When the bird is tender serve in a dish with the chopped coriander leaves and green chillies on top. Dove or wood-pigeon is eaten with rice.

Farmers, who consider pigeons a nuisance and shoot them, might relish them served this way.

One bird to each person

DISHES OF IRAN AND IRAQ

IRAN

IRAN is the name by which Persia is known officially in the West today, but it is the name by which Persia has always been known to Persians. Their cuisine has much in common with all food in the East but, like Turkish cookery, pungent spices are not used as heavily as in India, Pakistan, Ceylon, Burma, Indonesia and Malaya.

POLO

This has no connection with the game of the same name, which, incidentally, was invented in Persia (Iran).

METHOD

Wash 1 breakfast cup of rice twice in warm water and place in a bowl with *warm* water. Put into the bowl ½ teaspoon of salt in a cotton or muslin bag—it is important that the salt does not touch the rice. Leave for 24 hours. Then drain in a colander and tip the rice into a panful of boiling water. After 15 minutes test a few grains of rice between finger and thumb, and when tender, remove from the heat, drain and put into a dish.

Now place a knob of butter on the bottom of a pan, add about ½ pint of water and boil. Pour half the liquid away, leaving ¼ pint of the oily mixture at the bottom of the pan. Add the rice to this and cook fast till steam rises; this should happen in a matter of seconds. The drain off the liquid through the rice.

Decrease the heat almost to vanishing point, wrap the lid of the pan in cloth to prevent the steam from escaping and cook gently for 30 minutes. The *polo* is now ready to serve.

Enough for two

Polo can also be made with the addition of: lentils (*Addas Polo*); broad beans (*Baghela Polo*); kidney beans (*Loubia Polo*); vermicelli (*Reshteh Polo*); and black cherries (*Albalu Polo*).

For the first four, prepare the *polo* as above. Boil the alternative ingredients in a separate pan with salt to taste; then add the *polo* to the ingredient, or ingredients, and mix thoroughly, before the final steaming. At that stage also, onions, garlic, a little saffron or turmeric, paprika or other spices may be added (never sweet spices); but this is optional.

If fresh or dried cherries are used, boil and mix with sugar (sugar should be a little less than a tenth of the weight of cherries) and add a little vanilla. When the cherries are tender, put half the *polo* in the serving dish, then half the cherries, then the remainder of the *polo* and the rest of the cherries on top. Add the syrup.

If cherries are used, no other spices should be added.

Polo made with vegetables is a dish on its own, though it can be accompanied by mutton or chicken.

TAHCHIN BAREH (Lamb) and TAHCHIN ESFENADJ (Spinach)

METHOD

Prepare a dish of *polo* as instructed in the preceding recipe, but in the second stage, when boiling a knob of butter and a little water in a pan, do not drain off the butter-water but add the rice to it.

Take 1 lb. lamb, either from the saddle or leg, remove all fat and boil in water to cover till tender, adding salt only when the water *comes* to the boil. Then drain the water into a dish, cut the meat into cubes, put into the *polo* pan with a knob of butter and a little water, add the *polo*, cook gently for 30 minutes, and then pour in the stock in which the meat was cooked.

Boil 1 lb. spinach very fast for 8 minutes in just the water that clings to it after it has been washed and drained. Put half in the bottom of a serving dish, then the rice and meat, and finally the rest of the spinach on top.

Here again, spices may be cooked in with the *polo* and meat: onions finely sliced, cloves of garlic, paprika or pinches of turmeric, saffron, cummin seed or coriander; but these are optional.

Enough for four

KABAB BARG

INGREDIENTS

2 lb. good veal steak	2 medium-sized onions
Juice of 1 lemon	1 egg
3–4 cloves garlic (optional)	Salt to taste

METHOD

Remove as much fat as possible from the veal. Then cut into small pieces, add the lemon juice, salt, crushed onions and crushed garlic (if used). Mix well together and leave for 2 days in a refrigerator or ice-box. If you haven't one, make the mixture in the morning and cook at night.

When ready for cooking, bind the mixture with an egg, spear it on a *kabab* knife (skewer) and roast over a charcoal fire. As most housewives cook either by gas or electricity, the skewered meat will have to be placed under the grill and turned from time to time as each side cooks.

The meat can be minced instead of cut in pieces: egg and onions will bind the mixture which can then be moulded round the *kabab* knife or skewer.

Enough for six

CHELO KABAB

This is merely *polo* with two kinds of *kabab*: minced and cut in pieces.

KHORESH (Sauce)

Three kinds of sauce are very popular in Iran: *Bodemjan* (aubergine); *Karafs* (celery); and *Ghorme Sabzy* (vegetables obtainable only in Iran—there is no point, therefore, in discussing this version).

Bodemjan

INGREDIENTS

1 large aubergine   Pinches of paprika, cummin seed, coriander, fenugreek

1 tablespoon butter, margarine or oil for frying   and turmeric

1 medium-sized onion   Tomato sauce

3–4 cloves garlic (optional)

METHOD

Skin the aubergine and place the vegetable, whole, in a dish. Rub with $\frac{1}{2}$ teaspoon of salt and leave for 2 hours.

Now fry the aubergine in butter or oil till it is dark brown. Crush the onion and add it to the aubergine and butter and fry for a minute or two: then cover with water and boil fast for 15 minutes. The aubergine has by this time disintegrated, so add a couple of tablespoons of tomato sauce and such spices as you wish and cook slowly for 20 minutes.

This should be served with chicken, mutton or beef fried in butter and usually eaten with *polo*.

Karafs is prepared in the same way, substituting celery for aubergine.

Fasenjan

Take 1 lb. shelled walnuts, mince finely and fry with 2 chopped onions and 1 dessertspoon of butter. When the oil starts to ooze from the nuts, add 1 wineglass of grenadine juice and 1 dessertspoon of brown sugar. Simmer for 2 hours. Add salt, pepper or/and spices to taste, and serve with meat, chicken or duck.

These recipes were kindly supplied by

MR ESFANDIAR Y BOZORGMEER
THE COQ D'OR RESTAURANT
TEHERAN

PILO

INGREDIENTS

2 breakfast cups fine rice, Kashmiri, Burmese or Patna $\frac{1}{4}$ cup cooking oil

3 quarts boiling water

METHOD
Cover the rice with salt water and soak overnight, then drain.

Place the rice in a thick pan and add 3 quarts of boiling water and cook until almost done. Feel a few grains from time to time between finger and thumb, and if fairly soft but firm, the rice is nearly done.

When this state has been reached, drain off the water and put in the oil. Tilt the pan from side to side till the sides of the pan are coated with oil, then place a thin, clean cloth over the pan and jam on the lid over this.

Now place the pan in a very slow oven—No. 1 if a gas oven, just under 200° if electric; and cook for 3–4 hours.

Pilo may be eaten plain or garnished with chopped onion (raw or fried), garlic and parsley.

It is usually served with *kabab* or some other meat dish.

Enough for four to six

CHIRINE PILO (Sweet Rice)

INGREDIENTS

2 breakfast cups rice

1 breakfast cup candied or glazed
   orange peel, finely diced

¾ cup plump currants

½ breakfast cup blanched slivered almonds
   (pine kernels may be used instead)

¼ cup cooking oil

METHOD

Cook the rice as in the recipe for ordinary *pilo*, and when ready, divide it into 3 parts.

Divide the almonds, currants and peel also into 3 parts.

Spread 1 portion of the rice at the bottom of a thick pan, then a portion of the peel, almonds and currants. Then a second layer of rice with peel, almonds and currants, and finally the third layer of rice, with the third layer of peel, almonds and currants.

Then put in the oil, tilt the pan in every direction till the sides of the pan are coated, cover with a thin, clean cloth, and put on the lid. Bake in a slow oven, as before, for 3–4 hours.

Chirine Pilo may be garnished with splintered angelica and crystallized cherries, but if this is done it is eaten on its own, and never with flesh. Otherwise it is usually accompanied by a fried mutton dish.

Enough for four to six

IRAQ

SHISH KABAB

INGREDIENTS

('Shish'—Skewer: 'Kabab'—Broiled Meat)

1-lb. leg of very young lamb

½ teaspoon ground cinnamon

A good sprinkling of nutmeg

6 tomatoes, sliced

½ teaspoon black pepper   2 onions, sliced

6–10 cloves, ground   1 breakfast cup Patna, Burma, or other fine rice

1 teaspoon ground coriander   Stock or water

1 tablespoon butter, good oil or cooking fat   Salt to taste

  (butter is best)   Metal skewers

METHOD

Soak the rice overnight, then drain. Fry it in the butter till golden brown, then add 1 breakfast cup of stock or water, bring to the boil, then lower heat till the contents just simmer. Now put on a tight-fitting lid and cook till the water has evaporated entirely. The rice should be thoroughly cooked, with each grain separate from the others. If not, add a little more water and cook till this evaporates.

Turn out into a dish and place in a warm—not hot—oven to dry.

Cut the lamb into 1½-inch cubes, but before doing so, mix the ground spices in a little tomato juice so as to make a paste, and rub well into the meat. Put the lamb aside for an hour.

Now put the pieces of lamb on skewers: one piece of lamb, then a slice of onion and finally a slice of tomato; then another piece of lamb, and so on. Grill the skewered lamb over a charcoal fire or under a gas or electric grill till the flesh is tender. Turn the skewers from time to time so that the lamb is cooked on every side.

Serve with the rice and garnish with onions, nuts, sultanas, parsley and/or garlic sliced very finely.

Vary the quantities of ground spices to suit your taste.

The garnish is optional.

Enough for four

THE SARABIA RESTAURANT
9 OLD BROMPTON ROAD
LONDON, SW7

DISHES OF MALAYA

THE population of Malaya comprises mainly Malays, Chinese and Indians, the majority from South India and Ceylon, with a sprinkling of Sikhs and Pathans; and a small but influential Arab community, most of whom come from Hadramaut, in Arabia.

As a result there is a similarity between Indian and Malayan food, though Malayan curries have a distinct tang, appearance and even aroma of their own, and no one with a discriminating palate would mistake a Malayan curry for an Indian curry.

BANANA CURRY

INGREDIENTS

4 large, unripe bananas

1 tablespoon small onions, sliced

1 green chilli, sliced

1 tablespoon pounded Bombay duck

¼ teaspoon fenugreek

2 breakfast cups coconut milk, which can be extracted
    from ½ lb. desiccated coconut

A pinch (⅛ teaspoon) of ground saffron or turmeric

1-inch stick of cinnamon

1-inch piece of *rampe*

3–4 curry leaves

1 sprig fennel

2 tablespoons coconut oil, ghee, butter, mustard
    oil or margarine

1 teaspoon salt

METHOD

Skin the bananas; slit them lengthwise and then in half; rub them with the salt and saffron or turmeric and fry them in oil.

Now pour the coconut milk into a saucepan with the other ingredients, bring to the boil and simmer for 30 minutes. Then add the bananas and simmer till the gravy is thick.

Use bananas with the skin as green as possible, and use 2–3 chillies if you like it more pungent.

Enough for two

FRIED EGG CURRY

This is a popular curry and far more spicy than egg curries concocted in India, Turkey and elsewhere.

INGREDIENTS

8 large eggs	$\frac{1}{4}$ teaspoon sweet cummin seed
1 tablespoon onion, finely sliced	$\frac{1}{2}$ teaspoon fenugreek
4 cloves garlic, chopped	Juice of 1 lemon
1-inch slice of green ginger, chopped	$\frac{1}{2}$ lb. desiccated coconut—to make
1 small piece of *rampe*	2 breakfast cups coconut milk
$\frac{1}{2}$ stem lemon grass	2 dessertspoons Bombay duck, broken up
3–4 curry leaves	5 red chillies, ground
2-inch stick of cinnamon	$\frac{1}{2}$ teaspoon turmeric
1 sprig fennel	A pinch of salt
3 teaspoons coriander seed	1 tablespoon frying fat, butter or oil
$1\frac{1}{2}$ teaspoons white cummin seed	

METHOD

Boil eggs very hard, then shell and rub with the salt and turmeric, and fry to a light-brown colour. It is advisable to prick the eggs all over with a hat-pin or similar instrument, otherwise they are likely to explode when fried.

Now fry half the onion in a dessertspoon of fat, together with the *rampe*, lemon grass and curry leaves; then pour in the coconut milk and remainder of the ingredients—except the lemon juice.

Simmer till the gravy is thick, stirring the while; then add the eggs, cover with the gravy, spooning it over the eggs again and again, then put in the lemon juice. Simmer for 10 minutes, then serve.

Enough for four

YELLOW RICE

INGREDIENTS

2 breakfast cups table rice (Patna, Burma or Kashmiri)	3–4 curry leaves
$\frac{1}{4}$ lb. ghee, butter, dripping or best margarine	$\frac{1}{2}$ stem lemon grass
$\frac{1}{2}$ lb. onions, finely sliced	2-inch piece of *rampe*
$\frac{1}{4}$ lb. Bombay duck, pounded	1 *full* teaspoon ground turmeric for
10 cloves	colouring (or saffron)
20–30 peppercorns	Milk of 2 coconuts, or milk from 1 lb. desiccated
1 sprig fennel	coconut—2 breakfast cups
10 cardamoms, ground or powdered to bring out flavour	Salt to taste

METHOD

Heat the fat and fry in it about a third of the onions, *rampe* and lemon grass and the curry leaves.

When the onions are well browned, mix in the rice, cook briskly for about 5 minutes, stirring all the time; then add the coconut milk and the remainder of the ingredients except the cardamoms, which must be added when the rice is half cooked. Some prefer not to grind or powder the cardamoms, but to mix the seeds into the rice after it has been cooked.

If coconut milk is not available or you would rather not use milk made from desiccated coconut, the rice may be boiled either in meat or vegetable stock, or a mixture of both.

The rice is thoroughly cooked when each grain is separate from the others and yet soft enough to be eaten. If there is any stock or coconut milk left when this state is reached, drain it off; if there is not enough liquid, add a little boiling water.

Yellow rice is served with curry.

Enough for four to five

CHICKEN GRAVY CURRY WITH PULWAL

INGREDIENTS

1 chicken	2 blades lemon grass
2 oz. ghee, mustard oil, coconut oil or other cooking fat	$\frac{1}{4}$ teaspoon ground garlic
	2 large cups coconut milk (the milk from
1½ teaspoons salt	1 large coconut)
4 teaspoons ground onions	3–4 cloves—ground or whole
1 teaspoon ground turmeric	3–4 cardamoms—ground or whole
1 teaspoon ground chilli	3–4 1-inch sticks of cinnamon, ground
$\frac{1}{2}$ teaspoon ground ginger	can of *Pulwals*

METHOD

Take a plump chicken, bone it and mince the flesh as finely as possible, till it is reduced to a pulp. Mix the flesh and salt with the spices given, using onion, turmeric, chilli, ginger, garlic, cloves, cardamom and cinnamon, but first fry these spices in heated ghee or fat or oil, in a thick saucepan.

Then take a dozen or more large *pulwals* (the *pulwal* is a vegetable like a large squat pea, but much greater in diameter), slit them down one side, and scrape away the seeds from inside. Wash the *pulwals,* and stuff them with the forcemeat. This done, join the sides together and tie with cotton and cook in coconut milk (2 breakfast cups), adding a couple of blades of lemon grass to the liquid; these must be removed before serving. Bring to the boil; simmer for 30–40 minutes. Serve with rice.

Enough for four

Pulwals may be had in cans from any store that sells Indian curry spices, and, like okras (Lady's Fingers), have a flavour quite distinct from vegetables grown in Europe.

Either prawns or fish may be treated in much the same way and stuffed into *pulwal*, and both are favourite dishes.

LIVER CURRY

INGREDIENTS

2 lb. liver	1 tablespoon ghee, dripping, mustard oil or margarine
10–20 red chillies, ground	20 cardamoms, either whole or powdered
2 dessertspoons white cummin seed, ground	1 teaspoon fenugreek
1½ tablespoons small onions, sliced	3 pieces of aromatic ginger, powdered
8 cloves garlic, either whole or chopped	Salt to taste
3 1-inch slices of green ginger, chopped	1 wineglass (sherry size)
3 1-inch pieces of *rampe*	best wine vinegar
½ stem lemon grass	2 breakfast cups coconut milk; if this is made from
1 sprig curry leaves	desiccated coconut, use about 1 lb.

METHOD

Boil the liver till firm, then cut it lengthwise into strips, and chop the strips into pieces about 1 inch long.

Place the liver, coconut milk and all the ingredients, except the fat, into a saucepan with a thick bottom and boil till the liver is soft.

Now drain off the liquid, put in the fat and fry liver and ingredients till well browned; then pour back the liquid and simmer, stirring the while, till the gravy thickens. To be eaten with rice.

Enough for six

FISH PUDICHCHI

INGREDIENTS

2 large slices of cod or other coarse fish, each about 1 lb.	Salt to taste
10 red chillies, pounded (or less)	1-inch piece of *rampe*
1 teaspoon ground turmeric	½ stem lemon grass
1 tablespoon onion, finely sliced	1 sprig curry leaves
4–6 cloves garlic, chopped or whole	½ teaspoon fenugreek
3-inch stick of cinnamon	2 breakfast cups coconut milk
3 1-inch slices of green ginger, chopped	Juice of 1 lemon

METHOD

Quarter each slice of fish and place in a thick saucepan. Add all the ingredients except the lemon juice, and boil. When the fish is soft but not cooked through, add the lemon juice; then finish cooking.

This is one of the few Eastern dishes in which fat is not used.

Enough for four

PRAWN CURRY

INGREDIENTS

½ lb. dried prawns (if fresh, use double the quantity)   1-inch piece of *rampe*

10 large half-ripe tomatoes, sliced   ¼ stem lemon grass

10 dried chillies, pounded (as many as 40 are used in   4–5 curry leaves
   Malaya)   1 tablespoon ghee, butter, margarine, or coconut oil

2 tablespoons pounded Bombay duck   3 breakfast cups coconut milk

1 large onion, sliced finely   Juice from 1 oz. tamarind in hot water

1 teaspoon ground turmeric   6 cloves garlic, chopped

2-inch piece of green ginger, chopped

METHOD

Fry the *rampe*, lemon grass, curry leaves and onion in the fat. Mix the remainder of the ingredients together, and when the onion is golden brown, pour them in, and bring to the boil. When the prawns are nearly soft, turn down the heat and simmer till the gravy has almost all evaporated.

Eaten usually with yellow rice or *pilau*.

Enough for four

These recipes were kindly supplied by

MR K. THARMARATNAM
SECOND SECRETARY, MALAYA HOUSE
57 TRAFALGAR SQUARE
LONDON, WC2

FISH CURRY

INGREDIENTS

1 large teacup cooked fish   1 tablespoon grated coconut

1 small cooking apple   3 tablespoons rice

½ onion   A squeeze of lemon

1 tablespoon butter   Salt and pepper to taste

1 small teacup milk and water in equal amounts   1 teaspoon curry powder

1 teaspoon flour

METHOD

Peel and chop both the apple and onion. Melt the butter in a saucepan, add the apple and onion and fry till golden brown. Then stir in the curry powder and flour, pour in the milk and water and bring to the boil. Simmer for 30 minutes (this is the curry sauce).

Prepare the cooked fish in large flakes.

Boil the rice till soft, drain off water, and dry.

Now add the fish to the curry sauce and sprinkle in cayenne and salt, and squeeze in the lemon juice. If, after making this dish once, you find there is too little lemon, add more next time. Heat fish and curry sauce but do NOT boil.

To dish: make a border of the boiled rice, pour the curried fish into the middle and sprinkle with either white or browned coconut. Garnish with 'butterflies' of lemon, and/or parsley, and chilli skins. Serve with sweet mango chutney.

Enough for two

In Malaya this dish is served to the accompaniment of sliced banana (uncooked), sliced banana fried brown, pineapple diced small, salted ground-nuts (peanuts), grated coconut either raw or browned, ground red peppers, *brinjals*, okras and sultanas.

You can vary this curry by using ½ lb. fresh prawns, cooked beef, chicken or game instead of fish. It is an easy curry to prepare and specially suitable for beginners.

MRS G. K. RAMESHWAR
17-D LIM TUA TOW ROAD
SINGAPORE, 19
MALAYA

DISHES OF TURKEY

CURRIES proper—that is, curries rich in chilli, cummin, coriander, cardamom, cinnamon, fenugreek, turmeric and saffron—emanated doubtless from India (including what is now Pakistan), Ceylon, Burma, Malaya and Indonesia; but for 4000 years or more rice has been eaten as far west as Egypt and as far east as China, Japan and the Philippines.

As rice goes hand in hand with savoury foods, it is little wonder that Turkey, too, that land of Empire-builders, is the country where the *pilav* (*pilaf* or *pilao*) was born.

The Turks are noted gourmets. In Istanbul, Turkey's mysterious metropolis, men choose their drinking water as Parisians choose their wines, and a mere sip serves to identify the spring from whence it gushes.

This sensitivity to nuances reflects the Turk's aesthetic approach to life. He is easily the 'choosiest' eater in all Europe, with an Oriental rather than an Occidental outlook on food. The discriminating Turk never asks for an 'apple', but for an *Amasya* or a *Gumashane*; and if for a pear, when it was plucked from the tree!

His cuisine is the best balanced (from a dietetic point of view) in Europe, and the variety of his sauces, creams and blends of food would turn most Parisians electric green with envy. The aubergine, alone, is cooked in more than forty different ways.

In such a volume as this it is possible to give only a handful of Turkish recipes; and those the simplest and most easily concocted.

Turkey, once the cross-roads of the civilized world, has borrowed from both East and West and has contrived both kinds of cuisine into a blend that is distinctly her own.

If you dine with a Turk in his country he will start the meal with the salutation, 'May it give you good health,' adding the words, 'and happy eating, too'. Only thus can food benefit you to the utmost.

TURQUOISE (Yogurt Soup)

INGREDIENTS

3 medium-sized cucumbers	1 teaspoon dill
$\frac{1}{4}$ teaspoon salt	1 pint yogurt (4 bottles)
1–2 cloves garlic	1 onion (optional)
1 tablespoon best malt vinegar	2 tablespoons olive oil
1 tablespoon chopped mint or $\frac{1}{2}$ teaspoon dried mint leaves	

METHOD

Peel the cucumbers (some prefer them unpeeled), quarter lengthwise, and slice about ⅛ inch thick. Place in a bowl and sprinkle with salt.

Rub another bowl with the garlic and swish the vinegar around it to collect the flavour (discarding the garlic); or, preferably, slice or mash the garlic into the vinegar. The onion, if used, may be put in, finely chopped, at this stage. Next add the dill and yogurt and stir till the mixture has the consistency of thick soup. If too thick, add cold water. Pour over the cucumbers and stir.

Serve cold, sprinkled with the olive oil and garnished with the chopped mint. In winter the soup may be served hot, and for those who cannot stomach it, the olive oil may be omitted. In summer, chill before serving.

Enough for four

DOLMAS

Dolmas are a feature of Turkish food; *dolma* comes from *doldurmak*—to stuff.

INGREDIENTS

1 lb. ground lamb or beef free from fat	1 teaspoon chopped dill
1 large chopped onion	½ teaspoon cummin seed (optional)
3–4 cloves garlic, crushed	Salt and pepper
¼ cup rice	A pinch of chilli powder (optional)
1 teaspoon chopped mint	1 tablespoon tomato sauce (optional)
1 teaspoon ground coriander seed (optional)	

METHOD

These ingredients comprise the stuffing. Vary them, at times using the optional spices, at times leaving them out till you find which you like best.

Place the meat in a bowl and add the onion, garlic, rice, mint, dill, the remainder of the spices, and the tomato sauce, if you are going to use these. Knead well.

If aubergines are to be stuffed, choose short, fat, round specimens that will cook upright in a pan. Cut off the stem end and keep it for a cover. Peel the aubergine lengthwise, in strips, leaving alternate unpeeled layers to strengthen the aubergine. Scoop out the inside leaving a shell less than 1 inch thick. Fill with the stuffing and replace the stem-end cover.

Don't waste the inside of the aubergine, which has been scooped out; this, cooked with onion, garlic, tomato and a little lemon juice, forms an excellent addition to any dish such as *kabab*.

If green peppers are to be stuffed, slit through the tops but don't sever them. Then remove the seeds and membranes, fill with stuffing and close.

Tomato *dolmas* can be prepared in the same way as green pepper *dolmas*.

Zucchini Dolmas (Squash)

Clean the outside of the squash (or marrow), cut off the narrow end and use this as a cover. Scoop out the inside, leaving a ½-inch shell, then stuff and replace the cover, fastening it with toothpicks or cocktail sticks.

Sometimes one prepares all the *dolmas* together. When this is done place the aubergine and *zucchini dolmas* on the bottom of a large saucepan; on top, a layer of green pepper *dolmas*, and over them a layer of tomato *dolmas*.

Then put in 2 tablespoons of butter and a breakfast cup of water, put on a well-fitting cover and cook on a medium heat for 30–40 minutes, or until the vegetables are soft.

If any stuffing is left over, make it into meat balls and place between the stuffed *dolmas* in the saucepan.

All these *dolmas* may be cooked separately or together, but the quantities given for stuffing ingredients are enough only for four persons.

ROAST CHICKEN WITH PINE-NUT STUFFING

INGREDIENTS

1 roasting chicken	3–4 cardamoms, shelled (optional)
1 breakfast cup rice	3 tablespoons butter
¼ breakfast cup currants	¼ teaspoon ground ginger (optional)
¼ breakfast cup *pignolia* (pine kernels)	3–4 cloves garlic (optional)
A pinch each of ground coriander seed and chilli	2 cups water
powder (optional)	Salt to taste

METHOD

Prepare the chicken for roasting. Cover the rice with lukewarm water and allow it to stand. Take out the chicken liver and chop it into small pieces.

Clean the currants and nuts, then melt 1 tablespoon of butter in a large saucepan and *sauté* (fry quickly and lightly) the nuts until they turn pink.

Remove the nuts and *sauté* the chicken liver in the same butter. Now return the nuts to the pan (with liver) and add the currants, rice (washed and drained), salt (and ginger, cardamoms, garlic, coriander and chilli, if used) and 2 cups of boiling water.

Cover and stew slowly over a medium heat. When the water is absorbed, add 2 tablespoons of butter and mix well. Then remove from the stove and place in a warm oven (uncovered) for 15 minutes.

The rice should by this time be fluffy with every grain separate.

Fill the chicken loosely with this stuffing till it is about two-thirds full and sew or skewer the opening. Then roast as usual.

There is no hard and fast rule for this dish; experiment with the spices and leave out those you do not like—if any. Walnuts or chestnuts may be used instead of pine kernels.

Enough for six

KORISTCH

INGREDIENTS

2-lb. shoulder of mutton	4–6 cloves
1 teaspoon pepper	½ lb. stewed prunes—half stewed and still firm
½ teaspoon salt	5 1-inch sticks of cinnamon
8 finely sliced onions	4 tablespoons ghee, margarine or butter

Beef Curry on Sticks
(See recipe page 58)

METHOD

Bone the mutton, rub thoroughly with the salt and pepper, roll and tie with string.

Heat the fat in a thick saucepan and fry the onions till brown. Then put in the mutton and well brown all over.

Now add just enough water to prevent the onions from scorching, put in the cinnamon and cloves, cover the pan and simmer till the meat is tender and the liquid absorbed. If the meat is not tender and the liquid has evaporated, add a little more water or stock.

Then put in the half-stewed prunes and baste the meat with the prune syrup. Turn down the heat till the contents of the pan just simmer gently and keep on till the prunes are soft and mushy.

Sultanas may be added with the prunes, or half prunes and half sultanas; and 3–4 cloves of garlic may also be put in after the meat is tender, and before the prunes are added. Some like garlic and think that it improves the flavour; others think that the dish is much too strong with garlic and omit it.

Enough for six

SHISH KABAB

INGREDIENTS

2-lb. leg of lamb	2–3 bay leaves—or more. Green pepper (optional)
1 tablespoon olive oil	Pinches of other spices (optional)—cummin, chilli,
Juice of 1 lemon	coriander
1 medium-sized onion, thickly sliced	Aubergine (optional)
3 medium-sized tomatoes, sliced	Salt and pepper to taste
3–4 cloves garlic (optional)	Metal skewers or spits

METHOD

Cut the meat into 1-inch cubes. Mix the olive oil and lemon juice, and if garlic is used, mash this in. Rub this mixture into the meat. Place it in a dish, sprinkle with salt and pepper (and if other spices are used, with them, too), and put away for 6 hours.

Then take the spits or skewers, and spear on them in turn a piece of meat, slice of tomato, slice of onion, piece of bay leaf; and so on; meat, tomato, onion, bay leaf . . . .

If green peppers or aubergines are used, insert a piece of pepper or aubergine, or both, on to the skewers at intervals.

Grill slowly over a charcoal or wood fire, or an open coal fire. Where these are not available, an electric or gas grill will do. Turn the spits as you grill.

Enough for four

LADY MEAT BALLS

INGREDIENTS

1 lb. finely ground lean mutton	$\frac{1}{8}$ teaspoon chilli powder
3 large onions (diced)	$\frac{1}{2}$ cup flour
$\frac{1}{2}$ cup rice	4 eggs

½ cup grated cheese	2–3 cloves garlic
1 teaspoon chopped parsley	¼ cup shortening or lard
1 teaspoon chopped dill	Salt to taste
⅛ teaspoon pepper	

METHOD

Put the mutton (or lamb, if you like), onions and garlic through the grinder. Boil the rice till tender, drain away water, and mix with the onions and garlic, then with the cheese, parsley, dill, pepper, chilli powder and salt. Knead well for 5 minutes, form into egg-sized ovals and roll in flour. Beat the eggs till frothy, then dip the meat ovals into the egg and fry all over in the shortening.

Enough, with vegetables, for four

LENTIL MEAT STEW

INGREDIENTS

1 cup red lentils	⅛ teaspoon chilli powder
1 large onion, chopped	1 teaspoon turmeric
4 cloves garlic, whole	½ teaspoon cummin, ground
1 tablespoon butter	¼ cup rice
1 lb. beef or lamb cut into 1-inch cubes	2 cups water
1 teaspoon salt	Vinegar to taste (optional)
¼ teaspoon pepper	Juice of 1 lemon (optional)

METHOD

Wash the lentils, put into a thick saucepan and cover with water. Soak overnight and then drain. Brown the chopped onion and garlic in butter and add lentils; then the meat and enough water to cover (about a cupful), and salt, pepper, chilli, cummin and turmeric. Bring to the boil, then simmer gently (about an hour), add the rice and another cup of water. Simmer, stir well, then cook for 20–30 minutes till rice is cooked through. If you wish, add vinegar or lemon juice before serving.

Enough for four

PILAV

INGREDIENTS

2 breakfast cups rice	2 teaspoons salt—or less—to taste
4 medium-sized tomatoes (fresh or canned)	2 oz. butter
3½ breakfast cups vegetable or meat stock, or chicken broth	3 cloves garlic (optional)

METHOD

Wash the rice well, and drain, then set aside. Peel the tomatoes, then cut them into small chunks and seed them, though this is not essential.

Heat butter and tomatoes together till a tomato paste is obtained. If garlic is used, cook it with the butter and tomatoes. Add the stock and salt to this mixture and boil for 2 minutes.

While still boiling, pour in the rice, stir once, cover and simmer without stirring till the rice has absorbed all the liquid. Now turn the flame very low and simmer for another 20 minutes.

Remove from the stove and leave uncovered for 30 minutes—but do not stir.

When transferring rice to the serving dish, use a flat serving spoon and handle the rice gently to keep it fluffy.

Enough for six

Coffee is a beverage drunk in few Eastern countries outside the Arab zone, and generally speaking the making of good coffee is not understood in India, Ceylon, Burma, Malaya and Indonesia.

The Turks, however, are connoisseurs of coffee, and black coffee made in the Turkish way is well worth sampling.

TURKISH COFFEE

INGREDIENTS

2 tablespoons brown sugar	2 teaspoons pulverized coffee
(Demerara or Barbadoes)	$\frac{1}{2}$ breakfast cup water

METHOD

Turkish coffee is made in a *jezve*—a cylindrical pot with a long handle, sold in shops specializing in Mediterranean food. In London, a *jezve* may be bought in Soho.

Turkish coffee is roasted to a darker brown than coffee from the West Indies, Kenya, India or South America, and is far more bitter to the palate. It should be taken after breakfast or lunch when, according to Dr Bernard Aschner, it restores a flabby or hyper-acid stomach with no harm to the heart. It keeps you awake and enables you to conduct business, with all your faculties alert, even after a heavy lunch. It should NOT be taken at night.

Put cold water in the *jezve*. Add sugar and coffee. Stir well.

Place the *jezve* over a low flame and cook till the coffee and water rise to the boil. The surface will be covered by froth. Pour this off into two *demi-tasse* cups. Then bring the liquid to the boil again and remove from the fire, or stove. Pour the coffee over the froth to fill the cups, and serve.

Vary the proportions of coffee and sugar to suit your taste; but remember, Turkish coffee is NEVER taken with either milk or cream. It always has a froth on it. You can add milk or cream, but it won't be *Turkish* coffee.

Enough for two

THE FOURTH BOOK
OF CURRIES

EVEN MORE THOUGHTS ON CURRY

THERE are some who can't abide curry. I know a man, apparently civilized, who says, 'Give me a plate of corned beef and chips and you can keep your curry—or caviar!' There is no accounting for tastes. The Eskimo delights in *muk-tuk*, which is rancid blood and blubber mixed with putrefying fish.

Perhaps the idea persists that Indian cooks are dirty and their dishes permeated by disease germs, but in India cooking is a rite and before a Hindu lady enters her kitchen, she bathes and puts on clean clothing. The spices in which foods are curried have antiseptic value; and the *Sustras* lay it down that naught shall be eaten unless it has a protective skin or shell; that vegetables must not be left over from one meal to the next; and that onions, which harbour germs when peeled, shall be eaten at one sitting, unless curried.

Cooling and Heating Properties of Food

In India the temperature may vary in different parts, from 110°F. in the shade to below zero; so as you journey from place to place, you hear men discussing the 'cooling' and 'heating' properties of foods.

What they mean is that some foods induce a feeling of coolness in the body, whereas others appear to warm it. Steaming tea and pungent curries are cooling because they make you perspire; coffee, wheaten products, lentils, milk and all flesh have a heating effect. Europeans, who eat them to excess, get prickly heat; Indians rarely do.

Infinite Variety

Curries vary in areas where people speak different languages or dialects, and there are some dozen official languages and some 300 or more dialects in India and Pakistan. There is an infinite variety of curries, on which subject I shall touch later. According to the *Sustras* and the *Code of Manu*, meals should be planned to whip up the appetite, maintain it, and finally aid digestion. Curries convey richness and taste, rice softens the pungency, and so on. The cardamoms and cloves which finish off a meal cleanse the breath and help digestion too. Each dish should be complementary to the others and play its part in the general scheme.

Salt

Salt is meant to flavour, not poison, food. Far too much is eaten. Dr Victor Heiser says that Americans eat half an ounce of salt a day; the British consumption is *one tablespoon* a day! Medical experts say that too much salt aggravates many diseases, increases high blood pressure, coronary disease and constipation; and Professor Coirault, the famous French neuro-psychiatrist, has proved that when too much salt is eaten the body finds it difficult to rest and insomnia is the result.

THE FUNCTION OF RICE

IN INDIA, as elsewhere, there are many indiscriminate feeders; we do not base our standards on them but on the gourmets and epicures. We don't mix every article of food into one bowl on the principle that ultimately they will mingle in our stomachs, but keep them apart so that the various flavours may delight our palates. In Europe the French do this better than any nation; in Asia, the Indians.

It is generally understood that in India rice is meant to serve the purpose that bread or potatoes do in Britain, as a 'filler', but this is not quite so. Here, meat of various kinds imparts flavour, and bread and potatoes fill the vast empty spaces because they are bulkier and cheaper. In Italy spaghetti and macaroni do the same thing. At a well-planned Chinese dinner, rice is served last and it is a compliment to your host to confess that you are so full that you simply cannot touch it! This does not apply, of course, to the majority who are poor and depend on rice to fill their stomachs.

In India rice isn't supposed to be a filler, but a *neutral base* which helps to bring out the flavours of the various dishes. A little curry from one dish should be placed on an area of virgin rice; a little curry from another dish placed on another free area of rice; and so on. You sample one kind of curry with a little rice, then another, and another. If the curry is too pungent, a little more plain rice will subdue the burning pangs. It can be sweetened with chutney or given an acid tang with pickle.

Nutritional Value of Rice

The idea that plain white rice is coolie's food and that the well-to-do eat only *khichiri* or *pilau* is nonsense. Plain, well-cooked white rice, where every grain is separate, forms the base for some of the choicest meals. The best rice nutritionally is that from which the thin red skin—like that on the peanut—has not been removed. The red skin contains 17 I.U. (International units) of vitamin A, 15 I.U. of B_1 and 1.00% mineral matter; whereas polished (white) rice contains no vitamin A or B_1, and only 0.35% mineral matter.

Red rice is the staple food of the very poor, who, if they can afford it, add to rice a handful of lentils or a few vegetables. Those who can afford it eat pure (?) white rice, just as white bread, denuded of vitamins and minerals, is eaten by most people in Britain.

MORE RICE DISHES

TURKISH SHELLFISH PILAU

INGREDIENTS

½ breakfast cup olive oil

2 breakfast cups rice

1 cup shelled mussels or 1 cup scallops

a sprinkle of pepper

10 medium-sized onions

3 breakfast cups water

2 cups shelled oysters

3 teaspoons mixed herbs

salt—to taste

METHOD

Slice the onions finely and fry them to a golden colour in the oil. Put in the water and rice and bring them to the boil; then add the fish and green herbs and sprinkle liberally with pepper. Add salt, simmer gently till all water has evaporated, turn out into a flat dish and place in an oven preheated at 200 degrees F. Leave for ten minutes; then serve.

Enough for four

PORK PILAU

INGREDIENTS

1 breakfast cup of rice

6 bananas

1 inch of cinnamon (ground)

4 bay leaves

12 cloves (ground)

6 oz. butter

4 large onions, finely chopped

1½ lb. lean, boned pork

½ lb. brown sugar (pieces)

½ pint lemon juice *or* ½ pint apple cider vinegar

a generous pinch of basil

a generous pinch of origano (wild marjoram)

METHOD

Cut the pork into inch-pieces and brown in a smear of butter, together with onion and a squeeze of lemon juice. (Lime may be used if you wish.) When the pork is well browned, cover with water and boil till tender. Take the pan off the stove. Mix the sugar and lemon juice (or vinegar) in a small pan and cook till the mixture is thick, like syrup, and put aside the pan.

Place the rice, butter and bay leaves in a pan, add water till the level is an inch above the rice, and bring to the boil; then simmer. When the rice is ready (test by feeling individual grains), make a hollow in the mass, place the pork and chopped onions inside it, cover with rice and simmer for five minutes. Then turn into a large flat dish and place in a pre-heated oven (about 200°F.)

Now peel the bananas, split and cut them into pieces, roll them in flour, sprinkle with powdered cinnamon and cloves, pop them into the syrup and simmer for half an hour. Place them on top of the rice and pork, garnish with basil and origano and serve hot.

Enough for four

RICE SURPRISE

INGREDIENTS

1 breakfast cup of rice	6 chipolata sausages
½ cup fried bacon	½ cup Lancashire cheese
3 onions, finely sliced	¼ cup Parmesan cheese *or* ½ cup Leicester cheese
1 lb. of chicken pieces	2 tablespoons butter
½ lb. carrots	a pinch of tarragon
½ lb. peeled chestnuts	a pinch of coriander
4 cloves garlic	1 teaspoon jeera
a sprinkle of paprika	salt

METHOD

Grill the chicken pieces till they are tender enough to eat. Prick the sausages with a fork and grill them, too. Cut the carrots into cubes and cook carrots and onions in just enough water to soften them. Put aside. Cook chestnuts, jeera and coriander in water and a little salt, and put aside.

Place rice, garlic, butter and tarragon in a pan, add any water left from cooking carrots and onions, or chestnuts, jeera, etc.; bring to the boil and then simmer till done.

Turn the rice into a large dish. Make a hollow in the middle, put the chicken pieces in, cover with rice, arrange sausages and bacon on top, then chestnuts, and heat for a minute or two. The rice should be dry, tender and steaming. Garnish with onions and carrots and sprinkle with the two kinds of cheese, which will add colour and flavour.

Alternatively, the cheese can be added to the carrots and onions, cooked for a few minutes and poured over the rice. If this is done, sprinkle with paprika.

Enough for four

DUCK PILAU

INGREDIENTS

1 duck	juice of 2 oranges
1 breakfast cup of rice	the juice of 2 lemons or limes
½ cup raisins or sultanas	one inch cinnamon, crushed
6 cloves garlic	salt to taste
¼ teaspoon saffron *or* ¼ teaspoon turmeric	¼ lb. blanched almonds
12 cloves	¼ cup Barbadoes sugar
½ lb. carrots, grated	2 dessertspoons butter
1 pint milk	1 dessertspoon ground coriander seeds from 12 cardamoms

4 five-oz. cartons of yogurt

20 peppercorns

4 large onions, finely sliced

a pinch of aniseed—optional

METHOD

Wash the duck thoroughly in salt water, then swill with fresh and prick all over with a fork. Work coriander, garlic, aniseed and a little salt into a paste an hour before operations begin. Melt a little butter, brown the onion in it, add carrot, raisins, sugar and orange juice, and when thoroughly amalgamated, add this to the paste already made, and stuff the duck with the mixture. Now mash the almonds into a pulp, add milk, lemon juice and half of the butter and cook slowly into a thick sauce.

Place the duck in a tin in a medium-hot oven and baste with this sauce. When the duck is brown, place it in a deep casserole. Sprinkle the rice around it. Smear the duck with the remainder of the butter, strew it with cloves, cinnamon and cardamom seeds, put in enough water to cook the rice, and yogurt, saffron, peppercorns. Put on the cover of the casserole and cook for 5 minutes over high heat; then lower to just-simmering point and cook till rice is done. The water should have evaporated.

Enough for four

FISH KOFTA WITH RICE

INGREDIENTS

1 breakfast cup of rice

1 lb. filleted cod or haddock

3 egg yolks

1 tablespoon lemon or lime juice

6 oz. butter or ghee

1 wineglass of apple-cider vinegar,

    white wine or cooking sherry

1 teaspoon black pepper

$\frac{1}{2}$ cup mustard oil

$\frac{1}{2}$ teaspoon nutmeg

1 large onion, finely sliced

$\frac{1}{2}$ teaspoon ground cloves

$\frac{1}{4}$ cup wholemeal flour

$\frac{1}{2}$ cup chopped parsley

METHOD

Flake raw fish, mix with onion and fry in oil till golden brown. Do not put the fish in till the oil is well heated and a wisp of smoke rises from it. Fry till the fish is soft and a golden colour. Drain away oil and when the fish has cooled, mix it with egg yolk, nutmeg and parsley and mould it into balls with the help of flour.

Now melt the butter and at sizzling point sprinkle in the clove powder and fry for *10 seconds*. Add rice and stir over a medium heat for 7 minutes. Pour in cider or wine; cook for a minute longer, then add pepper, fish balls and lemon juice.

Pour in water slowly so that the rice is covered by at least an inch of water, bring to the boil, put on a tight-fitting lid and lower heat to simmering point. The rice should be tender by the time the water has evaporated; if not, add a little more. It is better to have too little than too much water, for water can always be added, and at simmering heat little damage can be done.

Apple cider vinegar imparts a tang that sherry or white wine does not—and is much cheaper. Try all three at different times.

Enough for four

PRAWN PILAU

INGREDIENTS

1 lb. shelled prawns	seeds from ½ doz. cardamoms
one inch of cinnamon	3 cloves of garlic
5 oz. bottle of cream	1 tablespoon lemon or lime juice
1 dessertspoon coriander powder	4 oz. butter
½ teaspoon black pepper	1 teaspoon turmeric
1 dessertspoon chopped mint	1 pint vegetable stock
2 breakfast cups rice	salt to taste
2 bay leaves	2 five-oz. cartons of yogurt

METHOD

Boil the stock, add salt, pour over the prawns and cook till tender. Only very little cooking is needed. Then drain, but keep the stock. Put the prawns in a casserole or shallow pan, pour the butter, well heated, over them, and cook for five minutes. Add bay leaves, yogurt, coriander, garlic crushed, and stock; bring to the boil and remove from the stove. Cover with cream.

Cook the rice in a generous quantity of boiling water for not more than 10 minutes and drain away water. Place in a large pan, add the prawns, etc., and mix gently. Now sprinkle in cardamom seeds, cinnamon (crushed), pepper, mint and turmeric and mix with a fork.

Put the mixture back into the casserole, put on the cover and cook in an oven pre-heated to about 200°F. for 20 minutes. Test rice for softness and if done, remove and sprinkle with lemon juice and serve. If not done, cook till soft. If moisture is needed, add more stock or water.

It is always best to test the rice because cookers, voltages and gas pressures vary in different parts of the country, and at different times of the day.

Enough for four

EGG PILAU

INGREDIENTS

8 hard-boiled eggs	2 teaspoons cummin seed
2 cups Patna rice	1 tablespoon fennel seed
2 onions, finely sliced	9 cloves
2 tablespoons butter	6 cardamoms, shelled
1½-inch stick green ginger, mashed	1 inch cinnamon
6 cloves garlic, ground	2 teaspoons ground turmeric
2 green chillis, mashed	parsley

METHOD

Fry onions till golden-brown in a fairly large saucepan, then put in two cups of water, the cloves, cardamom and cinnamon, mix, put on the lid and simmer for 10 minutes. Use a pan with a close-fitting lid. Add ginger, garlic, green chillis, cummin and fennel seed, mix, and place the rice on top. Add two cups of water, cover and simmer. Make a paste of the turmeric and a little boiling water, thin it down till liquid, and add to the contents of the pan. Cut the eggs into halves and place gently on the cooking rice.

Continue to simmer till the rice is soft, which should coincide with the evaporation of all the water, because any volume of rice, if simmered in a tightly closed pan with twice its volume of water, should be done by the time the water evaporates. In practice owing to many factors, this does not always work out, so it is best to test the rice from time to time.

Turn all carefully into a large open dish, garnish with parsley, and eat with poppadams (or pappadams), chutney or pickle, and if you like them, Bombay duck, either whole or crumbled.

Enough for four very generous helpings

RICE KOFTAS

INGREDIENTS

1 cup Patna rice	2 eggs
2½ cups milk	4 cloves garlic
2 oz. butter	1 tablespoon chopped parsley
½ teaspoon chilli powder	1 cup grated cheese
2 onions, minced	½ teaspoon ground cummin
4 tablespoons canned tomato or tomato sauce	½ teaspoon ground turmeric
breadcrumbs	salt
oil or fat, for frying	

METHOD

Cook the rice in milk, till milk has evaporated, when rice should be tender. (More milk is needed than if water alone were used, as milk contains fat and protein solids.) If rice is not tender, add more milk. When tender, remove from stove. Mix with butter, salt, chilli powder, cummin and turmeric. Chop parsley finely, and together with onion, garlic, cheese and tomato, add to the rice mixture. Mix thoroughly. Shape into balls, roll in beaten egg and then in breadcrumbs, and fry till golden brown in deep, boiling fat. Remove and drain. Enough for 2, if served alone. But rice koftas go well with grilled or baked herrings, in which case they will make a meal for 4.

Try tomato sauce the first time, and canned tomato the next, to find out which you prefer. Only half a teaspoon of chilli powder is given, but if you like it hotter, add to this quantity next time. It is better to be conservative at first.

Enough for two or four

KHICHIRI AND SAUCE

There are so many kinds of khichiri, and the ways in which they are made differ so vastly, that one often hears people say, 'Oh, but *that's* not khichiri!' It may not be one of the many kinds that they have tasted.

INGREDIENTS

½ lb. Patna rice	½ teaspoon cummin seed
¼ lb. lentils	½ teaspoon turmeric
salt	¼ lb. butter, dripping or other cooking fat or oil
1 large onion	1 pint water or stock

METHOD

Slice onion finely and fry till brown, then pour off half the fat into a small dish. Add turmeric and cummin seeds to the browned onions and fry for a couple of minutes. Turn the fried ingredients into a large pan, add rice and lentils, the remainder of fat, and mix well. Pour in the stock and salt. Put on close-fitting lid and simmer very gently till the rice is done. If there is still some water, pour it away. If the water has evaporated, and the rice still remains uncooked, add a little *boiling* water.

If the instructions are carried out, the rice should be just cooked to a turn when the last drops of water evaporate.

The khichiri part is easy to make; now for the sauce.

Ingredients for Khichiri Sauce

INGREDIENTS

2 cups of water or vegetable stock	a generous pinch of black pepper
1 pint fresh prawns or 1 lb. of any other fish	2 eggs
1 large onion	6 cloves garlic
4 oz. butter, dripping or margarine	a generous handful of parsley
½ lb. tomatoes	salt
4 tablespoons wine vinegar, or apple cider vinegar	

METHOD

Fry onions till golden brown, finely slice tomatoes and add, with parsley, garlic, pepper and salt. Fry till nearly dry. Pour on two cups of water or stock, bring to boil.

Clean prawns or fish (if fish, cut into pieces); put them in a saucepan, pour over the fried mixture and boil gently till soft.

Beat the eggs well, mix with vinegar and pour over prawns or fish just before serving.

The khichiri and the sauce must be served in separate dishes, and both should be piping hot.

Pappadams and sweet mango chutney go well with this dish; or a *saag* made with pounded green herbs, such as mint, to which a little sugar, vinegar etc., have been added.

If the sauce is too greasy, use less butter. Indians in the cities usually eat far more ghee or butter than Europeans, who sometimes find curries indigestible—and for no other reason.

Enough for four

MORE AND DIFFERENT CURRIES

CRAB KOFTAS

Koftas, of fish or meat minced or chopped very finely, mixed with seasoning and moulded into balls, are invariably tastier than fish or meat not so treated. And of all kofta curries, crab, lobster and prawn are the most delectable.

INGREDIENTS

1 lb. crab, lobster or prawn *meat*	4 red or 2 green chillis
1 dessertspoon chopped parsley	12 peppercorns
1 teaspoon chopped mint	1 breakfast cup tomato juice
1 teaspoon chopped tarragon	1 breakfast cup breadcrumbs
4 blades lemon grass	1 large egg, well beaten
6 bay leaves	1 teaspoon ground cummin
2 large onions, finely sliced	4 cloves garlic, chopped
1 dessertspoon coriander seeds	a pinch of ginger
8 oz. mustard oil or ghee	

METHOD

Half-cook the meat and break it up; if need be, pound it. Chop parsley, mint, tarragon and garlic finely and mix with the meat. Then add ginger, peppercorns and coriander seeds and again mix. Wet it with tomato juice (or water) and mould it into balls about $1\frac{1}{2}$ inches in diameter, dip in egg and roll in breadcrumbs. If the white of egg is first beaten stiff and yolk then added, the crumb will hold better.

Heat the mustard oil or ghee, add chopped chillis, cummin and onions and fry till the onions are light brown. Put in the lemon grass and bay leaves, gently roll in the meat balls and simmer till done (about 10–15 minutes).

Remove lemon grass and bay leaves before serving. Crab Koftas are best eaten with plain rice and lemon, lime or bamboo pickle.

Vegetarian koftas, which are also tasty, can be made by using all these ingredients, but substituting Granose Nut Meat, or Vegarian Savoury Meal for crab.

Enough for four

FISH KABAB

Kababs are traditional Muslim dishes and consist usually of beef, whole or minced, mutton, chicken, etc., and not fish. Fish Kabab is eaten, however, in Bengal, where fish and not flesh is the staple food of a riparian population.

INGREDIENTS

pan of deep fat or mustard oil	1 tablespoon chopped parsley
1 lb. cod or haddock	12 peppercorns
2 large onions, minced	$\frac{1}{2}$ teaspoon powdered cloves
2–3 onions, sliced	$\frac{1}{2}$ teaspoon chilli powder
1 teaspoon butter	2 eggs
2 inches green ginger	salt to taste
1 teaspoon cummin seed	1 dessertspoon chopped marjoram

METHOD

Boil fish till tender and set aside to cool. Heat a teaspoon of butter, toss in the onion and fry until golden. Chop parsley and marjoram very finely, and mix with ginger, cummin seed, peppercorns, cloves and chilli powder. Beat eggs well. Flake fish and mix with beaten egg, salt, spices and herbs. Form into two-inch balls.

Heat the fat till a wisp of smoke rises from the surface, then gently pop in the fish balls and cook till they are light brown. Remove, place on skewers with rounds of sliced onion between balls, and serve.

The fish balls may be rolled in breadcrumbs before cooking, but this is optional. Rolling in crumb gives a firm outside skin.

Enough for four

STUFFED BRINJAL WITH BOMBAY DUCK

INGREDIENTS

8 pieces of Bombay duck (a species of dried Indian fish)	lemon juice
4 medium-size brinjals (aubergines)	4 dessertspoons ground coriander
8 tablespoons fresh grated coconut,	2 teaspoons ground turmeric
or desiccated coconut	1 teaspoon ground cummin
4 large onions	1 teaspoon ground red chillis
8 cloves garlic	8 tablespoons mustard oil or ghee for frying. Oil is best

METHOD

Slice onions finely and fry, together with the garlic, till the onions are golden brown. Add coriander, cummin, turmeric and red chillis and cook briskly for 5 minutes.

Boil brinjals till soft; then hollow them out and cut off the tops. Mix the curry ingredients with the brinjal pulp and simmer for three minutes. Add grated coconut, mix well and stuff the pulp back into the hollowed brinjals. It should fit, as cooking evaporates a good deal of the moisture. Replace the tops and bake in moderate oven for 15 minutes (no fat is required—bake dry).

Serve with lemon juice. Each brinjal should be served on a small mound of boiled rice, or with two chappattis, and two sticks of fried, crumbled Bombay duck. Bombay duck can be bought in packets and cooked under a grill, or fried with a little fat.

Those unaccustomed to it may find the odour of Bombay duck a trifle overpowering, but if this initial distaste can be overcome, they may even acquire a passion for it.

Enough for four

CAMP FISH

The call of the outdoors is strong in Britain, even if the sun is not, and picnicking has a much stronger appeal to most of us than meals eaten sedately in the orthodox way. To fishermen there is no reward so great as a fresh trout, salmon—or even a coarse fish—whisked from a stream and cooked on a camp fire. What one needs is:

INGREDIENTS

1 fish 9 inches or more in length	1½ teaspoons coriander
garlic—6 cloves	½ teaspoon cummin
1 large onion	a handful of parsley
1 or two large tomatoes	a sheet of tinfoil or a ball of string
1 teaspoon turmeric	salt

METHOD

Open and clean the fish, using plenty of salt water. Chop onion, garlic, tomatoes and half the parsley and stuff inside the fish. Then close and lightly tie it. Rub fish all over (inside, too, if you wish, before stuffing) with paste made from coriander, cummin and turmeric.

Dig two holes, one on either side of the camp fire, and erect two stout stakes. Wait till the fire has died down and there are no flames. Then tie the fish, by head and tail, to the stakes, some distance above the still glowing embers; the distance above the fire to be regulated by the size of the fish. This will be gained by trial and error but in any case the fish will *ultimately* cook. Garnish with parsley.

An alternative method is to wrap the fish in tinfoil—double foil, if need be—and place it in the heart of the embers, under the dying fire. Continue fishing, and in an hour or so the fish will be ready—cooked in its own juices. All you then need is some bread with it.

DRY SHARK CURRY

INGREDIENTS

1 lb. shark or cod	enough coconut oil for cooking
2 tablespoons chilli powder	3 cloves garlic
1 teaspoon saffron or turmeric	3 slices green ginger
1½ tablespoons mustard	3 green chillis
2 or 3 curry leaves	1 inch piece rampe
1 tablespoon vinegar	1 inch piece sera
2 large onions, sliced	

METHOD

If new to curries, or if you've never tried this curry before, it would be advisable to start with 2 *teaspoons* of chilli powder and 1½ *teaspoons* of mustard, instead of *tablespoons*. You can always increase the quantities next time; and if you dislike cooking in coconut oil, as so many do, then use mustard oil, ghee or butter.

Wash and cut fish into slices, place in pan, cover with vinegar and a little water, and boil. When tender, remove fish. Mash ginger and garlic and mix with the chilli powder, turmeric (or saffron) and mustard, using a little water to form a paste. Smear this paste over the fish.

Heat a dessertspoon of oil or fat, fry the onions till golden brown, put in the rampe, sera and curry leaves, then fish and green chillis. Simmer the fish on one side, then turn and simmer again, altogether for 10 minutes. A little brown sugar may be sprinkled over the curry after it is taken from the stove. There is very little gravy in this curry; only if it tends to stick should you add a little water. Eat with rice and sweet mango chutney.

Enough for two

MRS VYVETTE LOOS
KINGSTON
NEGOMBO
CEYLON

CURRIED KIDNEYS

INGREDIENTS

2 oz. butter or margarine	salt to taste
8 kidneys	1 teaspoon chilli powder
4 large tomatoes or 1 can tomato pulp	1½ teaspoons coriander
4 onions, finely sliced	1 teaspoon turmeric
1 can of garden peas	½ teaspoon cummin
the juice of one lemon	¼ teaspoon ginger

METHOD

It is preferable to use one large can of tomato pulp for this dish instead of tomatoes, as tomato pulp is made from really sun-ripened tomatoes from Italy, Rumania or some country where tomatoes really do ripen in the sun.

Put the chilli, coriander, cummin, turmeric and ginger into a small bowl, add a little water and mix into a paste. Then add boiling water; keep mixing till the amount of water is about one breakfast cupful. Add the salt.

Slice the kidneys, which should already have been washed and cleaned.

Fry the onions in fat, till golden brown, add the curry spices; bring to the boil, put in the slices of kidney and turn each one.

Cover with the tomato pulp and continue cooking till the kidneys are soft. When that stage is reached, most of the tomato juice should have evaporated, leaving a thick gravy.

Put in the can of peas, shake till they are covered, cook for a minute and turn out into a dish.

Sprinkle with lemon juice and if you wish, garnish with parsley. Best eaten with chappattis or parrattas and sweet mango chutney.

Enough for four

DUCK RAICHATH

INGREDIENTS

1 fat duck	1 tablespoon Barbados sugar
2 tablespoons chopped onions	1 coconut
1 tablespoon chopped ginger	1 tablespoon ground coriander
1 tablespoon green chillis	2 tablespoons vinegar
1 dessertspoon chopped garlic	salt

METHOD

Wash, clean and cut duck into pieces. Grate coconut as finely as possible—if you can't buy a coconut, use desiccated coconut—and extract two lots of milk from it—a cupful each time.

Put pieces of duck into deep pan with the second extract of milk and a little water, and boil till tender. The water will evaporate and the fat from the duck will rise to the top. Pour this fat off, and fry the pieces of duck in it. If the duck is a good fat one, there will still be some fat in the frying pan or deep pan, whichever you use.

Remove the pieces of duck to a plate, and keep warm. Now add onions, ginger, chillis, garlic and coriander to the fat and fry them well for five minutes. Put in fried pieces of duck, sugar, vinegar and salt, cook for a further five minutes, or until the pieces are tender enough to be eaten, add the first extract of coconut milk, bring to the boil and remove from the stove.

Duck made in this way is extremely tasty without being too rich. If too pungent, use half the quantity of chillis. Serve with plain boiled rice, a lentil dish, and yogurt.

A satisfying meal for four

CURRIED TRIPE

Tripe, that is, the first and second stomach of a ruminant, is not a traditional Indian dish, and most Indians, especially Hindus, will not touch offal. Here one suspects the hand of the Anglo-Indian, who makes the best of both worlds.

INGREDIENTS

$\frac{1}{2}$ oz. of ghee, butter or mustard oil	1 lb. tripe
1 large onion, finely sliced	3 red chillis, seeded
1 oz. powdered coriander	6 peppercorns
1 teaspoon ground turmeric	4 large cloves garlic
1 teaspoon mustard (powder)	1 inch green ginger
a generous pinch of black pepper	1 lime or lemon or tamarind
$\frac{1}{2}$ pint coconut milk *or* $\frac{1}{4}$ lb. desiccated coconut	

METHOD

Cover the tripe with water, bring it to the boil and simmer till soft. Then drain off, but keep the liquor. Cut the tripe into $1\frac{1}{2}$ inch pieces. Heat butter or oil, add onion and fry till light

169

brown, then toss in ginger, mustard, turmeric and garlic, and brown. Now add the spices: coriander, black pepper, chillis and peppercorns. Simmer for a minute, put in the tripe, mix well and cover with the tripe water into which the desiccated coconut has been mixed. Stir gently and continue to simmer for five minutes. If coconut milk is used, do not keep the liquor from the tripe, but add coconut milk to the condiments.

Serve hot, with lime or lemon juice; or alternatively, with tamarind pulp mixed with a little water, and poured over the tripe. Tripe curry should be eaten with rice.

Enough for four

BRAIN CURRY

The ancient belief that eating certain organs will give you some of the qualities those organs possess no longer holds good but even so, brain curry is a favourite with many.

INGREDIENTS

3 whole sheep's brains	$\frac{1}{2}$–1 teaspoon chilli powder
2 large onions, sliced	the juice of one lemon
1 large tomato, sliced	1 teaspoon turmeric
1 dessertspoon cummin seed	1 small sprig rosemary
1 dessertspoon coriander seed	a handful of parsley
10 oz. yogurt	4 oz. mustard oil or ghee
salt to taste	

METHOD

After cleaning and washing the brains in salt water, plunge them into boiling water, remove and place them in a dish for half an hour, then cover with cold water to which the lemon juice and rosemary have been added. Heat the water, and when it boils, remove the brains. Heat the fat or oil, add first the onion and then the tomato, and fry till the onion is brown. Put in the cummin, coriander, chilli, turmeric, salt, and cook for five minutes, then add yogurt and cook for another ten till the mixture thickens. Then add the brains, and if need be, a little water, and simmer for 5–10 minutes.

The addition of rosemary to the water gives an unusual tang which some find very pleasant. Before serving, sprinkle with chopped parsley.

Brain curry can be eaten with rice, chappattis or parrattas, or on thick rounds of whole-meal bread, toasted.

Enough for four

MORE VEGETABLE AND FRUIT CURRIES

STUFFED BRINJALS

Brinjals or aubergines, the fruit of the Egg-plant *Solanum Esculentum,* may be prepared in many ways, some already described in the three previous curry books, but there are few tastier than stuffed brinjals.

INGREDIENTS

4 large brinjals	8 cloves
4 green chillis, chopped	seeds from 8 cardamoms
3 teacups of mixed vegetables—(carrots, potatoes, celery)	salt to taste
	2 oz. butter or ghee or mustard oil
4 large cloves of garlic	$\frac{1}{2}$ teaspoon powdered ginger
1 tablespoon coriander powder	1 large chopped onion
2 teaspoons powdered cummin	

METHOD

Dice and cook mixed vegetables until soft but firm. Cut the brinjals into halves, scoop out and simmer the middles in boiling water until soft. Fry onion in butter until golden, add chillis, garlic (mashed), coriander, cummin, cardamoms, cloves and ginger, and fry until brown. Mix the cooked spices, vegetables and scooped-out brinjal middles, add salt. Stuff brinjals with mixture.

If you have a steamer, place brinjals in it and steam until tender. If not, place in a casserole with a little butter and cook till tender. Serve with rice and some kind of acid pickle like lime or tamarind. Try both methods and see which you prefer.

Enough for four

KHATTA CURRY

Khatta (khut/ta) is the Hindi word for acid, and khatta curry has a piquancy which may not, perhaps, appeal to all at first, but like ripe Roquefort cheese, grows on one.

INGREDIENTS

¼ lb. carrots	1 tablespoon ground onion
¼ lb. potatoes	1 teaspoon turmeric
¼ lb. artichokes	½ teaspoon chilli powder
½ lb. pumpkins	4 cloves garlic, ground
1 lb. tomatoes, or a 1-lb. can of tomatoes	1½ teaspoons coriander
¼ lb. swedes	1 oz. tamarind
¼ lb. turnips	1 tablespoon *foot* sugar
1 teaspoon onion *seed*	4 green chillis
2 or 3 oz. mustard oil	

METHOD

This dish is made in two stages.

1. Mix tamarind into a paste with a little water; then keep adding and mixing till a pint has been put in. Sweeten with the foot sugar and mix thoroughly. In India *jaggery* is used, but as this is not easily bought, foot sugar (black Barbados sugar) is the best substitute. Ask any big grocer for foot sugar and he will know what you mean. Strain the liquid into a jug.

2. Chop hard vegetables into inch or 1½ inch cubes and add tomatoes or canned tomato, just cover with water; toss in the ground onion, turmeric, chilli powder, garlic and coriander, bring to the boil, then simmer till half cooked.

Bring the mustard oil to such a heat that it gives off a wisp of smoke, then pop in the onion seed and fry for two or three minutes. Use a deep saucepan. Now pour in the tamarind water, add the half-cooked vegetables and bring to the boil. As soon as boiling point is reached, turn down the heat and simmer till the vegetables are cooked. Can be eaten cold or hot, with plain rice. No pickle or chutney is needed. Garnish with chopped green chillis.

Enough for four

PUMPKIN CURRY

INGREDIENTS

1½ lb. pumpkin	2 green chillis
6 cloves garlic	1 large onion
1 inch of turmeric	½ coconut
2 red chillis	1 inch green ginger
ghee or mustard oil for frying or butter or margarine	salt to taste

METHOD

Cut pumpkin into inch or 1½-inch cubes. Grate coconut finely and mix well with one breakfast cup of cold water. Mash garlic, ginger and turmeric. Cut the red chillis into very fine pieces and add to this mash; then mix into the coconut water. Put the lot into a pan with the pumpkin and green chillis, which should be sliced lengthways, bring to the boil, then simmer till the pumpkin is tender.

Now fry the onion, which should also be sliced, and when brown, pour into pan. Stir, simmer for five minutes, season with salt and serve with plain white rice and crushed Bombay duck and pappadams; or alternatively, with lime pickle.

This is a very easily concocted dish. There is a tendency, however, to cook the pumpkin till it is too soft. If you do this, it becomes mushy and degenerates into a thick broth.

Enough for four

BEAN FOOGATH

INGREDIENTS

1 lb. French beans	8 small onions
1 large coconut	1-inch piece green ginger
8 cloves garlic	2 tablespoons butter or ghee
4 green chillis	1 teaspoon powdered turmeric
salt	

METHOD

Wash beans, strip the edges, slit and mince very finely. Place in a saucepan, with a small cupful of water, a shake of salt, 2 minced onions and the garlic. Boil till soft, simmer until all the water evaporates and remove from stove. Scrape coconut, mince remaining onions and chillis. In another saucepan, brown the onions in butter or ghee; then add the ginger, turmeric and chillis, finally the beans. Stir for three minutes and then remove. Now add the coconut, place on the stove again, stir for a minute or two and the foogath is ready. Eat with plain rice, or rice and lentils. Desiccated coconut may be used instead of a coconut: about 8–12 ounces.

Instead of beans, spinach or cabbage may be used. If so, substitute a teaspoon of black pepper for chillis. The use of turmeric is optional.

Enough for two

MIXED VEGETABLE CURRY

The mixed vegetable curry one gets in the average Indian restaurant—even in the West End of London—is a travesty of the real thing: a potato or two, a carrot, a bean and a lady's finger (*okra*) swimming in a tepid greeny-brown ooze. Try this:

INGREDIENTS

4 small aubergines	4 cloves garlic
4 potatoes	½ lb. carrots
4 large onions	1 can tomatoes (1 lb.)
½ lb. beans or green peas	6 red chillis
2 teaspoons coriander	1 teaspoon ground cummin
seeds of 3 cardamoms	1 inch turmeric
the flesh of one coconut	½ inch ginger
a small handful of coriander leaves	1 inch cinnamon
1 tablespoon butter or ghee	1 teaspoon asafoetida
1 dessertspoon cooking oil	

METHOD

Halve, then soak, the brinjals with the potatoes and carrots in cold water. Mash the turmeric and ginger; break up cinnamon finely, and mix into a paste with the coriander, cardamoms, cummin, garlic and chillis, and fry spices with two sliced onions in a tablespoon of butter or ghee. Scrape the coconut and add. If you can't get a coconut, use $\frac{1}{2}$ lb. desiccated coconut.

Put the cooking oil into a deep pan, bring to the boil and toss in the asafoetida. Now add the coconut mixed with curry spices, and the coriander leaves. Add $\frac{1}{2}$ pint of water, bring to the boil, put in the brinjals, carrots, potatoes, tomato and peas (or beans), and two halved onions. Bring to the boil again, close with a well-fitting lid, and simmer till the carrots, beans etc. are soft. Most of the liquid should evaporate, leaving a thick, rich gravy.

Eat with plain rice and acid pickle.

Enough for four

SIMPLE SPINACH CURRY

Spinach is not a vegetable that many try to curry, but if well curried, it makes an excellent supper dish. Incidentally, the top young leaves of ordinary stinging nettle—*urtica dioica*—can be treated in the same way, and taste like spinach, though a trifle stronger.

INGREDIENTS

3 lb. spinach or young nettle leaves	6 green chillis, sliced lengthways
6 cloves garlic, sliced lengthways	a little—6–12 spikes—rosemary
a sprig of fennel	1 tablespoon butter, mustard oil or olive oil
2 large onions, sliced, or 4 tablespoons	1 teaspoon cummin powder
minced spring onions or	1 teaspoon coriander powder
an equal quantity of shallots	salt

METHOD

Wash the spinach well. This is important as spinach is likely to gather grit. Take it out of the water and drop into a large, deep pan. Boil briskly without the addition of water, for about 8–10 minutes, by which time all the water clinging to the spinach will have evaporated and it will be cooked. Strain and squeeze dry. Cut the pulp into pieces. Fry the onions golden in oil or butter. The type of fat used will affect the flavour. Add garlic, chillis, cummin and coriander and fry for 3 minutes. Add this to the pan of spinach, together with fennel, rosemary and salt, cook for three minutes, then serve on toast or with chappattis and a little lime pickle.

The few drips of water squeezed from the spinach can be added during the final stages, and the spinach cooked till this becomes a thick gravy.

Enough for four

DHALL BHATH

This is a typical Bengali (or Bengalee) dish; simple, easily made, and satisfying. It is also tasty if well made.

INGREDIENTS

1 cup rice	4 cloves garlic
1 cup lentils	1 large sliced onion
3 green chillis	1-inch stick of green ginger
salt	1 teaspoon turmeric
1 dessertspoon ghee or butter or mustard oil	

METHOD

Boil the rice till soft, drain, and keep warm. Toss the lentils and salt into 1 pint of *boiling* water so that they break up quickly, and cook till fairly thick.

Brown the onion in fat, put in the chillis, garlic, ginger and turmeric, fry for 5 minutes, then mix with lentils and serve with rice, and pickle or chutney.

Enough for two

FRUIT CURRY

INGREDIENTS

2 large onions	1 teaspoon milk
1 small papaiya	$\frac{1}{2}$ teaspoon ginger
1 slice pineapple	1 teaspoon currants
1 dessertspoon scraped coconut	2 bananas
1 tablespoon coconut cream	$\frac{1}{2}$ lime or lemon
1 dessertspoon curry powder	1 teaspoon sultanas
1 cooking apple	pepper or chilli powder
1 dessertspoon butter	salt

METHOD

Slice the onions finely and brown them in butter. Add curry powder, a teaspoon of milk, and cook briskly for five minutes. Cut the pineapple, papaiya, bananas and cooking apple into pieces, squeeze the lime or lemon over them, put in pan together with the onions and curry and cook for 10 minutes. Now turn the ingredients from the frying-pan into a deep pan, add coconut cream, scraped coconut, ginger, currants, sultanas, pepper or chilli powder, salt, and simmer very gently for an hour and serve with boiled rice.

The papaiya is not common in England as yet, though it may be had from some of the bigger stores, such as Harrods, Fortnums, and Selfridges, when in season. The papaiya sold in Britain comes from the West Indies, where it is called a 'paw-paw'. The flesh is peachlike, and the middle filled with hundreds of small black seeds, like buckshot. These are easily scraped away with a spoon, and the green outside skin has to be discarded as well. It peels easily.

Serve with a border of boiled rice and pappadams.

Enough for four

BREADFRUIT CURRY (Yam Curry)

It is possible at certain times of the year to get breadfruit, a product of the South Seas, which is farinaceous and has a whitish pulp the consistency of new bread, at some of the

175

stores which sell exotic foods; and within the next decade, breadfruit should be as common as aubergines.

INGREDIENTS

1 medium-size breadfruit	oil for frying
2 cups thick milk (coconut milk)	1 small onion, sliced
1 cup thin coconut milk	3 green chillis, sliced
2 cloves garlic	2 slices green ginger
1 tablespoon Bombay duck	1 sprig curry leaves
½ teaspoon saffron or turmeric	salt
the juice of one lime or lemon	

METHOD

Clean and cut the breadfruit into round slices; then halve each slice and wash well. Put into a pan with a little oil and fry till golden. Add saffron (or turmeric) and lime (or lemon) juice and salt. Now add sliced onion, ginger, garlic, green chillis, powdered Bombay duck, curry leaves and the thin milk. Simmer. When the breadfruit is well cooked, add the 2 cups of thick coconut milk, stir well and remove from the stove.

This makes an excellent accompaniment to a beef curry. The thick coconut milk must be left till the dish is almost ready because coconut milk loses flavour if cooked too much.

Enough for four

MRS VYVETTE LOOS

PAPEETA CURRY

The *papeeta* (papaiya or paw-paw) already mentioned is a delicious fruit. In India it performs the same function as grapefruit in English homes and usually appears at breakfast. Lunches and dinners are often finished with *papeeta*, which has digestive properties. Here we eat melon. For those who are interested in such matters, *papeeta* contains 76% water (as much as the average potato), 5·2% protein, 0·9% fat, 16·8% carbohydrates, and 0·5% mineral matter. But, what no figures will convey, is its distinctive fragrant odour. Few Europeans realize that it can be concocted into curry; even fewer have tasted it in this guise. This is how it is made, and when, with the advance of quick-freezing, papaiyas flood our markets, you can try your hand. It won't be long.

INGREDIENTS

1½ breakfast cups of papaiya cut into small cubes	4 small onions, sliced
3 rounded tablespoons grated or desiccated coconut	6 curry leaves
1 inch of turmeric	1 tablespoon of butter or cooking oil
2 or 3 green chillis (start with two)	(butter much preferred)
½ teaspoon cummin powder	salt optional (in my opinion unnecessary)

METHOD

Put the papaiya pieces in a saucepan with 3 curry leaves and bring to the boil; then remove. Add salt, if you wish.

Mash turmeric, chillis and cummin, make into a paste with a little water, mix with grated coconut, add enough water to make a gravy, and simmer till thick. Add butter (or oil), onions and 3 curry leaves and bring to the boil; put in the curry-spice gravy, cook for a minute, pour over the papaiya and serve. To be eaten with plain rice.

Enough for two

TOMATO CURRY

INGREDIENTS

3 large tomatoes	1 sprig curry leaves
1 teaspoon chilli powder	1 dessertspoon Maldive fish or Bombay duck
¼ dessertspoon fenugreek	1 breakfast cup coconut milk
1 dessertspoon sliced onions	one 1-inch piece cinnamon
1 dessertspoon dripping	salt
1 or 2 cloves garlic	

METHOD

Select very large tomatoes; if you can't get very large ones, double the quantity. Cut them into thick slices—some like the pips removed. Sprinkle salt and chilli powder over them. Heat dripping in a small saucepan and add the fenugreek. Fry for five minutes. Put in garlic and fry for a further five minutes. Add sliced onions, cinnamon and curry leaves and fry till brown.

Slide in tomato slices and fry for another 15 minutes, stirring gently. Now add fish and coconut milk. Mix well, but try not to crush the tomato, and let the curry simmer gently till thick.

Tomato curry hasn't enough body to comprise the main dish of any meal; it is usually an adjunct in a dinner consisting of a number of dishes; or it can be eaten as a supper dish on a cold night. It is tasty and may be eaten with any type of rice, parrattas, chappattis, or bread from a loaf.

Enough for four

MRS DOROTHY THOMPSON
PANSALATENNE ESTATE
UKUWELA
CEYLON

SOME REGIONAL VARIATIONS

CURRIES VARY tremendously, and it would be quite wrong to assume that a mutton or chicken curry of one part of India will be cooked in much the same way in every other province (or in Ceylon or Malaya). There are other differences, too, in the cuisine.

In the North-West (now Pakistan) less rice is eaten than in other parts, much of it in the form of *pilau*. This is also true of Uttar Pradesh where *chappattis* (unleavened bread) and *dhall* are staple foods. Nor is fish highly regarded, though it may accompany the main dish. Milk, lentils, wholewheat bread and goat-mutton, with vegetables, comprise the meals of the North and North-West.

In Bombay, the most cosmopolitan city in India, the cuisine has infinite variety and some swear that the best food in India is to be had there.

But the Bengali will challenge that, for where can one eat fish and prawn curries like those made in the typical Bengali home: fish curries concocted with succulent bamboo shoots and the sweet, scented milk of young coconuts? Anglo-Indians will swear that their cookery comprises all that is best of East and West; but the Goanese bear the reputation of being the best cooks of all.

Whereas the food in Bombay, the North-West and the North is cooked in *ghee* (clarified butter), many Bengali dishes are prepared in mustard oil, and food in the South in coconut oil.

As one journeys South to Madras and then along the West coast, curries are prepared in ways peculiar to the region and flavoured differently. Here the accent is on pungency rather than on piquancy, and pepper-waters and chilli-curries make the newcomer—even those accustomed to curries all their lives—gasp and perspire.

CORNED-BEEF BHURTA

Corned-beef bhurta is, of course, an Anglo-Indian concoction, for corned-beef is a British or perhaps American invention. But it was a staple food of the British Army and of civilians who existed in the *mofussil* far from the amenities of civilized life. They acquired a taste for curry but were suspicious of meat bought locally. In fact, in some parts of India it is difficult to get flesh in any form but fowl. And corned-beef bhurta is a compromise effected by the great race of improvisers.

INGREDIENTS

1 tin corned-beef

2 onions

3 green chillis

the juice of 2 lemons

1 lb. floury potatoes

1 or 2 sprigs marjoram

1 large sprig mint

a little butter—optional

METHOD

Chop the onions and chillis very finely. Pound the beef or work it with a fork till it is broken. Wash, dry and grate the lemons and add the grated peel to the beef. Squeeze the lemons. Then mix lemon juice, chillis and onions with the beef.

If the potatoes are new, don't skin, but scrub and boil them, and mash—if you wish, with a little butter and chopped mint and marjoram. Place the mashed potato in a dish and pile the corned-beef on top of it.

This is best eaten on rounds of hot buttered toast with ripe tomatoes.

Enough for four

PINEAPPLE-BEEF

Pineapple-beef is another Anglo-Indian dish, for beef is not usually eaten where pineapples flourish, and it needs imagination to combine the two. The dish, it is believed, was invented by Count Benoît La Borgne, better known as General De Boigne, who was born at Chambéry, in Savoy, and was one of the famous military adventurers of Hindustan.

INGREDIENTS

1 lb. beef from the undercut of the sirloin	black pepper or chilli powder
1 tablespoon Worcester or similar sauce	2 oz. butter
salad oil—1 tablespoon	1 *ripe* pineapple (press to ensure it is soft)
salt	6 cloves of garlic

METHOD

Cut beef into rounds the size of pineapple slices, and trim off all fat and skin. Place on a flat dish, rub well with sliced garlic, sprinkle with salt and pepper (or chilli powder) and douse first with sauce, then with oil. Stand for four hours.

Now peel the pineapple, cut it into rounds, and fry lightly in the butter. Grill the rounds of beef. Put them on a large flat dish on a hot plate and place one pineapple slice on each round of grilled beef. Serve on fried bread.

Enough for four

SAVOURY BEEF (Ceylon)

INGREDIENTS

2 lb. beef from rump or round	1 pint vegetable or meat stock or
3 large onions, sliced	boiling water or meat extract
3 tablespoons fat or oil	3 tablespoons flour
$\frac{1}{2}$ teaspoon pepper	3 tablespoons vinegar
1 tablespoon ketchup	4 cloves garlic
$\frac{1}{2}$ teaspoon powdered cummin	$\frac{1}{2}$ teaspoon powdered turmeric
6 bay leaves	salt to taste

179

METHOD

Slowly brown the onions in fat or oil, then increase the heat.

Cut the beef into cubes and rub into them salt, pepper and vinegar.

Put the seasoned meat into the fat and onions. Fry.

Add the remainder of the spices: cummin, turmeric, garlic, bay leaves.

Make a paste with the flour and some more vinegar, and thin gradually with the stock, meat extract or plain boiling water. Add this to the meat, spices, etc., bring to the boil and then simmer till the meat is soft.

Add a tablespoon of ketchup, cook for a minute more, serve hot.

While cooking this curry, almost all the liquid should evaporate, so it is necessary to stir a good deal. If need be, a little water should be added to prevent sticking, but not enough to make a gravy. It should be a dry curry.

To be eaten with rice and mango chutney or brinjal pickle, or with yogurt.

MRS VYVETTE LOOS   *Enough for six*

HOT MEAT CURRY (Ceylon)

INGREDIENTS

1 lb. beef or mutton cut into ¾-inch cubes	1 oz. cummin paste
1 oz. pickling onions, sliced	3 oz. ground pepper
2 green chillis 3 oz. billin, sliced (a small, acid fruit), or lime or lemon	
½-inch piece of ginger, sliced	¼ teaspoon saffron or turmeric
1 piece of rampe leaf	1 oz. mustard or cooking oil
¼–½ teaspoon powdered nutmeg, cloves and cardamom	1 stick of celery
a few blades of lemon grass	1 oz. coriander paste
the milk of half a coconut, or milk made from	2 cloves garlic, sliced
½ lb. of desiccated coconut and boiling water	a few curry leaves

METHOD

Place the oil in a saucepan and heat it.

Mix the onion and chillis, coriander and cummin paste, pepper, billin, saffron (or turmeric), ginger, garlic, rampe, curry leaves, lemon grass and celery, and put them into the heated oil with the meat. Just cover with water, bring to the boil, and cook for half an hour. Stir from time to time to keep the ingredients from sticking or burning.

When the meat is tender, almost all the water should have evaporated, so pour over it the coconut milk. Simmer for two or three minutes, then remove from the stove and place in a heated dish.

Hot meat curry made this way should be eaten with plain boiled rice; and over the whole concoction should be sprinkled from ½ to ¼ teaspoon of roasted and powdered nutmeg, cloves and cardamom, which give it a delightful aroma and improve the taste.

The best pickle to accompany this curry is either lime or bamboo made from young shoots. Or eat with yogurt.

Enough for four

MRS VYVETTE LOOS

SHEIKH MAHSHI

This is a dish that has come by way of Iraq to India, and can be made either with aubergines, marrows or small pumpkins.

INGREDIENTS

4 aubergines (brinjals)	butter for cooking—4 oz.
$\frac{1}{2}$ lb. cold meat from previous meal	4 cloves garlic
1 cup boiled rice	4 sprigs parsley
1 large onion	1 teaspoon cummin
1 large tomato or $\frac{1}{2}$ tin tomatoes	1 teaspoon turmeric
salt optional	2 lemons

METHOD

Remove the top and stem from each aubergine, and peel lengthways in alternate strips; that is, peel one strip and leave some skin; then peel another strip, and so on.

Remove as much of the inside of the vegetable as you can without weakening the shell. Perforate with a fork or pointed knife and soak in salt water for 15 minutes, then fry gently in butter till a golden brown.

Fry the cold meat, garlic, cummin and turmeric briskly for two minutes in 1 oz. of butter; then mix with the following ingredients finely chopped: onion, tomato, and parsley. Add the boiled rice and mix again. Stuff this mixture into the aubergines, replacing the end pieces.

Put the remainder of the butter into a large pan, heat; add the stuffed aubergines with a little water, salt if you wish, and the juice from two lemons. The lemons may be grated before being squeezed, and the grated skin added to the pulped mixture used for stuffing.

Cook till the aubergines are soft enough to eat. Don't boil briskly; simmer. Melons may be similarly treated if stuffed with a sweet mixture: raisins, sultanas, currants, dried bananas, etc.

Enough for four

MALAY CUCUMBER CURRY

Though Indian influence may be seen in some Malay curries, these usually have a more delicate flavour and generally eschew coriander and cummin, which tend to overpower the flavour and perfume of coconut milk.

INGREDIENTS

2 pints of shelled prawns	2 blades lemon grass
6 cucumbers or $\frac{1}{4}$ of a pumpkin	$\frac{1}{2}$ teaspoon ground ginger
2 oz. ghee or butter	4 cloves mashed garlic
1 tablespoon ground onion	2 breakfast cups coconut milk
2 teaspoons turmeric powder	6 cloves
1 teaspoon chilli powder	seeds of 6 cardamoms
4 small sticks ($\frac{1}{2}$ inch) cinnamon	salt to taste

METHOD

Cut the cucumbers into 15–20 pieces. If pumpkin is used, remove the outer skin, cut it into 16 pieces each about two inches square, and steep in water for an hour. Fry all spices, except lemon grass, with onion in butter for 10 minutes on a medium heat, then add prawns and cook till soft. Put in cucumber pieces (or pumpkin) with water drained off, pour over this the coconut milk, add lemon grass, salt, and simmer gently for 30 minutes.

Before serving, remove the lemon grass.

Malay Cucumber (or Pumpkin) Curry is always eaten with rice, usually to the accompaniment of some acid pickle, like lime.

The quantity of chilli can be increased or decreased according to the sensitivity of your palate. I have been told by some who have been kind enough to use my books that my curries are not *hot* enough, but this can easily be remedied.

Enough for four

STUFFED SNAKE-GOURD CURRY

Snake gourds have not, as far as I am aware, appeared on the stalls in our market places in any quantity, but small round, or cylindrical pumpkins will do.

INGREDIENTS

1 snake gourd or pumpkin	ghee or butter for frying
milk from ½ a coconut	

Stuffing ingredients

4 oz. onions, finely sliced	1 green chilli, sliced
2 teaspoons chilli powder	3 curry leaves
½ lb. boiled potatoes, diced	1 stick celery, chopped
4 oz. tomato pulp	½ teaspoon fenugreek
½ lb. minced beef or beef left over from a previous meal	1-inch piece of rampe

METHOD

A cylindrical pumpkin is best. Peel and wash it, then cut into pieces 2–3 inches thick, scoop out the centres, scald in salt water and drain.

Fry onions till light brown. Add beef and ½ teaspoon of chilli powder and fry for a few minutes. Scrape flesh from coconut, pour ½ pint of boiling water over it, allow it to stand for 10 minutes, then squeeze through muslin. This is the *first* milk. Repeat the operation. This is the *second* milk. Put both aside.

Thoroughly mix remainder of stuffing ingredients, add fried beef, and fill this mixture into the scooped-out pieces of pumpkin or snake gourd.

Put the pumpkin pieces in a deep wide pan, add the second milk and boil. As soon as

Chicken Korma
(See recipe pages 63 and 128)

boiling point is reached, simmer till the pumpkin is soft enough to be eaten. Then bring to the boil again, add the first milk and remove the pan from the flame. Shake the pan occasionally in cooking; don't stir, or the stuffed pieces will break.

Enough for four

MRS NOELLE DENTROM
47/1 1ST CROSS STREET
PAGODA
NUGEGODA
CEYLON

CHICKEN WHITE CURRY

INGREDIENTS

1 chicken	1 dessertspoon sliced onion
2 sprigs fennel	2 cloves garlic
2 slices green ginger, chopped	$\frac{1}{2}$ teaspoon saffron or turmeric
10 red chillis, ground	1 dessertspoon coriander seed
$\frac{1}{2}$ teaspoon sweet cummin powder	1 teaspoon white cummin seed
$\frac{1}{4}$ teaspoon fenugreek	1 dessertspoon ghee
1-inch piece cinnamon	2-inch piece rampe
$\frac{1}{4}$ stem lemon grass	small sprig curry leaves
juice of $\frac{1}{2}$ lime or lemon	$\frac{1}{2}$ pint thick coconut milk
salt	$1\frac{1}{2}$ pints second extract coconut milk

METHOD

Dismember chicken and place pieces into a saucepan with the $1\frac{1}{2}$ pints—second extract—of coconut milk, fennel, garlic, ginger, saffron (or turmeric), red chillis, fenugreek, cinnamon, and half each of the onion, rampe, lemon grass and curry leaves.

Cook until chicken is parboiled, then make a paste of one dessertspoon of the thick coconut milk, coriander and cummin. Put in the remainder of the thick milk, stir, add lime (or lemon) juice and salt, and pour into saucepan. Simmer till chicken is tender. Now heat the ghee, put in remaining ingredients and fry them; then turn into pan with chicken. Simmer for two or three minutes and serve with either plain rice or pilau.

Usually accompanied by lime or bamboo pickle, or some kind of bhurta.

Enough for four

MRS VYVETTE LOOS

LIVER CURRY

INGREDIENTS

1 lb. liver	2 cloves chopped garlic
1 dessertspoon chilli powder	a 2-inch piece of cinnamon
1 dessertspoon curry powder	a small sprig of bay leaves

1 teaspoon saffron or turmeric	1 teacup thin coconut milk
1 clove garlic, chopped	$\frac{1}{2}$ teacup thick coconut milk
1 clove garlic, crushed	juice of one lemon
1 slice green ginger	1 dessertspoon dripping
$\frac{1}{2}$ teaspoon fenugreek	2 onions finely sliced
a 2-inch piece of screwpine	table-salt

METHOD

Wash and cut liver into slices or cubes, then season with table-salt, curry powder and chilli powder, and set them aside for 15 minutes. Heat the dripping in a saucepan and put in the fenugreek. Stir for five minutes. Add crushed garlic and fry till it turns pale yellow. Follow with sliced onions, bay leaves, screwpine, cinnamon, chopped garlic and ginger, and fry till the ingredients are dark brown.

Put the liver into this concoction and fry for 15 minutes, stirring constantly to prevent the curry from sticking to the pan. Then add thin coconut milk, cloves and turmeric; stir thoroughly, cover pan and simmer gently till the liver is tender. Finally, add thick coconut milk and lemon juice and continue to simmer gently till the gravy is thick. *Do not cover the pan after the thick milk has been added.*

If eaten with plain white rice—Patna or Kashmiri—the full flavour is brought out; add a *sambal* or *bhurta* but no pickle or chutney.

MRS DOROTHY THOMPSON   *Enough for four*

RABBIT CURRY

The British rabbit—rarer alas, than before the war—makes a tastier curry than chicken, especially broiler chickens mass-produced in factories, which are just about as tasteless as blotting paper.

INGREDIENTS

1 large rabbit	1 tablespoon sliced onion
$\frac{1}{2}$ oz. coriander seed	a teaspoon of turmeric
$\frac{1}{4}$ oz. white cummin seed	6 cloves
$\frac{1}{8}$ oz. sweet cummin seed	1 clove garlic, sliced
$\frac{1}{2}$ teaspoon fenugreek	2 slices green ginger, 1 inch each
a 2-inch piece of screw pine	a 2-inch piece of cinnamon
1 dessertspoon vinegar	a small sprig of bay or curry leaves
the milk of one coconut	1 tablespoon dripping
20 dry chillis—use less if a mild curry is wanted	

METHOD

Roast chillis, coriander and cummin seed till they are almost black, then grind them into a smooth paste. Cut the rabbit into neat joints, and place in a saucepan with sufficient coconut milk to cover. Add all the other ingredients except dripping and one teaspoonful of sliced onion. Mix thoroughly and let the curry boil gently till the rabbit is tender and the gravy fairly thick.

Heat the dripping in another saucepan and fry the remainder of the onion till it is golden brown. Add the pieces of rabbit and fry for about 15 minutes; then pour in the gravy and cook for a further five minutes, stirring the whole time.

Eat with white or yellow rice and pickle.

Enough for five

MRS DOROTHY THOMPSON

BHOONA GOAST

Bhoona goasts are great favourites among Europeans and Anglo-Indians, and Pakistanis in particular excel in making them. There are many varieties of *bhoona goasts*, and they are usually eaten by Europeans and Anglo-Indians with *khichiri* (kedgeree); by South Indians with pepper water or *mooligatanee* (mulligatawny).

INGREDIENTS

1 lb. mutton cut into cubes	1 dessertspoon vinegar
1 tablespoon ghee or other fat	4 cloves garlic, sliced
1 tablespoon finely minced onion	3 pickled chillis, sliced
1 tablespoon desiccated coconut	salt to taste
1 tablespoon curry powder	

METHOD

Fry onion to a golden brown in ghee or other fat, add garlic and chillis, cook gently for a minute and stir in curry powder. Mix well and simmer gently for 5 minutes. Add meat and vinegar. Stir well, bring to the boil, then lower heat and simmer, stirring occasionally to prevent ingredients sticking to pan. When the meat is tender, add the coconut and stir briskly. Coconut absorbs moisture.

Bhoona goast is a dry curry with little or no gravy. If too dry and any of the contents tend to stick to pan, add a *little* water.

Remove from the stove the moment the meat is tender and eat *hot*, with chappattis, parrattas or poorees.

Beef, pork and rabbit can also be cooked in the same way; so may leftover cold meats.

Enough for four

MOLEE CURRY (South Indian)

INGREDIENTS

8 small fish, such as herrings	2 teaspoons ground turmeric
½ coconut	1 tablespoon ground coriander
10 green chillis	1 teaspoon ground cummin
2 tablespoons sliced onions	4 cloves garlic
6 pickling onions	3 red chillis
1 tablespoon butter or cooking fat	6 curry leaves
1 tablespoon vinegar	1 teaspoon salt

185

METHOD

Grate coconut finely and extract milk, about half a pint. If there is any natural coconut milk reserve that. Clean fish and smear inside and out with paste made from ground turmeric, salt and a little warm water. Heat fat to boiling point, fry fish, and when done, place fish on flat dish on a hotplate. Throw sliced onions and curry leaves into the fat, and brown them; add coriander, cummin, garlic and dried chillis. Cook for 5 minutes. If too little fat is left over after cooking the fish, add a teaspoonful.

Put in coconut milk, pickling onions and green chillis sliced lengthwise, then raise the heat till milk boils, and put in the vinegar. As the mixture thickens, put in the natural milk of the coconut; if there is none, add a little water. The gravy should be ready when there is no sign of oil on top.

Pour over fish and serve.

The ten green chillis make Molee Curry very pungent, so eat plenty of plain rice with it, and accompany it with bhurta or saag; not pickle or chutney.

Enough for four

COCONUT PRAWN CURRY (South Indian)

INGREDIENTS

½ a coconut	4 small chopped onions
1 pint cleaned prawns	1 tablespoon oil or fat
8 green chillis	tamarind—about the size of two marbles
½ teaspoon ground cummin	6 curry leaves
4 cloves garlic	salt

METHOD

The prawns, when shelled and cleaned, should amount to about one pint.

Grind the coconut very finely (desiccated coconut will do), chop curry leaves into small pieces, and mix with coconut, chillis, cummin, onions and garlic into a paste with oil or fat. Mix the tamarind in water and strain to remove stringy pieces. Add tamarind water to the paste and increase the mixture to one pint, with warm water. Pour the mixture into a pan, and add prawns and salt. Cook and stir gently till the prawns are soft.

Serve with plain rice.

Enough for two

DHOPA (South Indian)

INGREDIENTS

A slice of fish weighing about 1 lb.	2 eggs
6 green chillis—sliced	½ coconut—or 1 packet desiccated coconut
1 tablespoon small onions—sliced	2 tablespoons vinegar
—or one large onion, sliced	1½ teaspoons turmeric
½ teaspoon black pepper	salt

186

METHOD

Clean and wash the fish, then rub it, inside and out, with a paste made of turmeric, salt and water, then steam or boil it in water till tender and put in a dish on a hotplate.

Grate coconut finely and extract the milk. If desiccated coconut is used, extract the milk with hot water. Beat eggs and add sliced chillis, onions and pepper. Heat the mixture and when it comes to the boil, pour in the coconut milk. Stir, and as it thickens, add vinegar. Keep stirring and cooking till it thickens once more. Remove from stove, add salt, stir well and pour over fish.

This is a somewhat pungent concoction, as are most South Indian curries, and should be approached with circumspection, as a little goes a long way. It is, however, very agreeable with plenty of plain boiled rice. Dhopa is usually followed by a slice of melon, a fruit which assuages the internal fires.

Enough for two

FRIED EELS

INGREDIENTS

2 eels	16 curry leaves
1 inch piece of turmeric	1 teacup mustard oil
6–8 garlic cloves	4 red chillis
a piece of tamarind the size of a marble	1 teaspoon cummin
salt	4 oz. butter

METHOD

Clean and cut eels into rounds. Grind turmeric, garlic, chillis, cummin, salt and 12 curry leaves into a paste, and rub this well into the eel slices. Heat oil in a deep frying pan. Put in the tamarind and 4 curry leaves. Boil till the tamarind is very dark brown, then remove it and the curry leaves and discard them. The oil has now absorbed the flavour of the tamarind and the leaves and is 'seasoned'. Put the butter into the pan of oil and when boiling, slide in the slices of eel and fry golden brown or perhaps a trifle darker.

Serve with plain rice plentifully garnished with parsley.

Prawns and sea fish may be cooked in the same way and are extremely tasty, but the fisherman's favourite is fried eels.

Enough for six

SOUPS, SAVOURIES, PICKLE CURRIES AND RELISHES

INDIAN CORN SOUP

'Indian' corn is a cereal not indigenous to India. It was taken there from America, for originally it came from Mexico. The real name is *maize*: Spanish *maiz*; Cuban *mahiz*, and in South American countries the maize-starch or flour used for food is known as *maizena*.

Maize or *bhootta*, as it is known in India, is a popular food, and the climate and soil suit it, for it is a deep-rooting plant that does not need much manure.

INGREDIENTS

1 breakfast cup lentils	2 onions, finely sliced
3 pints water	1 tin Mexican sweet corn
1 teaspoon turmeric	1 teaspoon cummin powder
2 tablespoons finely chopped parsley	2 cloves garlic
salt—very necessary	

METHOD

Mix the cummin and turmeric well in a couple of tablespoons of boiling water. Bring the 3 pints to the boil and pour in the lentils. Unless the water is boiling the lentils will not break up easily. Some soak lentils overnight in bicarbonate of soda to achieve this result, but this is harmful and usually causes heart-burn. Putting lentils into *boiling* water always breaks them up.

Now add turmeric, cummin, onions and garlic—and salt. Without salt, lentils are tasteless. Boil fairly hard for 10 minutes, then whisk till lentils are dissolved, and add the tin of sweet corn.

Ladle out in generous quantities in *bowls* and top with chopped parsley. This is a meal in itself, if eaten with brown bread or Ryvita or rye bread.

Enough for two

MULLIGATAWNY SOUP

In the *First Book of Curries*, one recipe for Mulligatawny Soup is given, but of course, there are many kinds; the liquor may be meat stock, the stock from pigs' trotters or the shin bones of sheep, or even water in which fish has been cooked. This recipe is for *one kind of Mulligatawny*.

INGREDIENTS

A quart of vegetable stock *or* a quart of beef or other meat stock	1 teaspoon mashed garlic
	$\frac{1}{2}$ teaspoon coriander powder
4 oz. butter or ghee	$\frac{1}{2}$ teaspoon cummin seed
1 large chicken	2 oz. ground poppyseed
2 large onions, finely sliced	6 kurreah fool leaves
1 teaspoon powdered turmeric	2 or 3 lemons, sliced
$\frac{1}{2}$ teaspoon ground chillis—or more, according to taste	salt
$\frac{1}{2}$ teaspoon ground or powdered ginger	

METHOD

Clean and cut the chicken into 15–20 pieces. Fry one of the sliced onions in little ghee or butter to a golden brown, and set it aside. Put the remainder of the butter or ghee into a deep, capacious pan, bring to sizzling point and add the second onion, ground into a pulp, the turmeric, chillis, ginger, garlic, coriander and cummin. As the mixture fries, add a tablespoon of water. After five minutes of stirring, put in the chicken and when the chicken is golden brown, add poppyseed, salt and stock, fried onion and *kurreah fool* leaves.

Place a close-fitting cover on the pot and simmer till the chicken is tender. Serve piping hot, and just before eating, squeeze lemon juice over the soup.

This soup may also be poured over rice that has been left over from a previous meal.

Enough for six

PUMPKIN SOUP

Very few people in Britain ever think of pumpkins in terms of soup, yet a delicious soup can be made with either pumpkins or marrows. In India it is also made with the squash, a vegetable of a similar species.

INGREDIENTS

1 lb. pumpkin or marrow	4 cloves garlic
3 oz. butter or ghee	1 teaspoon turmeric
4 small onions, finely sliced	$\frac{1}{2}$ teaspoon cummin
6 cloves	$\frac{1}{2}$ teaspoon chilli powder or 2 green chillis
12 peppercorns	salt
1 tablespoon Worcester sauce or 1 tablespoon vinegar	handful of parsley
2 pints vegetable stock	2 eggs

METHOD

Skin the marrow or pumpkin and remove the seeds, though some like the seeds. Slice or cut it into cubes. Wash and drain. Heat butter in a deep saucepan and fry the vegetable briskly for 5 minutes. Then add onions, turmeric, cummin and chilli powder and fry again for 5 minutes.

Now pour the vegetable stock over it, put in the cloves, garlic and peppercorns, bring to the boil and then simmer till the pumpkin (or marrow) is very soft and pulpy. Strain this into a large basin and add sauce (or vinegar) and salt.

189

While all this is being done, boil the eggs till hard; shell and halve them. Mince the yolk and cut the whites into strips. When the soup is strained and ready, add the eggs and serve, well garnished with parsley. Always use either butter or ghee, never margarine or other fat, for butter makes all the difference to the taste.

Enough for four

CURRIED POTATOES

INGREDIENTS

12 potatoes	1½ teaspoons turmeric
8 dry (red) chillis	1 teaspoon coriander
2 eggs	4 ounces butter or ghee
salt	

METHOD

Scrub, then boil potatoes in their jackets till soft but firm. Remove and peel, cut in halves. Beat eggs well. Grind or chop chillis very finely, mix with egg, a little salt. Mix the turmeric and coriander into a thick, smooth paste, thin with a tablespoon of boiling water, add egg mixture and beat rapidly till thick.

Boil the fat in a frying pan, dip the potato halves into the egg mixture and fry till brown. Remove, drain and serve either with parattas or chappattis, or with cold meat. A tasty savoury for supper on a cold winter's night.

Enough for four

POTATO BADUN

INGREDIENTS

½ lb. potatoes	1 dessertspoon Maldive fish or
½ teaspoon saffron or turmeric	1 dessertspoon Bombay Duck
1 dessertspoon chilli powder	a sprig of curry leaves
2-inch piece of rampe	1-inch slice of ginger
4 onions, finely sliced	3 cloves garlic, chopped
a breakfast cup of thick coconut milk	salt
3 tablespoons cooking oil	

METHOD

Boil and then peel the potatoes. Cut into thick slices, put into a saucepan and cover with coconut milk. Add remainder of ingredients, except the onions and oil, and cook till the potatoes are soft enough to eat, but firm. Then fry the onions in the oil in another pan, and when golden-brown, empty in the contents of the first pan. Continue to simmer till the liquid evaporates and the gravy is almost non-existent.

Eat with bread, chappattis, or plain rice and a little lime pickle.

A tit-bit for two

MRS VYVETTE LOOS

KALUPOL SAMBAL

INGREDIENTS

½ coconut or ½ lb. desiccated coconut	juice of 1 lime or lemon
3 onions	1 teaspoonful fat or oil
12 red chillis	salt
1 tablespoon Maldive fish or 1 tablespoon Bombay duck	

METHOD

Scrape the flesh from half a coconut, or use desiccated coconut, put it in a pan and roast over a low heat till light brown. Then turn out on to a flat dish. Peel and slice onions finely, and roast them, too, in a little fat or oil. Put into the dish with the coconut. Roast the fish (or Bombay duck) and the red chillis, and put them into the dish as well. Each item must be roasted separately.

Place all the ingredients on a *seel* or grinding stone and grind well. Then add salt, lime juice, mix and mould into a ball. Serve.

To be eaten with curry and rice.

MRS VYVETTE LOOS

BRAIN CUTLETS

INGREDIENTS

4 sheep's brains	1 teaspoon chilli powder
1 dessertspoon parsley	a pan of deep fat
1 dessertspoon thyme	1 large egg
1 large onion	wholemeal breadcrumbs
6 cloves garlic	1 floury potato
a little butter	

METHOD

Wash brains, then plunge into boiling water. Remove and plunge into cold water and bring to boil. Remove and allow to cool. Boil and mash the potato with a little butter, and mix in chilli powder. Whisk egg till stiff. This is best done by first whisking the white, then adding the yolk.

Chop brains, parsley, thyme, onion and garlic and mix all, with potato, thoroughly. Mould this mixture into cutlets and dip in the beaten egg; then roll in breadcrumbs. Fry in deep fat till light brown, remove and drain.

There are many variations of stuffing that can be used in making brain cutlets: tarragon, rosemary, marjoram, thyme, etc. Experiment with them, though *if rosemary is used, put in very little* as this herb is pungent and too much can spoil the dish.

Brain cutlets should be eaten with *chappattis* and one of many kinds of *bhurta*. Rice and brain cutlets do not make the best combination.

Enough for four

CHINGREE PUFFS

Chingree puffs or patties are a favourite with Anglo-Indians—especially for tea or picnics. 'Tea' in such establishments is really a high tea, in which left-overs from 'tiffin' (lunch) appear, as well as cheese, guava cheese, palm fruit in hot weather, and other delicacies to titillate the jaded palate.

INGREDIENTS

¾ lb. self-raising flour	½ pint shelled prawns
10 oz. ghee or butter	1 teaspoon ground coriander
2 oz. sliced onions	1 teaspoon ground turmeric
¼ teaspoon salt	½ teaspoon ground cummin

METHOD

Mince or pound prawns into a paste, having *first* removed heads, tails and shells. Heat 2 oz. of fat and fry the sliced onions till brown. Mix the coriander, turmeric and cummin with a little water, into a paste, add a cupful of *boiling* water, and stir. Pour over onions and keep stirring for 3 minutes on a medium heat. Add prawns and salt, and cook gently for 5 minutes.

Use 4 oz. of the fat with the flour to make either short or puff pastry. Roll it out very thin, cut into rounds or squares, fill the middles generously with curried prawns and fold over, as if making jam puffs. Close the edges carefully.

Put the remaining fat into a large frying pan, bring to the boil, slide in the puffs and fry till they are light brown in colour. Remove and drain. The puffs should be very light and tasty.

Alternatively, they can be put into a hot oven and cooked like pastry. Meat can be used instead of prawns, but is nothing like as tasty.

Enough for at least twelve puffs

OMELETTE CURRY

The omelette is not an Indian dish, but curried omelettes—and there are innumerable varieties—are an excellent compromise between East and West. There are few tastier dishes.

Note: To make omelettes well, very little fat is needed, but it is essential to have a thick, special omelette pan. A thick pan retains the heat, so that the heat can be turned off once the pan is hot, and there will be no fear of burning.

INGREDIENTS

6 eggs	½ teaspoon turmeric powder
2 onions—finely sliced	½ teaspoon coriander powder
2 green chillis—minced	¼ teaspoon cummin powder
½ lb. of any cold meat left over: mutton, liver,	a pinch of ginger
bacon, beef, or even parts of chicken, grouse, etc.	2 oz. butter
2 cloves garlic	salt

METHOD

Place 1 oz. butter in a frying pan and heat. Brown the onions in it, then add turmeric, coriander, cummin, chillis, garlic and ginger and cook for 5 minutes, stirring briskly. If too dry, add a little water.

Add the minced cold meat and cook for two or three minutes, till the meat is saturated. Add salt now, or after omelette is made.

Break the eggs into a bowl and mix till white and yolks are one—but not till stiff. Heat omelette pan well, melt butter, then pour in the eggs. Turn off the heat. Put the curried meat into the middle of the egg from north to south, or east to west, and when the egg starts to thicken and consolidate, use a flexible slice, and fold. Turn and heat for a few moments on the other side. Serve hot. Garnish with parsley and eat on hot toast.

Enough for four

Bhajjis

Bhajjis are vegetable curries that are fried, for *bhajji* means *fried*, and the two most popular bhajjis in India are probably made from *brinjals* (aubergines) and *pulwals*. Aubergines can be bought almost anywhere in England during the summer, for they are imported in large quantities from France; but the *pulwal*, a large, beanlike vegetable, is indigenous to the tropics.

BRINJAL BHAJJI

There are many kinds of brinjal bhajji and this is perhaps the simplest of all, and the easiest if you have never tried this delicious vegetable. When selecting brinjals, don't pick the biggest, as big vegetables are usually old and have the toughest skins.

INGREDIENTS

2 medium-size brinjals weighing $\frac{1}{2}$ lb. each	1 teaspoon powdered turmeric
1 breakfast cup of mustard oil or butter	$\frac{1}{2}$ teaspoon chilli powder
salt to taste	

METHOD

Wash the brinjals thoroughly and slice them into rounds no more than an eighth of an inch thick. If much thicker they will not cook easily and quickly. Do *not* skin them. Steep them in cold water for an hour, then remove and dry them. Mix the turmeric, salt and chilli into a paste with water, and apply this to both sides of each slice of brinjal.

Pour the mustard oil into a large frying pan and heat it till blue smoke issues; then pop in as many slices of brinjal as the pan will hold and fry till golden brown. Prod with a fork or sharp pointed knife to test whether they are tender. Fry on both sides.

When the slices are done, place them in a warm dish and eat with plain boiled rice accompanied by lime pickle; or with *poorees,* or rolled up in *chappattis.*

If sufficiently cooked, the skin is not only edible but tasty.

Enough for four

Pickle Curries

Pickle curries are made in India and the Far East because they will keep for a fortnight, in the hottest weather—though not as long as pickles. No more than a dessertspoon of pickle curry should be eaten with curry and rice; the beginner should start with half a teaspoon or so and proceed gingerly.

SALTED LIME CURRY

INGREDIENTS

20 limes cut open and well impregnated with salt. If limes are unobtainable, 15 lemons will do instead

25 dried chillis—(red)

1 dessertspoon of *maythi* (fenugreek)

1 teaspoon cummin seed

1 teaspoon mustard seed

salt to taste

1 stick saffron or turmeric

8 pods garlic

1 doz. green chillis

4 tablespoons mustard oil

1 tablespoon ground mustard

5 breakfast cups of vinegar

6 curry leaves

METHOD

Broil the dried chillis, fenugreek, mustard seed and cummin for 5 minutes, then powder finely. Also powder the saffron or turmeric. Halve each lime; peel the garlic; slit the green chillis lengthwise. Heat oil in the thick pan and put in the ground mustard and curry leaves. Add pounded curry spices, salt and other spiced ingredients; next the limes (or lemons), finally the vinegar. Bring gently to the boil, and simmer. When the liquid is thick and the oil clear on top (not frothy), the pickle curry is ready. Allow it to cool and put it into jars. Seal with *cork,* not metal, stoppers.

Salted lime curry is very, very pungent. The beginner should be warned to try not more than half a teaspoonful with curry and rice, and to take just a pinch with each mouthful.

As you grow accustomed to eating curries, you will like them hotter; though some (I am one) never grow to like very hot curries. They are an acquired taste—like whisky.

VINDE AULY

Vinde Auly is merely one kind of *vindaloo* or *bindaloo,* of which there are innumerable varieties. Vinde Auly, because it is made from pork, is rarely met in the Muslim North and North-West, but is a favourite in the South. It is a relish rather than a main dish, though a satisfying and tasty meal can be made of vinde auly and rice alone.

INGREDIENTS

2 lb. salt pork. This must be well and truly salted

30 large red, dried chillis

$1\frac{1}{2}$ heaped teaspoons of powdered cummin

1 pod garlic (comprising many cloves or segments)

1 piece of turmeric

$\frac{3}{4}$ teaspoon of ground mustard

$\frac{1}{2}$ pint vinegar

METHOD

Cut the pork into large cubes and dry them in the sun all day. If there is no sun, this can be done in the oven, though you must take care only to dry them, and *not* cook them.

Cut up and soak chillis overnight in vinegar, mash them into a paste with the turmeric, cummin, mustard and garlic. Gradually pour vinegar from chillis into paste, mixing well. Put the concoction into a large glass jar with a wide mouth.

Gently plop the pieces of pork into the jar, and if the liquid does not cover the pieces, add vinegar until it does. Seal the jar with an airtight cork or stopper. After two days, see whether the liquid has been absorbed by the pork. If so, top with more vinegar.

When wanted, remove as many pieces as you need; just cover in water and boil. When the liquid thickens and the fat clears, it is ready to eat—warm—with curry and rice, chappattis and rice, with plain rice, or chappattis only.

PUDDA (South Indian relish)

INGREDIENTS

2 lb. cod or similar fish	2 dessertspoons cummin—powdered
90 dried (red) chillis (why not 100?)	1½ bottles vinegar
2 one-inch pieces of turmeric	tamarind—the size of 4 ducks' eggs
1 pod of garlic (this contains many cloves)	salt

METHOD

Clean and cut the fish into round slices, each about 1½ inches thick. Rub well with salt and leave for two days. Fish will keep, even in India, if well salted. After that, wipe well with a clean cloth and put in the sun for two days. (This should be tried in midsummer in a year when the sun is less fickle than normal. The Meteorological Office should be consulted.)

Pound and make a fine paste of the chillis, turmeric, garlic, and cummin, using vinegar. Mix the tamarind and some vinegar, strain, and mix with paste. Add the remainder of the vinegar so that a gravy-like consistency is achieved. If too thick, add more vinegar.

Dip each slice of fish in this gravy and place in a wide-mouthed jar; or in more than one jar. Then pour the remaining gravy over the fish, and cover with an air-tight cork, or some other air-tight cover. In this way the fish keeps, even in the Indian summer—and not in a refrigerator!—for a month.

When wanted for consumption, remove a slice or two and fry on both sides in butter for a minute; then add some of the gravy and cook till soft. But never cook until the fish has soaked for 7 or 8 days. To be eaten with curry and rice.

PUMPKIN CHAKEE

Bhajjis, as explained earlier, are vegetables that are fried. Chakees are not, and are usually made from a number of vegetables. But occasionally a *chakee* may be made from one vegetable such as aubergine, pumpkin, marrow, or *pulbul* (sometimes pulwal), a large beanlike vegetable indigenous to the tropics.

INGREDIENTS

1 dessertspoon tamarind pulp or	2 dessertspoons ground onions
2 or 3 tamarinds	1 teaspoon ground chillis
4 oz. mustard oil	1 teaspoon ground turmeric
½ teaspoon ground garlic	1 breakfast cup water
One quarter of a pumpkin	10 tomatoes, or 1 tin pulp

METHOD

Remove stones from tamarind and mix the flesh with water. Cut the pumpkin into inch or inch-and-half cubes.

Heat the oil till a fine blue plume rises, then put in the ground onion and cook for 2 or 3 minutes, stirring briskly. Now add chillis, turmeric and garlic, cook for a further 5 minutes and fold in the tamarind water and tomatoes or tomato pulp. When the mixture comes to the boil, gently slide in the pumpkin cubes. Again bring to the boil then lower the heat till the mixture just simmers. Cover and cook till the pumpkin is tender.

Chakees are best served with plain boiled rice, without chutney or pickle as the tamarind conveys a tang that may be killed by chutney or pickle. This should make enough for a supper dish for four. Incidentally—this has nothing to do with cookery—the shiny tamarind seeds, if pierced, can be strung together to make an attractive necklace.

FRIED BRINJAL SAMBAL (Burmese Dish)

INGREDIENTS

6 large *brinjals* (aubergines)   6 cloves garlic

16 oz. boiled prawns   2 large onions

1 teaspoon turmeric or saffron   3 green chillis

1 teaspoon balachong (bally chow)   4 lemons

$\frac{1}{2}$ pint cooking oil or 8 oz. fat or butter

METHOD

Boil the brinjals till soft. If you have a wood fire, or use coals that leave plenty of ash, bury the brinjals under the ash till soft. This brings out their flavour better.

Mince onions, chillis and prawns, add the pulp of the brinjal, and mix thoroughly.

Chop the garlic into slices, heat the oil well, toss in the garlic, and cook till brown. Then add the brinjal mixture and fry till well cooked; about 10 minutes.

Fried brinjal sambal is eaten with rice; though it goes well with *poorees* and even baker's bread. Before serving, pour the juice of the lemons over the sambal.

POTATO SAMBAL

INGREDIENTS

$1\frac{1}{4}$ lb. floury potatoes   1 green or 2 red chillis

1 teaspoon butter   1 lemon

2 large onions $\frac{1}{2}$ teaspoon salt

$\frac{1}{2}$ cup of coconut milk   1 teaspoon *panch phora*

METHOD

Boil the potatoes till soft in water into which a teaspoon of *panch phora* has been tossed. Strain off the water and keep for soup stock. Keep the panch phora. Peel the potatoes and mash them.

Slice onions and chilli, add salt and the juice of the lemon. Put the potato into a bowl and mash it; then add onions, chillis, and salt. Mix thoroughly, add coconut milk; mix again and serve in a circular dish topped with sprigs of parsley.

HIN-CHYO (Burmese Vegetable Soup)

INGREDIENTS

1 lb. of any vegetable such as marrow, pumpkin or runner beans	1 teaspoon salt
	6 cloves garlic
5 or 6 large prawns, or $\frac{1}{2}$ lb. cod	4 curry leaves
3 medium size onions	1 teaspoon balachong

METHOD

Clean and cut the vegetable into cubes or small pieces, place in a pan with 2 quarts water and boil. Add prawns, balachong, garlic and curry leaves and boil till fish and vegetables have broken down and are very soft. Serve hot.

PLANNING MENUS WITH INDIAN DISHES

INDIAN meals are not planned on the same lines as they are in Europe today. In Indian households, lunch and dinner do not usually start with soup or *hors-d'oeuvres*. The appetite does not need whetting: the smell of the curries does that.

And—there is no breakfast in the British sense, even though Englishmen abroad insist on grapefruit, bacon and eggs, porridge and cream, marmalade and toast, followed by tea or coffee. Indians in the North break their fast with tea or water, in the South with coffee; this is followed by either a little fresh fruit or something light, like *falowries* or *bhajias*.

The vast mass of the population eats little throughout the day: a snack of curry and rice, or curry and chappattis, and water, sherbet or tea. Afternoon tea is an English meal, now copied by millions, which consists of biscuits, tea and Indian sweetmeats rather than the cakes, sandwiches and cress of the English. Cakes, biscuits and leaven bread were introduced by Europeans. The main meal in India is dinner, usually taken at a much later hour than in Britain, often about midnight.

Lentils and mulligatawny are never eaten as soups, but with rice and meat or vegetables. Lentils are cooked in a number of ways and eaten with rice or chappattis, often forming the most nutritious part of the meal. In the South, mulligatawny, which is a thin pepper water (described on page 32) is eaten with rice and sometimes accompanied by dry curries. The lentil and mulligatawny soups eaten at the start of a meal in Britain are adaptations from Indian cuisine—and there is no reason why Indian dishes should not be adapted. Below you will find a day's menus based on Indian food.

Breakfast:
Half a grapefruit, or a slice of melon or papaiya, a fruit which will soon become popular in England. Porridge or other breakfast cereal; or/and bacon and egg, toast and marmalade; tea, coffee or fruit juice.

Lunch:
Clear vegetable soup; vegetable or dhall curry accompanied by lime pickle or prawn sambal, followed by a slice of Madras hulva.

Tea:
This isn't, and never was, an Indian meal and the Indian sweets and savouries favoured do not, to the European palate, go well with tea. So, it would be safer to keep to sandwiches and pastries.

Dinner:
Soup (pumpkin, vermicelli, dhall, mulligatawny, mutton, chicken or rice soups); a fish curry made with coconut milk and eaten with bamboo pickle; or a white chicken curry with

lime pickle; or pork or beef korma with bhurta and onion and tomato sambal; followed by a sweet of jellabies or kalajamoons, or rasagoollas with clotted cream. (Keep the sweet in the refrigerator till wanted.)

Curries may be eaten either with rice—plain or pilau—or chappattis.

Thumb through the recipes, concoct your own menus, but never serve more than two curries at any one meal. Curry and rice, or curry and chappattis, served with dhall, yogurt, bhurtas and sambals, and eaten with pickles, chutneys or chillis, are filling and substantial. If you serve too many curries your guests will be apt to overeat because the dishes are tasty, but they won't thank you.

The curse of the curry is that it is *too* tasty and the idea that the heat of the tropics dissuades one from eating too much is a fallacy. Tom Hopkinson describes in *In The Fiery Continent* some of the gargantuan meals eaten by well-to-do Africans. The same is true of Indians. Millions may be underfed, but those who can, too often stuff themselves, for obesity and strength are considered synonymous, and the saying, 'He is fat and strong,' is a compliment!

Meals Should Be Planned

Food as cooked by Indians who adhere to the *Code of Manu*, or abide by the Sustras, has a purpose, and meals should be planned, in much the same way as a menu is planned by a French chef. One dish should aid the next; and every dish should be complementary to all the others.

Thus a good Indian meal has design. Curry and rice should not be mixed together and eaten *en masse*. A little curry conveys richness and flavour; the blandness of rice assuages its pungency, and a *soupçon* of pickle gives it acidity, or chutney, sweetness.

A little food should be eaten at each mouthful; the mouth not plugged full—like a Scot filling his pipe with someone else's tobacco—and the whole should not be plunged madly down one's gullet as if one were starving.

Food should be well chewed, thoroughly tasted, and the many ingredients savoured and relished.

Avoid Dyspepsia

Digestive troubles, which afflict so many curry eaters, could be avoided if people realized that the process of digestion starts not in the stomach, but in the mouth. As you chew, the salivary glands produce a fluid which contains the first of the digestive enzymes, salivary amylase, which hydrolyzes starch or dextrin by splitting off the molecules of maltose from the long carbohydrate chain. Then the lubricating action of saliva aids the swallowing of food as it passes from the mouth, through the oesophagus into the stomach, the duodenum and the intestines, where it is acted on by other enzymes and broken down so that it can be absorbed into the bloodstream.

If not chewed well, starches ferment when acted on by hydrochloric acid later, and give the feeling of a 'hard lump' on the chest. So, chew bread, rice, potatoes and all starches, well.

WHAT DOES ONE DRINK WITH CURRIES?

ONE is often asked, 'What are the right wines to go with curries?'

In this the ancient books give no guidance whatever, for curries are indigenous to India, and India has no wines or spirits of her own except rum distilled in places like Shahjehanpur; arrack (Arabic, *sweet juice*) brewed in the country from the water of the coconut; and a potent liquor made from date-palm toddy (*tari*), all of which are shunned by the respectable, Hindu and Muslim alike.

Indians don't usually drink while eating, for if curries are too pungent, liquid does little to assuage the burning pangs. Rice or bread serves far better. Incidentally, long drinks after eating rice are not advisable, as they create a feeling of excessive fullness.

Sherbet

After a meal, when betel, cardamom and a little *paan* (a pungent leaf of the cress family) have been chewed to clean the teeth, sweeten breath and aid digestion, guests in India usually sip glasses of sherbet (Arabic *sharbah* from *shariba, to drink*; or Hindi *sharbat*) or cups of spiced tea.

Originally sherbet was made from fruit juice and snow, but today from any fruit juice, cooled and sweetened and with possibly a little rose water added. Indian sherbet bears no resemblance to the fizzy concoctions sold to children under that name in Britain. The most popular sherbets are made from mango, bael (wood apple), palm fruit, pineapple, lime, etc. Unfortunately, only the pineapple is available everywhere in Britain.

Spiced Teas

Spiced teas usually have a cinnamon, cardamom or mint base and are taken either hot or very cold, usually with sugar but never with milk. They contain herbs and are often flavoured with lime or lemon, and in a hot climate are very refreshing.

Wines, Spirits and Beers

When the Portuguese, French and British went to India they took their drinking habits with them, habits which were regarded as barbarous, for the orthodox Hindu does not touch alcoholic liquor, and the Prophet (whose name be blessed) forbids his followers to indulge in such delights. But today there are many Hindus and Moslems who place elastic interpretations on all such injunctions.

A good dry sherry goes well before dinner. Try one of the 'finos': a pale Amontillado or salty Manzanilla.

Generally speaking, light beers are the best beverages to drink with or after curries. The Japanese, a great rice-eating nation, drink *sake*, which is 15–18% alcohol and similar to sherry in flavour and strength, but light beers, like lager, are equally suitable.

Sweet, heavy red wines do not go well with curries; and if you want to drink wines, those like Riesling, Hock, Chablis, Sauterne, Vermouth, Graves or very dry sherries are best. Better far, I think, are perry or cider (sweet or dry), vintage cider, and, if you can run to it, after a very special occasion, a good champagne.

Perry is excellent with curries and I can't understand why more is not drunk. But this is merely a personal predilection.

There is, of course, no hard and fast rule about either eating or drinking in spite of everything Mr Andre L. Simon, Dr Saintsbury, Messrs Raymond Postgate or Cyril Ray might say. If you fancy a Guinness before, and a vintage port after your meal of curry and rice—and if it agrees with you—then to perdition with the Food and Wine Society!

THE FIFTH BOOK
OF CURRIES

EVERY MEAL A POEM

AFTER returning from dinner at the Thrales' one evening in 1775, the Rev. Dr Campbell opened his diary and wrote: 'The dinner was excellent. The first course, soups at head and foot removed by fish and a saddle of mutton; second course, a fowl called Galena at head, and a capon larger than some of our Irish turkeys at foot; third course, four different sorts of ices, pineapple, grapes, raspberry and a fourth; in each remove there were, I think, fourteen dishes. The first two courses were served on massy plate.*

There was nothing extraordinary about this for Thrale was a man of substance who liked quantity as well as quality and his prize guest that evening was Dr Samuel Johnson, whose habit it was to pontificate on every subject under the sun. He posed as an expert on food and once made that very sound observation: 'He who does not mind his belly will hardly mind anything else.'

Johnson and Thrale had voracious appetites, but whereas Johnson interspersed his feats of gluttony with 'fasting', (he boasted one week that he had seen 'flesh but twice, and I think fish once, the rest was pease.') Thrale devoured gargantuan meals up to the hour of his death.

On that fatal day, records Mrs Thrale, 'He eat, however, more than enormously. Six things the day before and eight on this day, with strong beer in such quantities! the very servants were frighted.'

After the Restoration, England emerged from the Dark Ages of the culinary art. Till then beef and bread formed the main body of every meal for men who could afford to eat well.

Slowly the teachings of Brillat-Savarin, Grinod de la Reynière, Louis Count Zinzendorf and Gonthier d'Andernach (Father of French Cookery) percolated into English kitchens.

The Chevalier d'Albignac, who escaped the French Revolution, was renowned as a mixer of salads, charging £5 to mix a salad for a dinner at any great London house. His salads were the talk of the town and his services in such demand that he would drive up in coach and four, mix a salad and then hurry on to his next assignment. In a few years he returned to France with a fortune of 80,000 francs, bought a fine house in Limousin for 20,000, invested the remainder in Government Securities which stood at fifty per cent and retired to a life of ease.

Centuries earlier men in Indonesia, Thailand, China and Japan had learnt to eat with discrimination and with regard to their health. In China and Japan cooking was raised to a fine art. No meal was worth consuming unless the smell of the food caused the gastric juices to flow, the colour of the viands gave aesthetic pleasure, the vegetables were crisp and delicately combined, the meat tender and juicy, the herbs and sauces blended with the other ingredients but did not overpower them, and the entire combination such as to leave a fragrant memory.

* Plate of precious metal; usually silver.

MISCELLANEOUS HINTS

CHILLIS are not included in the lists of ingredients in Thai cookery. It has been left to the reader to use as much—or little—of this spice as he thinks fit.

Chilli is an extremely pungent spice, so it is wisest to introduce yourself to it gradually by using either tiny pinches of chilli powder, or small pieces of green chilli, remembering always that green chilli is invariably more pungent than red, which is the dried variety; and that the seeds of the chilli are more fiery than the flesh.

To get the utmost satisfaction from Chinese and Japanese cookery it is advisable to buy the colourful, dainty bowls and spoons used in those countries, which add to the decorative quality of their food. Their spoons, for instance, are made not of metal but porcelain. It is not usually necessary however to go so far as to practise eating rice with chopsticks. Remember the old Chinese saying: 'When you prepare a dish you must keep three things in mind: it must be pleasant to the eye, the aroma must be appealing, and it must be appetising.'

A set of dishes for each diner consists of a bowl for rice, a bowl for soup, a dish for main courses, a dessert dish, a wine cup, a porcelain soup spoon—and a pair of chopsticks. The shape of Chinese tables is usually round; in contrast the dishes are often placed in a square with a bowl of soup in the middle.

The guest of honour is seated opposite the door; the host and hostess with their backs to it—not as a precaution to prevent him escaping.

When the first main dish is served the host usually toasts his guests by saying; 'Kan Pei,' (Northern dialect) or 'Yum Shing,' (Cantonese dialect), which means 'Drink up.' The guests in return express their appreciation for the hospitality, for Orientals are more formal than we are.

Many of the ingredients in everyday Chinese cookery are strange to us: Chinese vinegar (Shan Kwang), concentrated soy chilli sauce, Chinese wine (Shaohsing), triple distilled Chinese wine, soy sauce dark, soy sauce light, salted black beans, Chinese rose wine, oyster sauce, sesame oil, salted soy bean paste, Chinese preserved crab apple slices, dried mushrooms, shrimp chips, white and black sesame, and Chinese preserved honey dates. They also use the well known stand-by, catsup, walnuts and dried shrimps, and scallops, which they call abalone. There are other exotic items beloved by the gourmet.

Every variety of vegetable familiar to us is grown in China, and there are some, such as celtuce, arrow-head and the water chestnut, which are not found in Europe.

THAI COOKERY

RAPPATAN ARHAN—The meal is served

THAILAND is a halfway house between India and China with Burma to the West and Viet Nam to the East. Inevitably its cuisine, though based on edibles grown in its soil, is influenced by Chinese technique as well as Indian spices, for these two schools of cookery are the most important in Asian gastronomy. Thai food varies to suit all Asian tastes and has even borrowed something from Europe.

The newcomer to Thai cookery realizes very quickly that Thais like their food spicey and pungent, and when using their recipes he would be well advised at first to cut down drastically the quantity of 'prik-kee-noo', or tiny green or red chillis, which are anything but chilly. They may be only half an inch long, but one bite and your mouth is transformed into a dragon's, breathing fire.

Like the Americans, the Thais don't use knives for eating. All the butchering, slicing and quartering is done in the kitchen. Food arrives on the table in morsels that can be popped into the mouth with the aid of a fork only, and the gravies may be mingled with rice till manageable, or eaten with a spoon.

As Thailand is a rice-growing country, the staple food is rice, which forms the main portion of every meal, and all the other dishes are placed either on this snowy mound, or arranged around it.

SUBGUM FRIED RICE

INGREDIENTS

4 cups cooked rice	1 cup diced chicken, cooked
3 eggs	1 cup diced ham, cooked
2 teaspoons salt	$\frac{1}{2}$ cup peas (fresh or canned)
3 tablespoons oil	$\frac{1}{4}$ teaspoon pepper
3 green onions	2 tablespoons soy* sauce

METHOD

As green onions are unobtainable in Britain, the common or garden variety will do.

Beat the eggs, add $\frac{1}{2}$ teaspoon of salt, pour into a pan with one tablespoon of oil. Scramble and set aside.

Chop the onions finely, heat the remaining oil, toss in the onion and fry briskly for a few seconds. Add the cooked rice to this and stir till heated through. Now mix in the chicken, ham, peas, $1\frac{1}{2}$ teaspoons of salt, and pepper. Heat through, then fork in the

* Sometimes spelt soya.

207

scrambled egg, sprinkle with soy sauce, and serve. Soy sauce can be bought in any shop dealing in Chinese or Indian food.

Enough for four or six

SHRIMP FRIED RICE

INGREDIENTS

1½ cups rice	1 lb. shrimps, shelled and chopped coarsely
2½ cups water	3 onions, chopped
4 tablespoons vegetable oil	½ lb. mushrooms, sliced
3 eggs	3 tablespoons soy sauce
1½ teaspoons salt	1¼ teaspoons sugar
½ teaspoon pepper	

METHOD

Wash the rice thoroughly, soak it in warm water for 15 minutes, then drain and rinse again. Place the rice in a saucepan with a well fitting lid, add 2½ cups of water, bring to the boil and cook over a low heat till all the water is absorbed. This should take about 14 minutes.

Now heat the oil in a large heavy pan, put in the eggs and fry till firm; then turn them over and fry for a minute. Remove the pan from the heat and slice the eggs very finely while still in the pan. Return the pan to the heat and add salt, pepper, shrimps, onion and mushrooms. Cook the whole over a slow heat for 5 minutes, stirring frequently. Add rice, soy sauce and sugar and cook over a medium heat for 5 minutes, stirring constantly.

Enough for two or four

SPANISH BEEF WITH RICE

Thais are not great beef eaters, preferring pork, chicken and fish and it is probable that this dish was concocted on Thai lines by a Spanish sea captain hankering after the fleshpots.

INGREDIENTS

¼ cup vegetable oil	1 cup rice
1 onion, finely sliced	2 8-oz. cans tomato purée
½ chopped green pepper	1¾ cups hot water
½ lb. beef, finely minced	Generous dash of pepper

METHOD

Heat oil in a deep pan, then add onion, green pepper, beef and rice. Stir till lightly browned, then put in tomato purée and remaining ingredients, bring to the boil, cover with tight-fitting lid and simmer for 25 minutes.

Enough for four

THAI RICE AND COCONUT PUDDING

INGREDIENTS

1 cup rice	$\frac{1}{4}$ cup fresh or dried grated coconut
3 cups water	2 teaspoons grated lemon rind
1 teaspoon salt	$2\frac{1}{4}$ teaspoons ground cinnamon
1 cup sugar	1 cup milk

METHOD

Wash the rice well and put into a saucepan with salt and water. Bring to the boil and cook for 15 minutes, by which time the grains should be soft. Then drain away the water and return the rice to the saucepan. Add sugar, coconut and milk.

Mix well and cook over a low heat till the mixture is thick and creamy. This should take about 15 minutes. Keep stirring from time to time, else the mixture will stick to the pan.

Now add lemon rind, mix lightly, pour into a serving dish and sprinkle with cinnamon. This sweet may be served either hot or cold.

Enough for four

MR MANIT VARIN
EMBASSY OF THAILAND

INDONESIAN FOOD

INDONESIA consists of a necklace of islands, stretching from Kota Raja at the western tip of what was once called Sumatra, the same longitude as Rangoon, to the Moluccas, 2,000 miles away, which are as far east as Japan.

As it lies in the heart of the rice belt, which starts in the plains of India and terminates in Japan, the main food of the people is rice, which takes the place of both bread and potatoes. It is not surprising therefore, that most Indonesians eat rice three times a day, with fish, chicken, meat and vegetables prepared in a variety of ways.

Indonesians are poor in terms of pounds, shillings and pence and as there is water almost everywhere, fish also form an important part of their diet. Every village has a fish-pond and fish are also bred in the flooded rice fields. They are usually dried and salted and concocted into tasty dishes.

Everything grows profusely in the islands: almost all the vegetables one finds in Europe, and many more quite unknown to us. Much use is also made of beansprouts, bamboo shoots, plantains (bananas) and pineapples—and of course, the chilli, which adds a fiery touch to food. It may seem odd that people living on the equator should so love pungent dishes, but chillis make one sweat and perspiration cools the surface of the body.

Before trying your hand at Indonesian cookery it would be well to lay in a stock of dried chillis or chilli powder (or fresh chillis), garlic powder or fresh garlic, soya sauce, peanut butter or peanuts, bay leaves, paprika, ground ginger, ground coriander, and turmeric, all of which may be obtained in the stores listed at the end of this book. Where tamarind is mentioned, lemon juice may be used, though tamarind can also be obtained from most stores which sell Eastern spices.

Sauces

Piquancy is added to Indonesian food by sauces which accompany the various dishes; for instance, a peanut sauce is eaten with a dish called *sate*, which consists of small chunks of meat grilled on a skewer, like the *kababs* of Turkey, Iran, India and Pakistan. Another type of peanut sauce is eaten with a vegetable dish called *gado-gado*, in which the ingredients are chopped into a salad. Most common of all is chilli sauce, which can be obtained in Britain from almost any good grocer.

Little meat is eaten, and that made to go a long way by the addition of tasty sauces and vegetables. Nor is much milk produced and Indonesians, like Chinese, Japanese and Russians, drink tea without it. Milk, butter, cheese and meat are luxuries but so appetising is Indonesian food that the foreigner does not notice their absence.

RIJST-TAVEL

For centuries the Dutch ruled Indonesia and though their culinary ideas made little impact on the millions in the villages, their presence in the country inspired some notable dishes, of which *rijst-tavel* is the most renowned. The Dutch in the East were gourmands, equalled by few trenchermen, except perhaps the Germans. The quantity a large Hollander could stow away would make one's eyes pop. It was for them that an ingenious restaurateur in Java invented *rijst-tavel*, which quickly became popular wherever Dutch planters, sea-captains or civil servants ate.

First a mountainous plate of snowy rice was planted in front of the luncher or diner, which formed the foundation on which the dish was built. To this a leg or wing of grilled chicken was added. Then came a waiter bearing a large circular blue china tray divided into a dozen or more compartments containing bits of raw fish, dry, shredded or chopped; slices of duck, beef in tiny buttons, curries, chutneys, spices, chips of coconut.

This was followed by a procession of waiters, each with a different dish from which the eater helped himself: pickles, salted almonds, grated Parmesan, slices of egg, strips of fried banana, tender palm shoots, fiery *sambals* based on Indian cookery, fish-roe, sweetbreads, and mysterious concoctions which had no translatable name, such as liver buried in jars till it became deliquescent, and fish buried till it decayed. It may sound nauseating, but these concoctions stank no more than Limburger cheese, and killed no one. There were some thirty or forty different items and if one took only a small piece from each dish the total amount was alarming.

A good Dutch settler would attack his *rijst-tavel* and follow it with meat and salad, then dessert and coffee, and perhaps a cooling lager! Digestion took place during the hours of *siesta*.

People like that deserved to lose their Empire. They had learnt nothing from the downfall of the Romans who, if rumour is to be believed, pampered their stomachs not a little.

COCONUT MILK

This is used in many Indonesian recipes and bequeaths a lingering memory to all who have eaten rice or curries cooked in it. Coconut oil does not always appeal to European palates, so fat, vegetable oils or butter may be used. It may be made by the following method:

Pour a breakfast cup of boiling water over a third of a pound of desiccated coconut. When the water is cool, squeeze the coconut with the fingers till the liquid is thick and creamy. Thicker or thinner milk may be made by varying either the quantities of coconut, or water.

SAJUR BENING (vegetable soup)

INGREDIENTS

5 oz. spinach (or silver beet), chopped	2 cobs sweet corn
Soup stock—preferably meat stock. If no stock	1 clove crushed garlic
has been made, 2 soup cubes will do	2 tablespoons brown sugar
3 cups water	1 teaspoon salt

Slice the corn from the cob and cook in the stock with all the other ingredients, except the spinach, till tender. Add the spinach, mix and cook fast on a high heat, for 2 minutes. Most people in Britain cook spinach till it becomes mush, but fast cooking for only 2 or at most 3 minutes, renders it crisp, tender and palatable.

Serve hot either on its own or with boiled rice and pickle. Incidentally, in spring the young tender leaves of the common stinging nettle are every bit as tasty, if a trifle stronger than spinach.

Enough for four

BAKMI GORENG (Fried Noodles)

INGREDIENTS

Soup stock or 2 cubes bouillon

$\frac{1}{2}$ lb. cooked thin egg noodles

4 cabbage leaves, shredded

1 stalk celery, chopped (or silver beet stalk)

1 cup chopped meat or chicken

4 oz. butter or margarine

2 tablespoons fried onion flakes

2 carrots sliced lengthways

1 medium size tomato, chopped

$\frac{1}{4}$ tablespoon garlic powder or 1 teaspoon chopped garlic

$\frac{1}{2}$ teaspoon salt

$\frac{1}{4}$ teaspoon pepper

1 cup chopped prawns (if dried, soak before chopping)

A pinch of ground ginger

METHOD

Mix the spices with the chopped meat and prawns, then fry briskly in the butter for 5 minutes, stirring all the time. Cover the pan and cook till tender, giving an occasional stir. Now add the fresh vegetables and mix well. Finally, put in the noodles and stock, mix and cook for 2 minutes, then reduce the heat and simmer for 5 minutes.

Top with fried onion flakes and serve hot with rice.

This dish always tastes better if butter is used instead of margarine, and soup stock instead of bouillon cubes.

Enough for two

AJAM GORENG (Fried Chicken)

INGREDIENTS

1 frying chicken

1 teaspoon vinegar

$\frac{1}{4}$ teaspoon pepper

Peanut oil or other fat for frying

METHOD

Cut the chicken into pieces and marinade in the vinegar and spices for two hours. Fry in deep fat and serve with boiled rice and pickle or chutney.

Enough for four

SAJUR LODEH (Thick Vegetable Soup)

4 cups shredded vegetables (cabbage, beans, cauliflower, carrots, celery, bean sprouts, lima beans, silver beet stalks or any other vegetables in season).

INGREDIENTS

2 fresh green or red chillis

1½ cups stock

1½ cups coconut milk

½ cup chopped meat or chicken

1 laurel or bay leaf

1 small onion, chopped

Salt to taste

METHOD

First cook the spices and chopped meat in the stock. Then add vegetables and cook till they are soft. Add the coconut milk and stir occasionally to prevent the liquid from coagulating. When meat and vegetables are thoroughly cooked, serve hot.

Enough for four

SATE AJAM (Chicken Sate)

INGREDIENTS

3 cups of chicken, chopped into ½ inch cubes

½ teaspoon vinegar

20–25 skewers

½ cup water

¼ teaspoon of garlic powder or ½ teaspoon chopped garlic

METHOD

Put five cubes of chicken on each skewer. Mix the other ingredients and dip the skewered chicken into this mixture. Grill for about 15 minutes, turning and basting frequently.

Sauce

INGREDIENTS

4 tablespoons peanut butter

½ teaspoon chopped garlic

½ cup coconut milk

1 teaspoon ground chilli

1 teaspoon soya sauce

1 teaspoon brown sugar

1 bay leaf

Salt to taste

METHOD

Mix all the ingredients and cook on a low heat, stirring constantly till sauce is thick. Pour over sate and serve.
Enough for four

SAMBAL KETJAB (Hot Soya Sauce)

INGREDIENTS

½ cup soya sauce

1 tablespoon crushed chilli or 1 teaspoon ground chilli powder

¼ teaspoon crushed garlic

1 teaspoon molasses or Fowler's West Indian Black Treacle

METHOD

Mix all the ingredients thoroughly and add to main dishes as you would pickles and chutneys. This can also be eaten with plain boiled rice.

Enough for four

PILUS (Sweet Potato Balls—dessert)

Sweet potatoes are now sold by all shops that deal in curried spices and tropical food. The smaller potatoes are as large as long-type beetroots and may be mistaken for them, because they have a pink skin. Large sweet potatoes may weigh three or four pounds each, or more. They can be boiled or baked like the ordinary potato, though they are sweeter and somewhat stringier.

INGREDIENTS

2 cups boiled, mashed sweet potatoes	1½ tablespoons brown sugar
1 tablespoon flour	Oil or fat for frying
1 egg	

METHOD

Mix the potato, flour, sugar and egg thoroughly. Form into balls 1½ to 2 inches in diameter, fry in deep fat and drain. Serve hot or cold. An unusual sweet.

(Sweet potatoes are often sold off barrows in street markets.)

Enough for four

TAHU GORENG (Fried Soya Bean Cakes with Sauce)

INGREDIENTS

6 soya bean cake cubes	1 cup cooked bean sprouts
½ cup shredded cabbage	1 tablespoon fried onion flakes

METHOD

Soya bean cakes are obtainable from most Health Food Stores as well as from stores which sell exotic foods.

Fry the soya bean cakes in deep fat. Serve on a hot plate and cover with bean sprouts and cabbage and top with chopped celery and fried onion flakes. As no salt is mixed into the cubes, a little should be sprinkled over them when fried.

Sauce

INGREDIENTS

¼ cup soya sauce	¼ teaspoon ground chilli
1 tablespoon peanut butter	½ teaspoon ground or chopped garlic
3 tablespoons brown sugar	½ cup water

Mixed Vegetable Curry
(See recipe page 173)

METHOD
Fry garlic and peanut butter together, then add sugar, chilli and soya sauce. Pour in the water gradually and stir the whole time. When thick, pour into a bowl or jug and serve with the fried soya bean cakes.

Enough for four

UDANG BUMBU GORENG (Spiced Fried Shrimps)

INGREDIENTS

1 cup peeled fresh prawns split up the back	1 teaspoon brown sugar
1 teaspoon ground coriander	¼ teaspoon ground ginger
¼ teaspoon garlic powder	Salt to taste
1 teaspoon vinegar	¼ teaspoon laos powder or ¼ teaspoon ground ginger

METHOD
Mix all the spices together, add the prawns and marinade for several hours. (In summer—if there is any sun!—spread the mixture on a fine strainer and dry in the sun.) Then fry in deep fat till brown. This is not a dish in itself, but an adjunct to main dishes, or can be sprinkled over rice and eaten.

Enough for four

SAMBAL BADJAK (Fried Hot Pepper Sauce)

INGREDIENTS

2 tablespoons chopped onion	1 teaspoon salt
2 tablespoons crushed chilli	2 teaspoons brown sugar
3 tablespoons chopped tomato	1 teaspoon shrimp sauce
½ teaspoon vietsin or flavouring powder	2 tablespoons oil or butter
1 tablespoon crushed garlic	

METHOD
Fry the onion in oil or butter over a low heat, then add the garlic and continue frying till golden brown. Put in the remaining ingredients, give them a good stir and cook for 10 minutes, stirring occasionally to prevent sticking.

An alternative sauce may be made by adding half a cup of chopped fried prawns to the mixture.

Enough for four

KOLAK UBI (Sweet Potatoes in Sauce)

INGREDIENTS

2 cups diced sweet potatoes	1-inch stick of cinnamon
3 cups coconut milk	½ teaspoon ground cloves
½ cup brown sugar	A pinch of salt

215

METHOD
Cook all the ingredients together till the sweet potatoes are soft, then serve either hot or cold. Pumpkin or marrow may be substituted for sweet potato.

Enough for four

KRUPUK UDANG (Prawn Slices)

Prawn slices can be bought at Chinese grocery stores. Fry them with peanut oil or copha, also obtained at these stores. The oil must be at boiling point, so that the slices puff up the instant they are dropped into it. Turn them rapidly and remove before they change colour and serve with rice, sauce and pickles.

SAMBAL KELAPA (Hot Coconut Sauce)

INGREDIENTS

1 tablespoon crushed chilli	2 tablespoons shredded coconut
1 teaspoon shrimp sauce	$\frac{1}{2}$ teaspoon salt

METHOD
This needs no cooking. Place the ingredients in a mortar and crush and mix them thoroughly and serve with prawn slices and rice.

LUMPIA (Egg rolls)

For the Pancake mixture:

INGREDIENTS

2 eggs	2 cups flour
$\frac{3}{4}$ cup of water	Oil for frying

METHOD
Mix eggs, water and flour and beat till smooth, then fry in a little oil, using a little of the batter for each pancake, so that they are as thin as possible. When made, put the pancakes aside.

For the filling:

INGREDIENTS

Meat or fish: ham, pork, chicken, prawns, shrimps, or any combinations of these	1 or 2 cloves garlic
A little salt, pepper, brown sugar and vietsin or maggi	Vegetables: Cabbage, carrots, mushrooms, onions, bamboo shoots, etc.

METHOD
Vietsin can be bought in shops that sell Chinese groceries.

Chop the meat (or fish) and shred the vegetables, both very finely. Fry 2 medium size chopped onions, add the seasoning, chopped meat (or fish) and finally the vegetables. All

216

the vegetables mentioned need not be used, but just those of your choice. When tender but crisp, allow the vegetables to cool.

Put a little of this filling into the pancakes—the smaller the pancakes, the better. Moisten the edges and fold over, then fry each pancake in oil till brown. The oil should be bubbling as they go in. Drain and serve with chilli sauce or sweet and sour sauce. Lumpia make an excellent *hors d'œuvre*. What is more they can be made well in advance of any dinner you may be preparing and will keep in a refrigerator for days. But, before putting into a 'frige, coat each pancake lightly with flour to prevent sticking. Lumpia are even tastier eaten hot.   *Enough for four*

LODEH TERONG (Egg-plant Soup)

INGREDIENTS

1 medium size egg-plant or aubergene	1 teaspoon chopped garlic
1 cup coconut milk	2 tablespoons chopped prawns or meat
1 cup stock	$\frac{1}{2}$ teaspoon brown sugar
1 tablespoon chopped onion	1 bay leaf
1 tablespoon chopped green pepper (not to be confused with chilli)	1 medium tomato, chopped
	Oil for frying

METHOD

Peel and cut the aubergene into small pieces and cover with water. Fry the onions and garlic, then add the chopped meat (or prawns) and green pepper. Fry briskly for 3 minutes then put in tomatoes, sugar, bay leaf and, last of all, pour in the stock. Bring to the boil. Now slide in the aubergene and cook till tender.

Finally, pour in the coconut milk. Simmer till the milk thickens, stir and serve hot.

Enough for two

LAPIS DAGING

INGREDIENTS

1 lb. beef, sliced	2 whole peppers, finely chopped
$\frac{1}{2}$ teaspoon grated nutmeg	One $\frac{1}{2}$-inch stick of cinnamon
2 medium size tomatoes, chopped into small pieces	2 eggs
1 large onion, finely chopped	Butter or margarine for frying
1 tablespoon soya sauce	

METHOD

Mix and mash onions, tomatoes and spices and rub them well into both sides of the beef. Beat the eggs, pour them over the meat and turn the slices. Melt the fat in a large shallow pan with a well fitting lid and put the meat and the spices into the hot fat. Cover the pan, reduce the heat and turn the beef from time to time. If necessary add a little water to prevent the meat from burning. When the meat is tender, remove the stick of cinnamon and serve hot. To be eaten with rice and pickle.

Enough for two or three

INDONESIAN EMBASSY

KOREAN COOKERY

OWING to her geographical position it is inevitable that Korean cookery should be influenced by the Chinese and Japanese. There are certain dishes, in particular *kooks* (soups) which are indigenous. To Europeans they bear a closer resemblance to stews than soups, for they are rich, thick and satisfying. Though Korean waters teem with fish, their fish recipes are usually indistinguishable from those of Japan. They have few purely national dishes, but are great trenchermen.

KOREAN BEEF SOUP

INGREDIENTS

2 lb. shin of beef	1 teaspoon black pepper
1 lb. turnip	1 tablespoon sesame seed, ground
2 quarts cold water	1 tablespoon or more Korean red pepper, chopped
1 tablespoon soy bean sauce light	fine
1 teaspoon salt	1 tablespoon spring onion, chopped
1 teaspoon garlic, minced	$\frac{1}{8}$ teaspoon MSG

METHOD

Prepare the meat, removing any fat. Place in a saucepan and add the water and allow to stand for half an hour. Then bring to the boil for a few minutes and put in the turnip. Skim well, add black pepper, keep the lid on the pan and simmer for 3 hours. Now take out the meat, mix with soy sauce light, garlic, sesame seed, spring onion, Korean red pepper (dry) and MSG and allow to stand for ten minutes. Finally, put the meat and the mixed ingredients into a casserole and pour the soup over it. Serve hot.

Enough for four

BULKOKO (Korean Fire Meat)

INGREDIENTS

8 oz. best fillet of beef (thin slices)	$\frac{1}{4}$ teaspoon salt or $\frac{1}{4}$ teaspoon sugar
1 tablespoon spring onion, or leek, minced	$\frac{1}{2}$ teaspoon garlic
2 oz. Japanese soy sauce light (Kikkoman)	1 tablespoon sesame oil
4 drops Tabasco	1 tablespoon shallots, finely chopped

Sauce Ingredients

¼ teaspoon salt	2 oz. Japanese soy sauce light (Kikkoman)
½ teaspoon red pepper powder	¼ teaspoon sugar
¼ teaspoon minced spring onion	1 teaspoon sesame seed
1 tablespoon sesame oil	½ teaspoon garlic
1 teaspoon bean paste (*mien chiang*)	

METHOD

Slice and pound the beef lightly, season with spring onion, sugar or salt, soy sauce light, sesame oil, shallot, garlic and Tabasco for 3–4 hours.

Mix the sauce ingredients thoroughly, place the Korean Roast Beef Stove on the table and brush with a little oil. Put the beef into the stove piece by piece, and when cooked, dip into the sauce and eat.

If you don't have a Korean Roasting Pot, use a thick cast iron frying pan that will take half a cup of hot peanut oil. Into this the beef slices are dipped, cooked, taken out and eaten piping hot. Pork may be cooked in the same way.

Enough for four

HONG KONG AND CHINA GAS CO.

KEEN CHEE (Vegetable Pickle)

INGREDIENTS

6 cucumbers	3 teaspoons ginger, finely chopped
2 tablespoons salt (or to taste)	¾ cup of water
2 spring onions, chopped	1 tablespoon soy sauce light
3 cloves garlic, minced	1 teaspoon monosodium glutamate (MSG)
2 teaspoons Korean dry red pepper	

METHOD

Scrub the cucumbers thoroughly. Cut in half lengthwise, then into pieces ½ inch thick. Sprinkle with one teaspoon of salt and set aside for 30 minutes. Wash and drain cucumbers. Chop spring onions coarsely. Add garlic, red pepper, ginger, soy sauce light, MSG and remaining salt. Combine these ingredients with cucumbers and place in a bowl. Add the water and stir. Cover and place in a warm spot. Marinade for at least 48 hours, though it may take several days for the ingredients to become pickled if the weather is cool. To prevent the smell of pickle from permeating the entire house, place in one corner of the kitchen and cover with several layers of cloth. Chill and serve cold as a relish.

Cabbage, Tientsin cabbage or turnip can be used instead of cucumber.

Enough for four

HONG KONG AND CHINA GAS CO.

BEEF STEW KOREAN STYLE

INGREDIENTS

2 lb. good stewing beef cut into 3-inch strips	1 teaspoon MSG
1 cup Japanese soy sauce (Kikkoman)	6 green peppers or more, to taste
2 stalks spring onions	A sprinkle of salt and a dash of sugar

METHOD

Place the beef, Japanese soy sauce, salt, spring onions, green peppers, sugar and MSG in a pot and bring to the boil. Simmer steadily for 4 hours. Do not use any water as sufficient liquid will be produced by the ingredients to give the dish its special flavour.

Enough for four

HONG KONG AND CHINA GAS CO.

CHICKEN STEW KOREAN STYLE

INGREDIENTS

1 fat chicken cut into pieces	2 tablespoons Korean red pepper (dry)
2 tablespoons sesame oil	$\frac{1}{2}$ head of garlic, minced
4 tablespoons Japanese soy sauce (Kikkoman)	1 teaspoon MSG
2 spring onion stalks, chopped	Salt to taste

METHOD

Place the chicken in a big bowl and season with sesame oil, Japanese soy sauce, salt, spring onions, Korean red pepper, garlic and MSG. Mix well and let the mixture stand for 2 hours.

Then place the chicken and ingredients in a thick pot and simmer steadily for 2 hours. Do not add water, for the reason stated in the previous recipe.

Enough for four

KOREAN STYLE DUMPLING

INGREDIENTS

1 chicken; use drumsticks and breast-meat for filling; the remainder for stock	A dash of MSG 1 tablespoon sesame oil
2 catties* bean sprout, boiled, drained of water and chopped fine	1 teaspoon Korean chilli powder—(or less if too pungent)
6 cubes of bean curd, boiled and drained	A sprinkle of salt and pepper
$\frac{1}{2}$ catty shrimps, shelled and minced	1 tablespoon soy sauce light

Mix these ingredients together thoroughly.

* 1 catty = $1\frac{1}{3}$ lb.

Ingredients for wrapping

1 catty* flour   1½ cups cold water

METHOD

Mix the flour with boiling water to make a soft dough. Knead well, sprinkle with dry flour and roll into a long sausage. Pinch off small pieces of uniform size, and with a small rolling pin roll out each piece into a circular shape about 3 inches in diameter, taking care to leave the centre thicker than the edges.

Place a teaspoon of the filling mixture in the middle of each circular piece of dough. Fold over to make a semi-circle, then press the opposite edges with the fingers and you have what the Chinese call *Chio Tzu*. Place these little dumplings on a damp cloth in a steamer, and steam for 10 minutes.

Enough for four

MR B. H. TELFER
HONG KONG AND CHINA GAS CO.

SOOKJU-NAMUL

INGREDIENTS

4 bags beanshoots   A little cooking oil
Salt and MSG to taste   2 cups chopped spring onion or common onion

METHOD

Fry the ingredients in a large pan with a small quantity of cooking oil and remove while the beans are still crunch. A very palatable and quickly made supper dish.

Enough for fifteen

MR KIRSTY SALVESEN
SECRETARY TO THE KOREAN EMBASSY, LONDON

* 1 catty=1⅓ lb.

CHINESE FOOD

MY interest in Chinese food was first stimulated when in Calcutta I suffered from the traditional disease of the normal active schoolboy—chronic hunger.

Our entire pocket money, the equivalent of fivepence a week (we were not allowed more) was spent on food, bought as we straddled the school wall and haggled with passing vendors—another forbidden ploy. We stuffed on *bhagias, piagees, fallowries, kut-kutti-goalies, spiced gram, aam-saat* (mango-juice solidified), hunks of *goor* (jaggery), and when ravenous and down to the last *anna* (penny), *suttoo*, a pea flour which, when mixed with cane sugar, packed the empty crevices.

When affluent and rupees had passed between some indulgent relative or friend and ourselves, a nocturnal expedition would be organized to The Chinese Restaurant in Blackburn Lane. To be caught climbing out of school at night meant a public flogging, for ours was a truly Christian institution where the rod was never spared for fear of spoiling the child; but so magnetic was the attraction that we braved even this.

Once in the Promised Land, *chow* would be parcelled in greaseproof paper, stuffed into pillowcases or haversacks and conveyed to school through much-forbidden terrain in stealthy haste. Then in the gloom of our immense vaulted dormitories we would gorge to our fill and then replete fall into contented slumber on our iron-sheeted beds, for we slept on iron sheets (not mattresses), covered with a cotton overlay.

When friends and relatives invited us out The Chinese Restaurant was favoured above Vado's, Peliti's or any other caravanserai where the food made one's mouth water.

Chinese Food Never Palls

Since then I have sampled many kinds of Chinese food but my interest in it has never waned. As with Cleopatra, age cannot wither or custom stale its infinite variety.

Chinese restaurants have sprung up in Britain like mushrooms after rain, and those who haven't visited them must not be put off by tales about *bêche-de-mer* (sea slugs, which incidentally, are a delicacy), bird's nest soup, eggs a hundred years old, sharks' fins, wild ducks' feet, pigs' feet in honey, cocks' combs, snakes, frogs, dogs and almost anything that runs, swims or flies. They're all tasty if you know how to prepare them. And why not? Professor F. S. Bodenheimer of the Hebrew University, Jerusalem, recently published a work called *Insects as Human Food* in which he refers to a book by V. M. Holt, in the University Library at Oxford, in which the author says: 'Cheese-mites are freely eaten by many persons "a part of the cheese". In the same way cabbage worms are only part of the cabbage,' and relates how delicious are grasshoppers, cock-chafers and wasp grubs. A menu he gives for a gentleman's dinner consists of: snail soup, fried soles with woodlice sauce, curried cockchafers, fricassee of chicken with chrysalids, boiled neck of mutton with wireworm sauce, duckling with green peas, cauliflower garnished with caterpillars, and moths on toast.

Chow and Chop-Suey

The word *chow* is an abbreviation of *chow-chow* and refers to an assortment of food; a mixture. As for *chop suey;* there isn't any Chinese dish of that name. Peh der Chen relates in *Honorable and Peculiar Ways* that when the first Chinese ambassador to America was dining, reporters swarmed into the room, disturbing his privacy, to ask what he was eating. He was so annoyed that he snapped: 'Chop suey!' meaning 'dirty mixed fragments'. Whatever else it may be *chop suey* is not the Chinese national dish.

Colonel E. T. Etherton, who was a puisne judge in China in the bad old days of the Treaty Ports, told me that he was once guest of honour at a banquet in Manchuria where the *pièce-de-résistance* was a boiled sheep's eye. As Chief Guest, he was expected to set the ball rolling by swallowing it—like an oyster. Such delicacies, however, are for the gourmet and the recipes given here are for the average housewife with no aspirations towards a *cordon bleu*.

Rice is the Basis of Chinese Food

Like all food in the Far East, Chinese dishes revolve around rice. But there the resemblance to Indian food, for instance, ends. No violently pungent spices are used and the preparation is quite different. Chinese cuisine has a variety of sauces and soups which Indian lacks. The vegetables are chopped finely and cooked rapidly at high temperature, thus retaining most of the valuable vitamin C.

The Ubiquitous Soya Bean

The Chinese make surprising use of the soya bean. A traveller who accepted the hospitality of a Buddhist monk, wrote: 'The feast is worthy of host and guest. First from the kitchen temple spreads the aroma of dishes rich and spiced. They are followed by fish, done to a turn. A sharp sauce accompanies it. A chicken comes after it, swimming in golden chicken soup. Vegetables and delicate spices are on every hand. Is this the way, the guest asks himself, that the Buddhist monks preserve their vows of abstinence from fish and fowl? He tastes the fish, the sauce, the chicken, and his unworthy suspicions vanish. They are all beans; the fish, like the chicken, is moulded out of bean curd. The skilled cook of the monastry is master of a thousand tastes and flavours and colours. He can make soya bean look like anything and very nearly taste like it. A meal of beans, and beans alone can be had, with every dish different and none of them tiresome. What other vegetable can do as much?'

Both the Indian peasant and the Chinese peasant are poor. The first is under-nourished because he has so many tabus and does not get enough protein (body building food). The Chinese peasant is a tough resilient specimen, though his food costs no more than the Indian diet. His soya bean is richer in protein than any food, including flesh and fish. An ounce of lean mutton contains 5.97 grams of protein; fish 5.50; chicken 6.74; egg 3.79; wheat 3.90, dried peas 1.58, soya bean 9.60. And the calories in these foods are 43, 32, 30, 42, 28 and 119.

223

Major-General Sir Robert McCarrison, I.M.S., said that if the soya bean were to become the staple food of India her nutritional problems would vanish, and Dr McCollum of Johns Hopkins University, stated that if Americans tempered their food with soya beans there would be a drop of at least 20 per cent in the mortality rate, because it alkalinises the blood and helps to prevent hardening of the arteries and the advent of senility in middle age.

Spices and Flavourings

Foods peculiar to Chinese cooking are pea and bean sprouts, bean curd, dried mushrooms and fungi, bamboo shoots, snow peas or *mang tout*. Taste powders are used sparingly to enhance the natural flavours of ingredients, to stimulate appetite and aid digestion. The *Five Spices of Fragrance* or *Ngung Heung* which can be bought at any Chinese grocery store are also used. The five can be obtained separately. They are:

(1) Star Anise (Illicium Anisatum) called *Pa Chiao* or *Baat Gok,* a dark brown fruit shaped like an eight-pointed star, about an inch in diameter. At the tip of each star is a tiny seed which, when crushed produces a fragrant volatile oil. Star Anise is used in 'red cooking', and is sold in powdered form.

(2) *Wu Heung* or fennel (Foeniculum Vulgare); pale green eliptical seeds.

(3) *Hua Chian* or Chinese Anise-pepper (Xanthoxlum Piperitum); small reddish seeds, popular for fish.

(4) *Ding Heung* (Jambosa Caryophyllus); dark brown cloves from which a volatile oil is produced.

(5) *Yook Gwey* (Cinnamonum Assia); the Chinese cinnamon; coarser and more fragrant than the Ceylon variety.

MRS M. R. LAERUM

Sauces

Three sauces are widely used: Soy sauce, Oyster sauce and *Hoi Sin*. Many types of soy sauce are used, the most popular in Britain being Amoy Soy sauce. Oyster sauce, though an extract of oysters, is not fishy and may be used for meat and vegetables. *Hoi Sin* resembles ketchup, is used for cooking as well as a dip and popular with dishes such as Peking Roast Duck or Shell Fish. It is red, thick and tasty and is sold in cans.

MRS M. R. LAERUM

BEAN CURD

Because bean curd forms the bases of so many Chinese dishes it is as well to know how to make it. All that is needed is a quart (or less) of yellow beans. Either add a little water and grind them into paste, or put them through a coffee grinder and mix them into a paste with water. Put the paste into a pan and boil for an hour. Then add a quantity of *ke lao* (gelatine made from seaweed; agar-agar or kelp will do) and the bean curd will coagulate and settle on the bottom of the pan.

Strain off the water, put the curd in a cheese cloth and press it between boards. When solid, cut into squares ready for use.

When needed, cut as much as you want into half-inch cubes, soak in hot water for 10 minutes, fry in oil or fat and eat while hot with onions, leeks, chives or garlic sprinkled on it.

BEAN SPROUTS

Bean sprouts are universally used by the Chinese especially in the winter months when fresh vegetables are not available. They are not only tasty but an excellent source of vitamin C.

Soak a quart of beans in a bowl for 24 hours, then strain and put a cover on the beans, with a weight on top to press them down. Put the bowl in a warm place, such as an airing cupboard or the warmest corner of the kitchen. Cover with tepid water for half an hour every day, then strain. Soon the beans will sprout. When the sprouts are an inch long they are ready for use.

Bring a pan of water to the boil, then turn off the heat and put in the beans. When cool, take out as many beans as you need, shell them, soak the sprouts for 10 minutes, add oil, vinegar and a little chopped onion. Serve hot or cold, with meat, fish, bean curd or vegetables.

MIEN-TIAO (Noodles)

1 lb of any kind of flour: wheat, bean, pea, millet or soya, add water and mix it into dough, then roll out to about $\frac{1}{8}$ inch thick. Fold the dough; then fold it again and again till the pile is about 3 inches wide. Cut into fine strips.

Bring a pan of water to the boil and drop the strips in. The water will go off the boil; but as soon as it comes to the boil again, take them out.

Put the noodles into individual bowls and add salt, vinegar, oil and finely chopped vegetables—or meat.

Enough for four

BIRD'S NEST SOUP

This is made from the nests of swallows who build their homes in caves on the islands in the China Seas and the South Seas of the Pacific. When the nests are collected the tiny feathers, which adhere to the gelatinous substances binding the twigs together, are removed.

Because the task of collecting these nests involves great risk, they have always been costly and the Chinese regard this soup as a luxury to be served at banquets and important functions. Both Bird's Nest Soup and Shark's Fin Soup are considered health foods as they are easily digestible and nutritious. Nests are sold either whole or in pieces, a half-ounce piece being sufficient for six people. Incidentally, the nest itself is tasteless, flavour being obtained from the chicken stock which accompanies it.

INGREDIENTS

$\frac{1}{2}$ oz. bird's nest	2 slices smoked ham, finely chopped
3 pints chicken stock	Salt and pepper to taste
2 pieces chicken-breast, finely chopped	

225

METHOD
Soak the bird's nest in 1 pint of boiling water overnight, then drain away the water. Place the chicken stock in a soup pot, add chopped chicken-breast and the soft bird's nest, pepper and salt, and simmer for about 40 minutes.

When serving, sprinkle a little chopped ham over each bowl of soup.

Enough for six

MRS M. R. LAERUM
243 CREIGHTON AVENUE
EAST FINCHLEY
LONDON N.2

CHOW MEIN (Fried Noodles)

INGREDIENTS

½ lb. Chinese egg noodles	3 tablespoons cooking oil or lard
½ lb. pork, shredded	3 tablespoons stock, preferably pork
3 small onions or shallots, thinly sliced	2 hard boiled eggs, sliced
5 dried Chinese mushrooms, soaked and sliced, or 5	4–6 pints of water
medium size fresh mushrooms	Salt and pepper to taste
2 tablespoons soy sauce	

METHOD
Bring the water to the boil in a saucepan 8–9 inches in diameter. Add salt. Drop in the noodles and continue to boil till noodles are tender and float to the surface. Strain in a colander, pour cold water over the noodles and set them aside to drain.

Fry the sliced onions in a tablespoon of oil or lard till the colour starts to change. Now lower the heat and sauté the pork and mushrooms in the pan with the onions, for 10 minutes and set aside. Add salt and pepper.

Put the remainder of the fat into the pan used for boiling the noodles and when simmering, lower heat, add drained noodles and soy sauce, stir for 5 minutes, put in pork mixture and cook for a few minutes more. Now add stock and stir to prevent sticking. Serve hot, garnished with sliced boiled eggs.

Instead of pork you can use a cup of chopped chicken and ham; or one cup chopped pieces of chicken liver, one cup pea sprouts and shredded omelette; or one cup crab meat, one cup shredded or sliced bamboo shoots, or sliced bean curd.

Noodles are a staple food in Northern China, but in Southern and Central China they form snacks or supper dishes.

Enough for four

MRS M. R. LAERUM

CHOP SUEY (Odds and Ends)

Though virtually unknown to the Chinese housewife, this dish which originated in the United States, is popular in restaurants throughout the Far East. It is both appetising and easy to prepare.

INGREDIENTS

1 lb. shredded pork	2 cups chicken or pork stock
1 cup pea or bean sprouts	6 water chestnuts, shredded, (optional)
2 cups shredded celery stalks	2 tablespoons soy sauce
1 cup chopped onions	3 tablespoons cooking oil or lard
8 small mushrooms, shredded	Salt and pepper to taste

METHOD

Bring the fat to a high heat in the pan and sauté the pork for a couple of minutes; then lower heat and add onions, celery, mushrooms, water chestnuts and soy sauce and sauté for 5 minutes, stirring all the time. Add stock and the pea or bean sprouts, mix well, cover the pan and simmer for 10 minutes. Add salt and pepper, mix well and serve in soup bowls.

Chop suey can be varied by adding a thickening made by mixing into a paste a teaspoon of cornflour and a little water or stock. Mix well, stir in and cook for a couple of minutes. Garnish with sliced hard-boiled eggs and serve.

Beef, lamb or chicken can be substituted for pork, and any vegetables added. It's an an odds and ends dish.

White fish and fish stock may be used instead of pork and pork stock, and oyster sauce instead of soy. 2 or 3 slices of finely chopped ginger, or powdered ginger may be added.

Chop suey may be made entirely of vegetables such as potatoes, carrots, string beans, red and green peppers Julienned, and instead of meat stock, vegetable water to which Marmite or similar flavouring is added.

MRS M. R. LAERUM *Enough for four*

EGG FOO YONG (Chinese Omelette)

INGREDIENTS

4 eggs	¼ cup chopped onions
1 cup chopped cooked meat or fish—chicken, pork, crab or shrimps	1 tablespoon soy sauce
	2 tablespoons cooking oil
1 breakfast cup pea or bean sprouts	1 teaspoon salt
½ cup chopped fresh mushrooms	¼ teaspoon pepper
½ cup chopped celery stalk	¼ teaspoon monosodium glutamate, if desired

METHOD

Fry onions, celery and mushrooms over a high heat in one tablespoon of oil; then lower heat, add sprouts, cooked meat, soy sauce, a little salt and pepper, continue cooking and stirring for a few minutes. Put aside to cool.

Beat eggs and pour the cooled mixture into it, folding well.

Use an omelette pan about 5 inches in diameter, put in 2 teaspoons of oil, heat gradually, and when very hot use a ladle and put in a quarter of the egg-and-meat mixture. As soon as it shrinks from the sides of the pan and starts to brown at the bottom, turn, using a spatula. Fry again for a minute or two, then loosen edges and turn into a *warm* dish. Make three more and serve hot, or with a sauce made from the following ingredients:

INGREDIENTS

½ cup stock	1 tablespoon cornflour
1 teaspoon soy sauce	¼ teaspoon MSG
Salt and pepper	(mono-sodium glutamate)

METHOD

Put the stock in a pan on medium heat. Make a smooth paste with cornflour and a little stock, pour into the pan, stir rapidly and add soy sauce, MSG and seasoning. Stir, bring to the boil, remove and serve separately, and pour over the omelettes.

Enough for four

MRS M. R. LAERUM

SWEET AND SOUR SPARE RIBS

INGREDIENTS

1½ spare ribs cut into about 20 lengths, with ample meat on the bones	1 tablespoon cornflour
	2 small slices ginger, finely minced
2 tablespoons soy sauce	1 tablespoon sherry
1 tablespoon good vinegar	3 tablespoons cooking oil
1 teaspoon brown sugar	Some mixed prepared vegetables
1 clove garlic, well crushed	Salt and pepper to taste

METHOD

Chop the spare ribs into 1½ inch lengths and soak for 2 hours in a marinade of soy sauce, vinegar, sugar, sherry, garlic and ginger, with salt and pepper to taste. After 2 hours remove the ribs, dredge with cornflour and fry or roast.

To fry, heat the oil until very hot and fry for 10 minutes till well done. Remove and keep warm in a large dish.

To roast, place the ribs in a roasting pan and pour a little of the marinade and oil over them. Place the pan in the middle shelf of a moderate oven (350°F.) and roast for 30 minutes. Turn and baste from time to time, with remaining marinade and oil, if necessary. Serve in the same way as fried ribs, with vegetables.

Use vegetables in season: leeks, carrots, sweet peppers or Chinese vegetables, sliced, shredded or diced; enough to fill three breakfast cups. Put them into the frying pan after the spare ribs have been removed and sauté *quickly* till they are crisp, but not overdone. Remove and place them in the serving dish beside the spare ribs.

Instead of spare ribs you may use (1) 1½ .lb. lean pork—fillet or tenderloin—cut into 1½-inch pieces (2) pork balls with sauté green and red peppers and pineapple chunks (3) 1½ lb. plaice, halibut or cod, whole or cut into large pieces and fried in batter and garnished with chopped parsley.

Enough for four

SWEET AND SOUR SAUCE

INGREDIENTS

2 tablespoons soy sauce

1 tablespoon vinegar

1 tablespoon sugar or honey

½ breakfast cup hot water or stock

1 teaspoon minced ginger

½ teaspoon Accent or other taste powder

1 clove garlic, minced

2 tablespoons cornflour

1 teaspoon cooking oil

½ teaspoon salt

½ teaspoon pepper

METHOD

Make a smooth paste with cornflour, vinegar and soy sauce. Place over a moderate heat in a saucepan, add sugar, ginger and garlic and stir well. Slowly pour in the hot water or stock, stir till the mixture thickens and flavour with salt, pepper and Accent or taste powder.

Remove from the heat and stir in a teaspoon of oil to give it a glaze. This sauce may be used for any sweet and sour dish of meat, fish, fowl or vegetables and may be stored in the 'frige for use when needed.

Enough for four

FRIED PRAWNS WITH CHILLI SAUCE

INGREDIENTS

1 lb. prawns

2 eggs beaten slightly

½ teaspoon salt

A dash of pepper

A dash of MSG

Oil for deep frying

2 tablespoons flour

1 tablespoon starch

1 teaspoon soy sauce light

1 teaspoon Chinese wine

Sauce Ingredients:

1 tablespoon lard

1 clove garlic, sliced

6 slices of Pekin spring onion

2 tablespoons Chinese wine sauce

A dash of soy sauce dark

3–4 thin slices of ginger

¼ teaspoon starch mixed with ½ teaspoon cold gravy stock

2 dry red chillis

2 teaspoons sugar

1 teaspoon soy sauce light

A dash of MSG

METHOD

Mix the tablespoon of starch with a little water to form a thin paste. Remove shells and heads of prawns and black veins. Wash and dry thoroughly and set aside. Season with salt, Chinese wine, soy sauce light, MSG* and pepper, then sprinkle flour on top, add egg and 1 tablespoon of starch.

* Monosodium Glutamate.

229

Heat oil and deep fry for a few seconds; then remove from oil and drain.

Mix sauce ingredients, put into the hot oil and mix. When the mixture thickens, add prawns. Cook on a high heat and stir constantly.

Enough for four

CHINESE WINE SAUCE

To make one catty† of Chinese wine sauce, use one catty of Chinese wine, 2 tablespoons Chinese wine cake, 1 teaspoon flower seasoning, 2 teaspoons sugar, ½ teaspoon salt, soak for a few hours, then sift three times and add 1 teaspoon MSG.

MR B. H. TELFER

HONG KONG AND CHINA GAS CO.

HUNG SHAO NIU JOU (Stewed Shin of Beef)

INGREDIENTS

2 lb. shin beef	Salt and pepper to taste
1 stalk spring onion cut into three	1 large slice ginger
4 tablespoons soy sauce dark	1 clove garlic
2 tablespoons Chinese wine	1 teaspoon sesame oil
2 teaspoons sugar	2 teaspoons star anise
½ teaspoon Faah Jui-Anise pepper	1 tablespoon Chinese brown vinegar

METHOD

Heat oil, add ginger, onion and garlic, fry till brown and remove. Put in the beef, fry for 2 or 3 minutes, then add all the above ingredients and fry for a few minutes.

Turn into a deep saucepan, pour in sufficient water to cover the beef and bring to the boil. Remove from heat, skim, and simmer for 3 hours. Slice and serve with gravy.

Enough for four

STEWED CHESTNUT CHICKEN

INGREDIENTS

1 spring chicken cut into 1½-inch pieces, including bone	2 slices ginger
1 stalk spring onion, chopped	1 teaspoon salt
1 lb. chestnuts, boiled and shelled	1 teaspoon sugar
3 tablespoons soy sauce dark	3 tablespoons oil
2 tablespoons Chinese wine	

† One catty = 1⅓ lb.

METHOD

Heat the oil and fry ginger and spring onion. Then add the chicken and when the chicken changes colour, add salt, sugar, soy sauce dark, and wine. Cover and simmer for 10 minutes; then add half a cup of water and simmer for 30 minutes. Put in chestnuts, simmer for 15 minutes more and serve hot.

As chestnuts are sweet, boil them separately and drain off the water before adding them, otherwise the dish will be too sweet.

Enough for four

MR B. H. TELFER
HONG KONG AND CHINA GAS CO.

SHIH TZU T'OU (Lion's Head)

This is one version of Lion's Head, a Cantonese speciality, popular at Labour Day celebrations.

INGREDIENTS

2 lb. cabbage	2 lb. tenderloin of pork
1 cup crab meat (optional)	10 small cooked mushrooms, chopped fine
1 cup finely chopped onions	1 egg, well beaten
3 cups good pork stock	1 tablespoon cornflour
1 teaspoon finely chopped ginger	3 tablespoons soy sauce
1 tablespoon pork fat (lard)	3 tablespoons cooking oil
Salt and pepper to taste	

METHOD

Bone the pork and use the bones (with chicken bones, if available) to make the stock.

Mince very finely, or grind, the pork, then place it in a bowl with onions, ginger, mushroom, beaten egg, cornflour, soy sauce and one tablespoon of oil. Mix well and allow it to stand for at least 30 minutes, giving it an occasional stir in that time.

Remove the outer coarse leaves of the cabbage and cut it into 16 sections, or remove each leaf carefully, but leave the centre, which should be sliced.

Grease a casserole with lard or pork fat and line the bottom and sides with cabbage leaves, or fill with about 10 sections of cut cabbage. Sprinkle with salt and pepper and set aside.

Now make the meat balls. Stir the mixture well and shape four large, or eight small meat balls. Then heat 2 tablespoons of oil and sauté the meat balls in a frying pan, browning them all over. Remove from the pan, place them neatly over the cabbage, and place the remaining sections of cabbage on top of the meat balls.

Add three cups of stock to bring the level of the liquid halfway up the casserole, and cook slowly (275°F.) for 2 hours. Serve hot, with small bowls of steamed or boiled rice.

Enough for four

MRS M. R. LAERUM

HUN T'UN (Chinese Ravioli)

INGREDIENTS

½ lb. pork (minced)   Soy sauce light

½ lb. cooked spinach (finely chopped)   1 teaspoon sesame oil

1 stalk spring onion (finely chopped)   1 teaspoon Chinese wine

1 slice ginger (finely chopped)   1 dash MSG

1 tablespoon stock

Mix the ingredients thoroughly in a bowl.

Ingredients for wrapping: (Can be bought ready-made)

1 cup flour   A little starch

2 eggs

METHOD

Mix the ingredients well and knead into a dough. Sprinkle cornflour on a rolling board and roll out the dough till very thin and about 20 inches wide. Cut into strips. Place the strips one on top of the other and cut them into squares.

In the middle of each piece of dough place half a teaspoon of the filling, then fold diagonally to make a triangle. Join the extreme ends together by brushing with egg. The amount of filling given in this recipe should be sufficient for 50 or 60 ravioli. Put into boiling water and cook and when ready, serve with good stock.

Enough for four

MR B. H. TELFER
HONG KONG AND CHINA GAS CO.

JAPANESE FOOD

THE Japanese are an artistic race who don't regard edibles merely as fillers. Food must have an aesthetic appeal. The foundation of every *gohan* (meal) is boiled rice, of which there are many varieties.

They also make imaginative use of the many kinds of potatoes, especially sweet potatoes, which may be bought in British markets.

Seaweed
Before the war the only kind of seaweed obtainable in Britain was agar-agar, used mainly in hospitals for germ culture, and by a few vegetarians for making jellies and mixing into soups. It came from Japan, where many kinds of seaweed are eaten: *nori* (seasoned laver like that found off the Welsh coast); *kombu* (kelp, which is made into tablets); *wakame* (lobe-shaped undaria); and *hijiki* (spindle-shaped bladder leaf, like bladderwrack—*Fucus Vesiculosus*—a variety of kelp), all rich in minerals, especially iodine.

All Japanese food is chopped small so that it may be dealt with easily with chopsticks or a fork. Vegetables are cooked rapidly on a high heat for a few minutes, till parboiled, remaining crisp and succulent. Soggy cabbage cooked for hours in soda, as in Britain, till the life has been boiled out of it, and smelling of drains, would not be countenanced for a moment in Japan.

The Soya Bean
Though a native of China, the soya bean has been adopted by the Japanese. When they invaded Manchuria they realized the value of the soya bean and it was this crop that put Manchuria on the industrial map. As long ago as 1930 she produced 5,200,000 tons of soya beans, most of which was exported to Japan to feed her rapidly expanding population.

From the bean they produced vegetable milk, flour for bread, margarine, cheese, a coffee substitute, infants' food, custard powder and salad oil. The pressed cake was used as cattle feed and some of the oil for lighting as well as soap, paint, enamel, varnish, printing ink, rubber substitute, and glycerine for high explosives. But for the Manchurian soya bean, Japan would not have been able to go to war.

Hiya-Yakko (Cold tofu—bean curd)
Soya beans are immersed in water for from 10 to 24 hours, according to the season, for when young they are softer than when old. The soaked beans are strained and then pulped in stone grinders, after which the liquid is filtered away through cotton cloths. The residue is used as pig or cattle feed. A little water is added to the liquid, which is then heated over a slow fire. Then the heated liquid is poured into a perforated wooden tub, lined with cotton cloths. The remaining curd serves as a foundation for many dishes.

233

Somen

Somen is an under-sized *udon* (noodle), but because of the process by which it is made, is much whiter and finer. Somen is eaten cold in summer in the same way as the cold *soba*, and is often added to soups, together with vegetables, meat and fish.

It isn't necessary to know how to make *tofu* and somen for both can be bought; the information is given as a matter of interest.

Tempura

The *tempura* is a feature of Japanese cooking, the word being a relic of the visit of Portuguese priests to Japan centuries ago. They planted the seed of Christianity and left their mark on the country. *Tempura* is derived from the Latin *temporarious*, relating to time, and refers to the fast days on which no meat was eaten.

There are innumerable *tempura*, once vegetarian in character, though with the passage of time fish, shell fish, beef, mutton and pork have insinuated themselves into the recipes.

GLOSSARY

Aji-no-moto: Monosodium glutamate. A seasoning invented in America, often called 'taste powder', and sold under various brand names. A pinch added to most cooking develops the natural flavour of the ingredients—or so the Americans say. If food is made with the best available materials, however, and conservatively cooked, there is no need for aji-no-moto, which plays no part in the ancient Japanese cuisine.

Bancha: An egg custard prepared with meat or sea food, vegetables and *dashi*.

Daikon: A large white radish, usually carrot-shaped.

Dashi: A broth prepared by steeping *kombu* and *katsoubushi* in hot water. A mild fish stock or bouillon used in soups and as the foundation of many dishes.

Kaguto-age: Literally, 'fried armour'. The 'armour' usually refers to a shell in which the ingredients are fried.

Katsoubushi: Dried bonito, shaved or flaked and used for flavouring.

Kombu: A species of kelp or seaweed called tangle.

Matsutake: *Aramellaria edodes*. A species of mushroom.

Sake: A Japanese rice wine made from white rice, malt mold and water. Usually drunk warm and often used in cooking.

Sancho: *Kanthoxylum piperitum*. A variety of Japanese pepper.

Sachimi: Raw seafood.

Shiitake: *Cortinellis shiitake*. A Japanese mushroom cultivated in oak logs, like the Oyster mushroom (Pleurotus ostreatus) found growing on tree trunks in British woods—usually on fallen trees and stumps. The Oyster mushroom is excellent, cut into pieces and stewed or fried with a coating of egg and crumbs or butter, and, if Shiitake cannot be obtained, is a good substitute.

Shioyaki: 'Salt broiling'.

Shirataki: Translucent threads of gelatinous starch extracted from a root plant.

Shoyu: Soy or soya sauce; a flavouring made from wheat, soya beans and salt.

Sukiyaki: Beef, vegetables and other ingredients cooked in *shoyu*, sake and sugar.

MRS R. N. GOWAN, JAPANESE EMBASSY

SUKIYAKI

These recipes have been selected because they appeal most strongly to Europeans, particularly Americans. With Americans sukiyaki is the most popular of all; perhaps because the main ingredients are familiar, and because the meat and vegetables are cooked in sauces which make them particularly appetising. It is also generally agreed that the preparation and eating of sukiyaki in the traditional Japanese way gives added pleasure to both hostess and diners. In Japan it is prepared at the table over a *hibachi* (charcoal brazier) but, in Britain where charcoal braziers—or for that matter, charcoal—cannot be bought for table use, an electric hotplate, or a table burner of the chafing dish variety, may be used instead.

Use a heavy saucepan, preferably enamel over cast-iron—such as the French and Norwegians use—which can be bought in most big stores. Once hot they hold the heat and need only a low flame. And when the dish is ready the diners, using chopsticks, transfer the food directly from the cooking pot to their plates. In this way they can also select ingredients cooked exactly to the degree they prefer.

Arrange the following ingredients on a large serving platter and bring to the table:

INGREDIENTS

4 oz. beef suet	2 cups shirataki
2 lb. tender loin of beef sliced very thin	12 large mushrooms
12 scallions* cut into 2-inch lengths	12 pieces of tofu in 1-inch cubes
½ Chinese cabbage cut into 2-inch lengths	1 can bamboo shoots
½ lb. fresh spinach cut into 1-inch strips	in large bite-sizes

Sauce:

½ cup shoyu	¼ cup sake
⅓ cup of sugar	

METHOD

To prepare sauce, mix shoyu, sugar and sake. Pour into a small pitcher.

Cut the suet into small pieces and place in the saucepan while it is being heated. The guests will watch with interest and perhaps impatience. When the suet has melted, take a slice of beef and dip it in the sauce, coating both sides, then put it into the saucepan. When one side browns, turn and brown the other. This should take but a moment as finely sliced beef is most delicious when 'rare'. When cooked, dip in freshly prepared mustard sauce (made with water not vinegar) and eat. About a third of the beef is consumed in this way.

There will still be some fat in the saucepan, so put in enough sauce to cover the bottom of the pan, add the remaining slices and cook lightly till the beef turns colour, then place all the other ingredients on top of the beef slices. Cook for a few minutes, then with tongs or chopsticks, transfer the beef to the top of the vegetables, but *don't* stir.

* Shallots: shoots of old onions planted a second year.

Continue cooking gently over a medium heat till the vegetables are tender but crisp, then eat with bowls of hot rice. The juices in the saucepan should be spooned over the rice.

Most Japanese like dipping sukiyaki in beaten raw egg before eating, for they think the coating of egg cools the steaming sukiyaki and brings out its full flavour, but this is optional.

In Japan—and China—vegetables are never 'cooked to death'. In this dish the vegetables are 'done' when they are thoroughly heated through and the sukiyaki is kept on the hotplate till the dish is empty or the guests have had enough.

More of all, or some, of the ingredients may be added—according to taste—while sukiyaki is being cooked. Thin sauce, in the proportion of three parts of sauce to one of water, for instance, may be put in to cover the bottom of the pan.

Shirataki may be bought in cans and used without further preparation, and so can cold cooked egg noodles, which may be substituted for *shirataki*. One can also get canned bamboo shoots; and *tofu*, which has the consistency of thick custard and must be handled with care, otherwise it will disintegrate.

Fresh mushrooms are used widely, when in season, and when out of season canned button mushrooms, canned *matsutake* or dried *shiitake* may be used. The Japanese use a variety of mushrooms, together, which add flavour. Most mushrooms can be used without advanced preparation, but the *shiitake* must first be soaked in water for a few hours.
MRS R. N. GOWAN

Mushrooms

Incidentally, while on the subject of mushrooms, Britain has many varieties which are ignored by almost the entire population, who will risk only two kinds: the field mushroom and the cultivated variety. But other excellent eaters are Shaggy Caps (Coprinus comatus), The Blusher (Amanita rubescens), Tawny Grisette (Amanitopsis fulva), Parasol Mushroom (Lepiota procera), Ragged Parasol (Lepiota rhacodes), Blewits (Tricoloma personatum), The Chanterelle (Cantharellus cibarius), Saffron Milk Cap (Lactarius deliciosus), Ceps or Edible Boletus (Boletus edulis), Rough Stalked Boletus (Boletus scaber and Boletus versipellis), Common Morel (Morchella esculenta), Giant Puffball (Lycoperdon giganteum) and commonest of all, Fairy Ring Champignon (Marasmius oreades), which is seen in every lawn and field.

DASHI (First)

Dashi is indispensible to Japanese cookery for it is used as a soup base and as the liquid ingredient in many dishes, so it is as well to know how to prepare it. It is best described as a light, clear fish stock or bouillon. You will notice that *Kabuto-age*, *Tempura* and *Chawanmushi* all contain *dashi*.

INGREDIENTS

1 cup not quite full, of *katsoubushi*	1 teaspoon *shoyu*
1 square inch *kombu*	1 teaspoon salt
5 cups water	

METHOD

Sand is sometimes found in *kombu*, so rinse it well and place it in the water. Bring the water to the boil, then remove *kombu* immediately; it should not be allowed to boil. Remove the broth from the stove. Add *katsoubushi* and allow it to steep for a couple of minutes, then strain through a cloth and season with salt and *shoyu*. The *katsoubushi* and *kombu* are also used for preparing 'second *dashi*'.

'First *dashi*' is mainly used for soups. When ready *dashi* should be clear and the colour of weak tea (without milk, of course). *Dashi* may be kept indefinitely if bottled, corked, and placed in a refrigerator.

MRS R. N. GOWAN

DASHI (Second)

One third of a cup flaked *katsoubushi*
Also *katsoubushi* saved from the first *dashi*
Kombu saved from the first *dashi*
3 cups water

Put the *katsoubushi* and *kombu* in the water, then bring to the boil and remove from heat. Strain through a cloth.

'Second *dashi*' is used for preparing *Kabuto-age*, *Chawanmushi* and *Tempura* sauce. In appearance it is the same as 'first *dashi*', and if the flavour is too thin, add half a teaspoon of *aji-no-moto*.

MRS R. N. GOWAN

KABUTO-AGE

Kabuto-age, as explained, means fried armour, because the ingredients are fried in the shell of the lobster that is being eaten. Kabuto-age may be served with the main course of a western-style dinner, or in combination with any of the other dishes given here.

Quantities of all the ingredients are not specified for they vary with the size of the lobster, but the total volume of all the vegetables used (each in roughly equal amounts) should amount to about a third of the lobster meat.

INGREDIENTS

1 lobster body	$\frac{1}{8}$ teaspoon *aji-no-moto* (optional)
A few bamboo shoots sliced in thin 1-inch strips	Green peas
Carrots sliced in thin 1-inch strips	$\frac{1}{4}$ cup bread crumbs
1 teaspoon *shoyu*	1 slice lemon
1 teaspoon *sake*	Cooking oil
1 tablespoon *dashi* (second)	Pinch of salt
1 egg	*Shiitake* sliced in thin long strips

237

METHOD

Place the lobster in boiling water and cook for 15 minutes, or till cooked. Remove meat from body and claws, discarding the stomach, intestines and lungs. Shred.

Boil bamboo shoots, *shiitake* and carrots lightly, then drain and replace in saucepan. Mix *shoyu*, sugar and *dashi* and add to the vegetables, then stir till all the vegetables are coated with the mixture. Beat the egg and add salt and aji-no-moto; put the mixture into a lightly greased saucepan and stir over a low flame till the egg thickens but does not set. Now fold in cooked vegetables, green peas and lobster meat. Mix well, replace in the lobster shell, cover with breadcrumbs and pat. Fry in deep hot oil (about 390°F.) till brown and thoroughly heated through. Serve with sliced lemon.

Shiitake should be soaked for an hour or more before being cut into strips. When they are in season, fresh mushrooms may be served in place of *shiitake*, or canned *matsutake* or canned button mushrooms.

The stomach of the lobster is a small sac just behind the head; the lungs are the spongy tissue between shell and meat. Don't discard the green liver or red 'coral'.

MRS R. N. GOWAN *Enough for one*

TEMPURA

Tempura, like *sukiyaki*, is a great favourite in America, and in fact, with all foreigners who visit Japan. It is a delicious fritter made with shrimps, and the Japanese are very partial to other foods fried in this way, which include not only seafoods of every kind, but vegetables, mushrooms, roots, seaweeds and certain fresh herbs.

Here again, specific quantities are not given for the amount will depend upon the capacity and preference of the diners, but the batter should prove sufficient for four people of normal appetite. When properly prepared, however, tempura stimulates the appetite and one can consume more than usual. Recently it was reported that a student in Tokyo set a record by gorging 52 large shrimps during one tempura sitting. We've known guests like that, especially when, through some unforeseen contingency, too little has been prepared. So one should allow six shrimps for most adults sound in wind and limb.

INGREDIENTS

24 large green shrimps	About 1 inch of ginger root, freshly grated
A variety of vegetables in season: string beans,	Horseradish, freshly grated
aubergine, parsley, mint, etc.	Daikon or radishes, freshly grated

For the Batter:

1⅛ of a cup of flour	1 cup of water
1 egg	

For the Sauce:

¼ cup *shoyu*	Pinch of *aji-no-moto* (optional)
½ cup *dashi* (second)	

METHOD

Shell the shrimps, leaving the tail fins attached to the flesh, but remove the black veins and slit the underneath of the shrimps to prevent excessive curling; then wash and dry them thoroughly.

Wash the vegetables, dry thoroughly and cut into pieces about the same length as the shrimps.

Make the batter by beating the egg and water together, then adding the flour and mixing lightly (only 2 or 3 stirs are needed). Then fill a deep saucepan, or a deep frying pan to a third of its depth with cooking oil and then heat it. When very hot, dip each shrimp and each piece of vegetable into the batter and drop into hot oil. Large bubbles will form but when these become small it is a sign that the tempura is done. Drain and serve hot with warm sauce.

The sauce is made by mixing *shoyu, dashi* and *aji-no-moto,* and served in separate bowls, with separate condiment dishes of horse-radish, *daikon* (or radish) and ginger. It is left to each diner to stir in just as much of the condiments into his bowl of sauce as he wishes. He then dips hot tempura into the sauce condiment mixture and eats.

If you are not quite sure whether the oil is hot enough, make a small ball of flour and water and drop it into the oil. If the temperature is right, the ball will float immediately; otherwise it will sink.

MRS R. N. GOWAN

Enough for four

TERIYAKI

Teriyaki is fish marinated in a sauce containing *shoyu,* and then grilled. This dish illustrates the versatility of *shoyu,* which is an excellent general-purpose flavouring. It could well be utilized widely in Western cooking and sauces, much to their improvement.

1 lb. filleted salmon, tuna, mackerel or rockfish.

Sauce:

INGREDIENTS

¾ cup *shoyu*   ¾ cup *sake*

¼ cup sugar

METHOD

Mix *shoyu,* sugar and *sake.* Cut the fillets into small steaks and marinate in the sauce for 10 minutes, then remove from marinade and place in a hot broiler or under a grill. Broil one side for 4 minutes then turn and broil the other for 6 minutes; and while broiling baste 3 or 4 times with sauce. When nicely browned, serve hot, sprinkled with a little of the warm sauce.

In Japan the broiling is done over charcoal on three slender skewers each 10 inches long, with the fish held about 7 inches from the coals.

A *shoyu* coating tends to burn easily, so if the *teriyaki* is in danger of browning too rapidly, remove it further from the heat, or turn down the heat. The 6 to 4 minute ratio is the normal cooking time over a charcoal fire, so housewives who don't use charcoal (and one or two don't), should experiment with heat and distance and use their commonsense, which all housewives, of course, have in abundance. Serve with the lightly-browned surface uppermost.

Enough for four

CHAWANMUSHI

This is a steamed egg dish, resembling custard, but with certain differences. Unlike custard, it is served as one of the main courses in a Japanese dinner and not as a sweet. In Japan fresh fruit is usually served as dessert.

INGREDIENTS

3 eggs	4 small shrimps
2 cups *dashi*	4 button mushrooms
5 teaspoons *shoyu*	4 half-slices of bamboo shoots
8 bite-size pieces of chicken	½ teaspoon *aji-no-moto*

METHOD

Beat the eggs. Add *dashi* and 4 teaspoons *shoyu*. Then put the mixture through a fine strainer to blend the whites and yolks thoroughly. Add *aji-no-moto*.

Now mix chicken, shrimps, mushrooms and bamboo shoots with the remaining *shoyu* until it is evenly distributed over these ingredients. When this is done, put one shrimp, one mushroom, two pieces of chicken and one piece of bamboo shoot into each of 4 small bowls. The Japanese use special bowls with lids but if you haven't got these, cover each bowl with aluminium foil. Place them in a steamer and steam for about 15 minutes over a medium heat, but make sure that the water is boiling before putting the bowls into the steamer.

To test whether *chawanmushi* is done, pierce the surface with a toothpick. If juices do not run out of the hole it is ready to be served. Don't steam too long as *chawanmushi* cracks and separates just as custard does. Serve in the same bowls.

Pieces of fish fillet may be used instead of shrimps, and bite-size pieces of pork in place of chicken. Canned water chestnuts may be used as a substitute for bamboo shoots, and *shiitake* or *matsutake* instead of button mushrooms.

Sometimes a sort of 'egg tofu' is made by preparing *chawanmushi* without solid ingredients, and is used chiefly as one of the ingredients in soup.

Enough for four

MRS R. N. GOWAN

SHOYU

Shoyu or soy sauce is extensively used throughout Japan and is, indeed, an indispensable ingredient. Made of wheat, soya beans and salt, it adds flavour to almost every dish. There are many kinds of shoyu but the best obtainable in Britain is that bottled by The Yamasha Shoyu Co., which can be had from Mikadoya. Shoyu will also add piquancy to western dishes. Below are some typical ways of using shoyu.

INGREDIENTS

1½ lb. beef, pork, chicken,	1 lb. potatoes, onions
clam or prawn	or green peppers

METHOD

You may use either one kind of vegetable, or all three. Thread meat and vegetables alternately on skewers.

Seasoning:

INGREDIENTS

1 cup *shoyu*

2 tablespoons minced onion

¼ teaspoon red pepper

¼ teaspoon white pepper

1 teaspoon mustard

1 teaspoon minced parsley well soaked in water

METHOD

In Japan a charcoal brazier is always used, but a gas cooker or an electric stove will do. Light or switch on the grill and broil the vegetables till light brown on both sides. Then dip them in *shoyu* and place on a plate. Sprinkle with any seasoning desired and serve hot. The seasoning given here is best. The parsley must be chopped finely and mixed with the other ingredients. Some recommend dipping the skewered food in *shoyu* when light brown, and broiling again.

Enough for five

INGREDIENTS

1 lb. prawn, white fish fillet or oyster

½ lb. asparagus, aubergine, green peas, string beans, squash, potatoes, sweet
    potatoes, mushrooms or any other vegetables.

Tempura Batter

INGREDIENTS

½ cup flour, ½ cup water and one egg

METHOD

Beat the egg well. Add flour and water and stir lightly with a spoon no more than 4 or 5 times.

Tempura Sauce

INGREDIENTS

3 tablespoons *shoyu*

5 cups water

¼ teaspoon salt

½ cup dried-bonito flakes

4 pieces 4 inch square, *tangle*

3 tablespoons *mirin* (Japanese sweet sake)

METHOD

Put the *tangle* and water in a saucepan and bring to the boil. Remove the *tangle* and add dried-bonito flakes. Turn off the heat and wait till the bonito flakes sink to the bottom of the pot, then strain the liquid through a cloth strainer. Add *shoyu* and salt to the liquid and bring to the boil again. Skim off floating foam and keep on the boil for 2 minutes.

Now fill a pan with vegetable oil to a depth of 2 inches and heat it to 356°F., which is much hotter than boiling point (212°F.). Dip the ingredients one by one in the *tempura* batter and then place several of them in the heated oil; just before you think they are thoroughly cooked, remove them. To be eaten with rice and sauce, which is placed in individual bowls in front of each plate.

Enough for five

MRS R. N. GOWAN

INGREDIENTS

1½ lb. top sirloin steak 4 inches long,
    sliced thinly like bacon

½ lb. spring onions cut into 1-inch strips

½ lb. fresh spinach cut into 2-inch strips

1/5 lb. carrots cut into strips 1 inch by ¼ inch

2 or 3 large pieces of beef suet

1/5 lb. fresh or canned mushrooms
    sliced ⅛ inch thick

5 eggs (optional but will improve
    the dish vastly)

Sukiyaki Sauce

INGREDIENTS

1 cup *shoyu*   3 cups water

1 piece *tangle* 9 inches square   ¾ cup granulated sugar

METHOD

Put ripped *tangle* and water into a saucepan and bring to the boil, then pour the broth into a container.

Place a portable stove on the dining table. Heat a thick-bottomed pot on it and oil the inside thoroughly with beef suet. Place the strips of meat in it, side by side and cook until the juices start to ooze, then turn the slices of meat. Sprinkle the meat with sugar; then pour *shoyu* and tangle broth—in that order—over it. When the meat is done, toss in the vegetables and cook briskly.

Beat the eggs and place them in a bowl. As soon as the vegetables are done, the diners dip their chopsticks (or forks) into the dish, take out meat and vegetables, dip them in beaten egg, and eat. As the pot empties, more meat and vegetables are cooked, in the same way, more shoyu and broth are added, and when cooked, meat and vegetables are dipped in egg and eaten. If necessary, the pot must again be greased with beef suet to prevent meat from sticking.

Enough for five

MRS R. N. GOWAN

NIGIRI-ZUSHI

This, the most common of the *sushi*, is a ball of sticky boiled rice, treated with vinegar, topped with a bit of raw fish after being smeared with grated *wasabi* (Japanese horseradish), a greenish strong-tasting condiment to be used with considerable reserve.

This rice-ball, with its garnishings, is painted lightly with sugared *shoyu* and eaten with either chopsticks or fingers. It is usually served with small slices of yellow ginger.

The fish (sometimes shellfish) used to make *nigiri-zushi* are: sea-bream, tuna, prawn, shrimp, earshell, abalone, cuttlefish, flounder, sardine, etc., but fish found in European waters can be used.

SASHIMI

Sashimi or sliced raw fish, though strange to European palates, is the most characteristic of Japanese dishes. The custom of eating sliced raw fish is one, perhaps, introduced by the early settlers who doubtless came from the South Seas. Almost all varieties of fish may be made into *sashimi* but the most popular *sashimi* are made from *tai* (sea-bream), *koi* (carp), *maguro* (tuna), *katsuo* (bonito), and *hirame* (flatfish), though *same* (shark), *kujira* (whale), *ebi* (lobster), and the flesh of other shellfish make excellent *sashimi*. The fish is finely sliced and served on top of rice patties, or mixed with rice and vegetables. Octopus, clam, mussel and prawn are delicious served in this way, and there are restaurants all over Japan which specialize in serving raw-fish dishes.

MRS R. N. GOWAN

TEA

Tea, the national beverage of Japan, is served with all meals and between meals. In winter it is consumed piping hot because of the glow it imparts; and hot also in summer, for its cooling effect. In Japan, as in the West, there are different varieties of tea, some credited with medicinal properties, while others, used in ceremonies, are supposed to benefit the spirit as well as the body. Japanese tea is always taken without milk or sugar, and is most refreshing.

Put one tablespoon of *bancha* (coarse green tea of inferior quality) into the pot, pour over it three cups of boiling water and infuse for a minute or two. The strength of the tea will depend on the time it stands. Serve hot. Experiment with varieties of Japanese tea.

Japanese food ingredients can be had from:
Mikadoya
21 Lawrie Park Road, London S.E.26

MRS R. N. GOWAN

There is no Japanese restaurant in Britain, but if you would like to sample Japanese food, you can do so at the Yangtze, a Chinese restaurant at 222 Kensington High Street, London W.8, which has a section, the Edo Room, where only Japanese food is served. The only other place is the Nippon Club, 13 Chelsea Embankment, London S.W.3, where one has to be invited by a member.

MRS R. N. GOWAN

MALAYSIAN FOOD

IT WOULD be impossible, in one section of a small book, to give a true idea of Malaysian food because the recipes for their dishes are handed down, from generation to generation, by word of mouth and so they vary from district to district. Malaysian food has also changed enormously with the times and the conversion of the people to the Muslim religion in the thirteenth century did much to change their eating habits. They cut animals' throats, or beheaded them, according to Islamic tradition; the wild pig became tabu; and the wild dog unclean beast. Both are still eaten with relish by millions in the archipelago who have not embraced the religion and teachings of The Prophet.

Fish-eating Races

As rivers and lakes abound, and the sea washes thousands of miles of coastline, the people eat fish, turtles and their eggs, and seaweed, too, forms a prominent part of the diet. The country is green, for rainfall is plentiful; so fruit and vegetables abound, and are cheap. Some of the fish they eat would seem strange to British eyes: large pomfrets (bawal tambak, bawal chermin); Senangin, large Spanish mackerel (tenggiri); large kurau, Chermin, large dorab (parangparang), Terubok, Jenahak, Siakap; all suitable for making curry. Then there are smaller varieties, such as selar, kembong, chencharu, selangat, puput, and tamban, all equally delicious.

Some fish, such as Jewfish and sting rays, do not curry well; others—sembilang (cat fish) and the smaller varieties of the shark—do. They taste extraordinarily like fishy beef.

Pungency of Malaysian Food

Curries in rural areas hardly touched by civilization are more pungent than food anywhere except on the Madras and Malabar coasts of India, where food doesn't seem to be worth eating unless it scorches the palate. Britons who sample some of their dishes never get past the first mouthful.

CURRIED FISH

Let me, for example, give one recipe for currying a portion of fish weighing one *kati* (1⅓ lb.). The recipe involves two operations and the end product is somewhat similar to the fiery pepper water of Madras.

244

Mixture No. 1

INGREDIENTS

25 dried chillis

60 peppercorns

Dried turmeric 1 inch by $\frac{3}{4}$ inch

5 teaspoons coriander

1 teaspoon cummin seed

3 cloves garlic

6 small onions of the pickling variety

METHOD

Grind the chillis, pepper, turmeric, cummin and coriander on a grinding stone, or in a mortar. Mash the garlic and onions and mix them in.

Mixture No. 2

INGREDIENTS

$\frac{1}{2}$ teaspoon mustard seed

1 teaspoon dill

25 karuapillay leaves

1 clove garlic

2 medium-sized onions, sliced

5 tablespoons coconut oil

METHOD

Bring the coconut oil to the boil, drop in these ingredients and cook till they turn yellow.

Now mash half a *tahil* of tamarind and pour half a pint of boiling water over it. Mix it with Mixture No. 1. (tahil$=1\frac{1}{3}$ oz.).

Put Mixture No. 2 in a thick pan 9 inches in diameter and at least 5 inches deep, and simmer. Mix the tamarind water with Mixture No. 1, add a dessertspoon of coarse salt and pour this into the pan already simmering. Cook for 5 minutes, stirring well.

Now make a pint of tamarind water with a *tahil* of tamarind. Boil for 5 minutes and then pour in a pint of coconut milk made from the flesh of a quarter of a coconut, and boil for a further 5 minutes.

Wash the fish, cut it into 6 slices or cutlets, and if it is a small fish, include the head. Boil for a further 10 minutes, when the dish should be ready for the table. This dish should be eaten in a soup plate on which rice is piled, the fish placed on top and a ladle or two of liquid poured on.

In Malaysia more salt is advocated than that in this recipe, but even a dessertspoon may be too much for British palates, so perhaps it would be as well to use only a *teaspoon* of salt, for salt can be added but not taken away.

Enough for four

FRIED FISH

Fish isn't fried in a batter, as in Britain. For a piece of fresh fish weighing from a quarter to half a *kati* all that is needed is a pinch of coarse salt and a piece of dried turmeric about a half by a quarter of an inch. Grind the salt and turmeric finely and smear the fish with this; then cook in 5 tablespoons of coconut oil in a thick frying-pan.

Enough for four

MASAK ASAM

INGREDIENTS

1 tablespoon tamarind	5 small onions
3 cloves garlic	2 or 3 chillis
1 stalk serai (curry leaf)	1 teaspoon blachan
A few slices langkuas (optional)	1 teaspoon turmeric
1 lb. white fish	Salt
6 fresh chillis	

METHOD

The fish used is *ikan tennggeri*, tropical variety, but cod, hake or haddock can be used. Spanish mackerel is the nearest to this species. *Blachan* is a paste made with prawns, which can be bought in shops dealing in oriental food. If unobtainable, *ballychow* can be used.

Chop all the ingredients (except the fish and fresh chillis) finely and put them into a saucepan with two cups of cold water.

Clean and cut the fish into 2-inch pieces, put them into the pot and bring to the boil. When the fish is tender, split the chillis and add them to the boiling mixture. Serve with rice.

Enough for two

CURRY MINANGKABAU

Ribs of the buffalo are usually used for this dish, but ribs of beef will do.

INGREDIENTS

4 ribs of beef	4 buah kras (optional)
6 fresh chillis	2 cloves garlic
1 teaspoon blachan	A few pieces serai or a 1-inch
3 onions	piece of ginger
1½ inches of turmeric	1½ cups coconut milk
Oil for frying	A few blimbings
3 cups water	Salt

METHOD

Buah kras are the roasted seeds of the candle nut and may be obtainable in Oriental food stores, but one doubts whether *blimbing* (carambola to Europeans) is to be found. This is a yellow fruit which has sweet and acid varieties, the second of which is used in curries.

Strip the meat from the bone, cut into 1-inch lengths and put into a pan with the water and all the other ingredients except the *blimbings*. Bring to the boil and simmer till the meat is done. When nearly tender, slit the *blimbings*, throw them in and simmer for a couple of minutes.

Serve with rice.

Enough for two

Mixed Sambal Tray
(See pages 120–131)

LAKSA (Vermicelli)

INGREDIENTS

1 boiling chicken or 2 lb. fish	1 cucumber
4 oz. bean sprouts	1 bean cake
1 sprig mint	1 pint coconut milk
¼ lb. vermicelli	1 large onion

Curry Spices

4 chillis	1 breakfast cup small onions
1-inch piece of turmeric	2 cloves garlic
2 stalks serai leaves	1 teaspoon blachan
½ cup roasted coriander seeds	½-inch piece of ginger
8 buah kras (optional)	Salt
Oil for frying	

METHOD

Make a broth with the neck and feet of the chicken and add a piece of bruised *serai* stalk.

Grind all the curry spices together and fry them. Put them into the chicken broth. Rinse the vessel in which they were ground in a little water, and add that, too. Bring to the boil and pour in coconut milk.

Now add the chicken and boil gently till tender.

If fish is used instead of chicken, grate the raw flesh, mould into little balls and slip gently into the cooking curry spices, a few at a time.

While the curry is simmering, shred the cucumber and put it in a dish. Parboil the bean sprouts and fry the bean cake. Then shred a large onion and fry till brown and crisp. The cucumber, bean sprouts, bean cake, onion chips and mint will be used to garnish the finished dish.

Boil the vermicelli till soft but firm. There is nothing worse than clogging, soggy vermicelli. Drain away the water, place on a flat dish and garnish.

When the chicken (or fish) is ready, place on a separate dish. This is one of the few dishes with which rice is not eaten. It is usual to have a dish of pounded chillis mixed with salt to go with this—as if it were not hot enough already!

Enough for four

LAKSA (Vermicelli)

INGREDIENTS

4 oz. bean sprouts	1 lb. prawns (shelled)
4 oz. vermicelli	12 dried chillis
5 candlenuts	1 dessertspoon blachan
2 teaspoons salt	2 pieces serai
2 inches saffron (or turmeric)	2 cloves garlic
12 pickling onions	2 pints coconut milk
1-inch stick of ginger	4 tablespoons oil for frying
A sprig of mint or parsley	

Bake the *blachan* till brown. Grind chillis, saffron (or turmeric), ginger, serai, and onions together. Mix thoroughly with *blachan*.

Heat the oil and when boiling, put in the ground spices. Fry for 3 minutes.

Wash and clean the prawns and add them to the spices, with a little salt. Add coconut milk and boil for 10 minutes.

Cut the vermicelli into lengths, boil it till soft but firm, and drain away the water. Boil the bean sprouts till soft; then drain.

Serve the curry and vermicelli in separate dishes and garnish with bean sprouts and mint.

In Malaysia prawns are cheap and the food of the poor as well as the rich, but in Britain where prawns are costly, a pound of shelled prawns makes an expensive dish, so a smaller quantity may be used; but remember there is no substitute for prawns.

Enough for four

CURRY SPICES MAY BE OBTAINED FROM:

William Jones Ltd.
48/50 Bridge Street
Chester

John Little & Son
Eastgate Row
Chester

A. Abdullah & Son
2 Helmet Court
London E.C.2

Army & Navy Stores
105 Victoria Street
London S.W.1

The Bombay Emporium
70 Grafton Way
London W.1

R. Brooks & Co.
27 Maiden Lane
London W.C.2

M. O. & E. A. Dell
431 North End Road
London S.W.6

Dell & Holt Ltd.
33 Tachbrook Street
London S.W.1

Percy C. Richardson & Sons
33a Brigstock Road
Thornton Heath
Surrey

Fortnum & Mason Ltd.
181 Piccadilly
London W.1

Lal Jolly
70 Warwick Road
Earls Court
London S.W.5

Selfridges (Food Store)
Oxford Street
London W.1

L. Palm (Delicatessen) Ltd.
The Market
Oxford

Cottle Brothers
20/22 Queen Victoria Street
Reading

Cheong-Leen
22 Lyle Street
London W.C.2

Cydilda & Co.
61 Wimbledon High Street
London S.W.19

Chinese Emporium
22 Rupert Street
London W.1

Hongkong Emporium
53 Rupert Street
London W.1

Mohan Brothers
32 Holloway Road
London N.7

Harrods (Food Department)
Knightsbridge
London S.W.1

Premier Supermarkets Ltd.
210/212 Earls Court Road
London S.W.5

Mikadoya
21 Lawrie Park Road
London S.E.26

Wesley Lloyd
20 New Inn Hall Street
Oxford

Indian Emporium
8 Great Russell Street
London W.C.1

Culpepper House Ltd.
21 Bruton Street
London W.1

Patak (Spices) Ltd.
134 Drummond Street
London N.W.1

Continental Food Stores
167 Shepards Bush Market
London W.12

Continental Food Stores
208 Church Road
London N.W.10

Dein's Food Stores Ltd.,
191 Shepards Bush
London W.12

All Heath and Heather Stores

INDEX